# Taste of Home

# WHAT CAN I COOK IN MY...
## INSTANT POT®, AIR FRYER, WAFFLE IRON & MORE

TASTE OF HOME BOOKS • RDA ENTHUSIAST BRANDS, LLC • MILWAUKEE, WI

BLT WAFFLE
SLIDERS, 127

**International Standard Book Number:**
978-1-61765-788-7

**Library of Congress Control Number:**
2018951854

**Deputy Editor:** Mark Hagen
**Senior Art Director:** Raeann Thompson
**Editor:** Christine Rukavena
**Designers:** Arielle Jardine, Jazmin Delgado
**Copy Editor:** Ann Walter

**Pictured on front cover:**
Pizza Crust Tots, p. 112; Mini Teriyaki Turkey
Sandwiches, p. 80; Chocolate Pecan Skillet
Cookie, p. 272; Sweet & Tangy Chicken
Wings, p. 76

**Pictured on back cover:**
Avocado Crab Boats, p. 174; Deep-Dish
Sausage Pizza, p. 263; Air-Fried Pickles, p. 48;
Egg Baskets Benedict, p. 216; Arugula Pesto
Chicken, p. 298; Dutch Waffle Cookies, p. 129

Printed in China
1 3 5 7 9 10 8 6 4 2

SHEET-PAN CHICKEN
PARMESAN, 198

MELT-IN-YOUR-MOUTH
CHUCK ROAST, 39

SOUTHWESTERN EGGS BENEDICT
WITH AVOCADO SAUCE, 134

HAZELNUT
MACARONS, 306

## WHAT CAN I COOK IN MY...

GET GEARED UP

# GEAR UP FOR GREAT COOKING

**We cooks love our gadgets . . . and now there's finally a book that celebrates them all!**

Whether you're looking for fun muffin-tin lunches to feed the family or pressure-cooked meals that hit the dinner table fast, you'll find them in this exciting collection of 200+ innovative recipes.

Use this cookbook as a rally point around all the kitchen gear you love: Instant Pot®, air fryer, waffle iron, stand mixer, blender and more. There's even a special section on the best-loved bakeware. After all, muffin tins, cast-iron skillets and sheet pans are some of the most versatile pans in a well-equipped kitchen. Discover dozens of delicious new ways to put supper on the table fast and in style, too!

This book is also packed with valuable tips and how-tos.

Inside you'll learn:

- The best way to clean your pressure cooker
- How to make grimy sheet pans and rusty cast iron look like new
- Tips for perfect air-frying from our Test Kitchen experts
- Favorite hacks from staffers to inspire you

Make the most of your kitchen tools today. With *What Can I Cook In My . . .* the ideal dinners, snacks, sides, desserts and treats are always at your fingertips.

BACONY ROLLS
IN MINUTES

PERFECTLY BOILED
EGGS EACH TIME

ROOT BEER
PULLED PORK

GORGEOUS
SPIRALS

IRON-CLAD
COOKING
TECHNIQUES

KID-SIZED
CREATIONS

RISE & SHINE
PANCAKES

MEALS ON YOUR
SCHEDULE

SHEET-PAN
TRICKS

# INSTANT POT®

The Instant Pot is a busy cook's best friend. It's perfect for those days when you have to stop on the way home to pick up ingredients for a fast meal. And because pressure-cooker recipes cook hands-free, they're a terrific choice when you're working around the house, too.

# PRESSURE COOKER TIPS

Using a multipurpose cooker requires some reading and practice, so be patient. It will definitely be worth it in the end. Keep these hints in mind when using your cooker.

- Read the instruction manual that came with your electric pressure cooker before you make anything. Not all brands and models are the same, so get to know your pot!

- For food safety and efficiency, the total amount of food and liquid should never exceed the maximum level (also known as the max line or the fill line) indicated in the pot.

- Make sure the steam-release valve is closed before you start cooking. Even the pros at the *Taste of Home* Test Kitchen have forgotten to close the valve and returned to see the pot venting instead of building pressure.

- The steam-release valve should feel loose to the touch. The steam-release handle works by simply applying pressure on the steam-release pipe. Because the contact between the handle and the pipe is not fully sealed, the valve may release a little bit of steam while the food cooks.

- The power cord on some models is removable, which makes the appliance easier to store. If you plug it in and the light doesn't go on, check the cord. Is it attached securely? When the cooker isn't in use, consider storing the cord in the inner pot.

- After each use, remove and clean the sealing ring, steam-release valve and anti-block shield. See the facing page for more cleaning tips.

- If your pot starts to smell like food even after cleaning it, put the sealing ring through the dishwasher. If that doesn't work, try steam-cleaning: Pour 2 cups water and 1 Tbsp. lemon zest into the inner pot. Place the lid on and run the steam program for 2 minutes. Carefully remove the sealing ring and let it air dry.

## HERE'S HOW TO ADAPT YOUR OWN RECIPES:

**PASTA.** Cook for half the time called for on the package for boiling to al dente.

**RICE.** To substitute brown rice for white, increase liquid by ¼ cup and cook time by 5 minutes.

**GRAVY.** Increase the amount of cornstarch or flour a bit, since liquid won't evaporate in the cooker as it does with traditional cooking methods.

**A.** Appliance
**B.** Inner pot
**C.** Lid
**D.** Sealing ring
**E.** Anti-block shield
**F.** Condensation cup
**G.** Steam rack

# CLEANING TIPS

**STEAM-RELEASE VALVE AND FLOAT VALVE:** It's important to wipe food particles off these valves. You don't want anything blocking them, because that would hinder the steam from releasing when you are cooking future meals.

**ANTI-BLOCK SHIELD:** This is something that many cooks forget. Remove the shield from the lid. After hand-washing it, wipe it with a soft cloth and dry completely. Make sure to secure it in place on the lid before using the appliance.

**SEALING RING:** The sealing ring can absorb food odors, so you'll want to clean it after every use. Wash by hand or in the dishwasher. Ensure it's completely dry before placing in the lid.

**EXTERIOR:** Wipe the exterior of your Instant Pot with a damp cloth as needed. It's important not to submerge the cooker in water since it contains the heating element. When you need to clean the inside of the cooker (not to be confused with the inner pot), use a damp cloth.

**LID:** After carefully removing the sealing ring and the anti-block shield, wash the lid on the top rack of your dishwasher. It is not necessary to clean the lid after every use, but it's not a bad idea to simply give it a good wipe with a clean towel between washes.

**CONDENSATION CUP:** This little cup collects the moisture that's created during the cooling process. It doesn't get particularly dirty, so a periodic wash is all it needs. You should check the cup regularly, however, and keep it clean with a quick wipe every now and again.

# APPLE-CRANBERRY GRAINS

*These delicious pressure-cooker grains are perfect. A hearty breakfast is ready fast in the morning, making this quick and healthy recipe a favorite in my home.*
*—Sherisse Dawe, Black Diamond, AB*

**PREP:** 10 min. • **COOK:** 25 min. + releasing • **MAKES:** 10 servings

2 medium apples, peeled and chopped
1 cup sugar
1 cup fresh cranberries
½ cup wheat berries
½ cup quinoa, rinsed
½ cup oat bran
½ cup medium pearl barley
½ cup chopped walnuts
½ cup packed brown sugar
1½ to 2 tsp. ground cinnamon
6 cups water
   Milk, brown sugar, chopped nuts and apple slices, optional

1. In a 6-qt. electric pressure cooker, combine the first 11 ingredients. Lock lid; make sure vent is closed. Select manual setting; adjust pressure to high and set time for 25 minutes. When finished cooking, allow pressure to naturally release for 10 minutes, then quick-release any remaining pressure according to the manufacturer's directions.

2. Serve with optional ingredients as desired.

**1 SERVING:** 286 cal., 5g fat (1g sat. fat), 0 chol., 8mg sod., 60g carb. (34g sugars, 5g fiber), 5g pro.

## PURCHASE EXTRA SEALING RINGS

Use one for your curries, tacos and other spicy dishes, and save the other for cheesecakes and other dishes with delicate flavors. Color-coded sets are available so you can always tell your savory and sweet sealing rings apart.

# MAPLE FRENCH TOAST

*My family and friends all love it when I make this scrumptious French toast in the morning. And it's so easy!*
—*Cindy Steffen, Cedarburg, WI*

**PREP:** 10 min. + standing ● **COOK:** 20 min. + releasing ● **MAKES:** 4 servings

6 cups cubed bread (about 6 oz.)
4 oz. cream cheese, cubed
4 large eggs
½ cup 2% milk
¼ cup maple syrup
1 cup water
  Additional maple syrup

1. Arrange half of the bread cubes in a greased 1½-qt. baking dish. Top with cream cheese and remaining bread. In a large bowl, whisk eggs, milk and syrup; pour over bread. Let stand 30 minutes.

2. Pour water into a 6-qt. electric pressure cooker. Cover baking dish with foil; place on a trivet with handles; lower into pressure cooker. Lock lid; make sure vent is closed. Select the manual setting; adjust pressure to high and set time to 20 minutes.

3. When finished cooking, allow pressure to naturally release for 10 minutes, then quick-release remaining pressure according to manufacturer's directions. Remove lid; carefully remove baking dish using handles. Serve with syrup.

**1 CUP:** 378 cal., 17g fat (8g sat. fat), 217mg chol., 434mg sod., 43g carb. (18g sugars, 1g fiber), 14g pro.

# APPLE-PEAR COMPOTE

*Apples and pears are almost always popular, so this warm, comforting recipe is great for potlucks or other get-togethers. I also like to add raisins or chopped nuts to the compote, and for a more grown-up flavor I add ⅓ cup brandy or rum.*
—*Nancy Heishman, Las Vegas, NV*

**PREP:** 20 min. ● **COOK:** 10 min. + releasing ● **MAKES:** 8 cups

5 medium apples, peeled and chopped
3 medium pears, chopped
1 medium orange, thinly sliced
½ cup dried cranberries
½ cup packed brown sugar
½ cup maple syrup
⅓ cup butter, cubed
2 Tbsp. lemon juice
2 tsp. ground cinnamon
1 tsp. ground ginger
5 Tbsp. orange juice, divided
4 tsp. cornstarch

1. In a 6-qt. electric pressure cooker, combine the first 10 ingredients. Stir in 2 Tbsp. orange juice. Lock lid; make sure vent is closed. Select manual setting; adjust pressure to high and set time for 6 minutes. When finished cooking, allow pressure to naturally release for 5 minutes, then quick-release any remaining pressure according to the manufacturer's directions.

2. Select saute setting and adjust for high heat; bring liquid to a boil. In a small bowl, mix cornstarch and remaining orange juice until smooth; gradually stir into fruit mixture. Cook and stir until the sauce is thickened, 1-2 minutes.

**½ CUP:** 149 cal., 4g fat (2g sat. fat), 10mg chol., 34mg sod., 30g carb. (25g sugars, 2g fiber), 0 pro.

# MARINATED MUSHROOMS

Here's a terrific, healthy addition to any buffet spread. Mushrooms and pearl onions seasoned with herbs, balsamic vinegar and red wine are fantastic on their own or alongside a tenderloin roast.
—Courtney Wilson, Fresno, CA

**TAKES:** 20 min. ● **MAKES:** 5 cups

2 lbs. medium fresh mushrooms
1 pkg. (14.40 oz.) frozen pearl onions
4 garlic cloves, minced
¾ cup reduced-sodium beef broth
¼ cup dry red wine
3 Tbsp. balsamic vinegar
3 Tbsp. olive oil
1 tsp. salt
1 tsp. dried basil
½ tsp. dried thyme
½ tsp. pepper
¼ tsp. crushed red pepper flakes

Place mushrooms, onions and garlic in a 6-qt. electric pressure cooker. In a small bowl, whisk remaining ingredients; pour over mushrooms. Lock lid; make sure vent is closed. Select the manual setting; adjust pressure to high and set time for 4 minutes. When finished cooking, quick-release pressure according to manufacturer's directions.

**¼ CUP:** 43 cal., 2g fat (0 sat. fat), 0 chol., 138mg sod., 4g carb. (2g sugars, 0 fiber), 1g pro.

# PEACH SALSA

Fresh peaches and tomatoes make my salsa a hands-down winner over store versions. As a treat, I give my co-workers several jars throughout the year.
—Peggi Stahnke, Cleveland, OH

**TAKES:** 25 min. ● **MAKES:** 11 cups

4 lbs. (about 12) medium tomatoes, chopped
1 medium onion, chopped
4 jalapeno peppers, seeded and finely chopped
½ to ⅔ cup packed brown sugar
¼ cup minced fresh cilantro
4 garlic cloves, minced
1 tsp. salt
4 each chopped peeled fresh peaches (about 4 medium), divided
1 can (6 oz.) tomato paste

1. In a 6-qt. electric pressure cooker, combine the first seven ingredients; stir in 2 cups peaches. Lock lid; make sure vent is closed. Select manual setting; adjust pressure to high and set time for 3 minutes. When finished cooking, quick-release pressure according to the manufacturer's directions.

2. Stir tomato paste and remaining peaches into pressure cooker. Cool. Transfer to covered containers. (If freezing, use freezer-safe containers and fill to within ½ in. of tops.) Refrigerate up to 1 week or freeze up to 12 months. Thaw salsa in refrigerator before serving.

**¼ CUP:** 28 cal., 0 fat (0 sat. fat), 0 chol., 59mg sod., 7g carb. (5g sugars, 0 fiber), 1g pro.

# CRANBERRY HOT WINGS

*Cranberry wings remind me of all the wonderful celebrations and parties we've had through the years. My daughter's friends can't get enough of them.*
*—Noreen McCormick Danek, Cromwell, CT*

**PREP:** 45 min. • **COOK:** 35 min. + broiling • **MAKES:** about 4 dozen

1 can (14 oz.) jellied cranberry sauce
½ cup orange juice
¼ cup Louisiana-style hot sauce
2 Tbsp. soy sauce
2 Tbsp. honey
1 Tbsp. brown sugar
1 Tbsp. Dijon mustard
2 tsp. garlic powder
1 tsp. dried minced onion
1 garlic clove, minced
5 lbs. chicken wings (about 24 wings)
1 tsp. salt
4 tsp. cornstarch
2 Tbsp. cold water

### ✳ TEST KITCHEN TIP

You can substitute Sriracha sauce for the hot pepper sauce to switch it up.

**1.** Whisk together first 10 ingredients. For the chicken, use a sharp knife to cut through two wing joints; discard wing tips. Place the wing pieces in a 6-qt. electric pressure cooker; sprinkle with salt. Pour the cranberry mixture over top. Lock lid; make sure vent is closed. Select manual setting; adjust pressure to high and set time for 10 minutes. When finished cooking, quick-release pressure according to manufacturer's directions.

**2.** Remove wings to a 15x10x1-in. pan; arrange in a single layer. Preheat broiler. Meanwhile, skim fat from cooking juices in pressure cooker. Select saute setting and adjust for high heat. Bring juices to a boil; cook, stirring occasionally, until mixture is reduced by half, 20-25 minutes. In a small bowl, mix cornstarch and water until smooth; stir into juices. Return to a boil, stirring constantly; cook and stir until glaze is thickened, 1-2 minutes.

**3.** Broil wings 3-4 in. from heat until lightly browned, 2-3 minutes. Brush with glaze before serving. Serve with remaining glaze.

**NOTE:** Uncooked chicken wing sections (wingettes) may be substituted for whole chicken wings.

**1 PIECE:** 71 cal., 4g fat (1g sat. fat), 15mg chol., 122mg sod., 5g carb. (3g sugars, 0 fiber), 5g pro.

## HOW TO CUT CHICKEN WINGS

- With chicken wing on a cutting board, use a sharp knife to cut between the joint at the top of the tip end. Discard tips. (If you want to be resourceful, you can keep them for preparing a batch of homemade chicken broth.)

- Take the remaining wing and cut between the joints. Proceed with recipe as directed.

# HEARTY PORK & BLACK BEAN NACHOS

My husband and I are both graduate students right now, so we don't have a lot of time to cook dinner. Our family loves this incredible nacho platter, and I love how easy it is to prepare.
—*Faith Stokes, Chickamauga, GA*

**PREP:** 15 min. ● **COOK:** 40 min./batch + releasing ● **MAKES:** 10 servings

1 pkg. (4 oz.) beef jerky
3 lbs. pork spareribs, cut into 2-rib sections
4 cans (15 oz. each) black beans, rinsed and drained
1 cup chopped onion
6 bacon strips, cooked and crumbled
4 tsp. minced garlic
1 tsp. crushed red pepper flakes
4 cups beef broth, divided
Tortilla chips
Optional toppings: shredded cheddar cheese, sour cream, thinly sliced green onions, pickled jalapeno slices and chopped tomatoes

1. Pulse beef jerky in a food processor until finely ground. Working in batches, place 1½ pounds ribs in a 6-qt. electric pressure cooker; top with half the jerky, two cans beans, ½ cup onion, three bacon strips, 2 tsp. garlic and ½ tsp. red pepper flakes. Pour in 2 cups of the broth. Lock lid; make sure vent is closed. Select manual setting; adjust pressure to high and set time for 40 minutes.

2. When finished cooking, allow pressure to naturally release for 10 minutes, then quick-release any remaining pressure according to manufacturer's directions. Remove from pressure cooker; make second batch by adding remaining ingredients to cooker. Repeat previous procedure.

3. When cool enough to handle, remove meat from bones; discard bones. Shred meat with two forks; return to pressure cooker. Select saute setting and adjust for high heat; heat through. Strain pork mixture; discard juices. Serve with chips and toppings as desired.

¾ **CUP MEAT MIXTURE:** 469 cal., 24g fat (9g sat. fat), 87mg chol., 1055mg sod., 27g carb. (3g sugars, 7g fiber), 33g pro.

✷ **TEST KITCHEN TIP**
Pinto and kidney beans work well in place of black beans. Try turkey jerky instead of beef jerky.

# WHITE BEAN CHICKEN CHILI

My sister shared this chili recipe with me. The jalapeno adds just enough heat to notice but not too much for my children.
—*Kristine Bowles, Rio Rancho, NM*

**PREP:** 25 min. • **COOK:** 20 min. • **MAKES:** 6 servings (1½ qt.)

¾ lb. boneless skinless chicken breasts, cut into 1¼-in. pieces
¼ tsp. salt
¼ tsp. pepper
2 Tbsp. olive oil, divided
1 medium onion, chopped
1 jalapeno pepper, seeded and chopped
4 garlic cloves, minced
2 tsp. dried oregano
1 tsp. ground cumin
2 cans (15 oz. each) cannellini beans, rinsed and drained, divided
2½ cups chicken broth, divided
1½ cups shredded cheddar cheese
Optional toppings: sliced avocado, quartered cherry tomatoes and chopped fresh cilantro

1. Toss chicken with salt and pepper. Select saute setting and adjust for high heat on a 6-qt. electric pressure cooker. Heat 1 Tbsp. olive oil. Add the chicken; brown on all sides. Remove chicken.

2. Add the remaining oil to pressure cooker. Saute onion until tender. Add jalapeno, garlic, oregano and cumin; cook and stir 2 minutes. Return the chicken to pressure cooker.

3. In a bowl, mash 1 cup beans; stir in ½ cup broth. Stir bean mixture and remaining whole beans and broth into chicken mixture.

4. Lock lid; make sure vent is closed. Select manual setting; adjust pressure to high, and set time for 10 minutes. When finished cooking, quick-release pressure according to manufacturer's directions. Stir before serving. Sprinkle with cheese; add desired toppings.

**1 CUP:** 344 cal., 16g fat (6g sat. fat), 62mg chol., 894mg sod., 23g carb. (1g sugars, 6g fiber), 25g pro.

❊ **TEST KITCHEN TIP**

Wear disposable gloves when cutting hot peppers; the oils can burn skin. Avoid touching your face.

# PROVENCAL HAM & BEAN SOUP

There is nothing quite like the wonderful smell of this delicious stew bubbling away in the pressure cooker. To make preparation even easier, I like to start it the night before. Then all I have to do is put everything in the pressure cooker the following evening, and dinner is ready before I know it.
—*Lyndsay Wells, Ladysmith, BC*

**PREP:** 15 min. + soaking ● **COOK:** 10 min. + releasing ● **MAKES:** 10 servings (3½ qt.)

2 cups assorted dried beans for soup
1 can (28 oz.) whole plum tomatoes, undrained
2 cups cubed fully cooked ham
1 large Yukon Gold potato, peeled and chopped
1 medium onion, chopped
1 cup chopped carrot
1 celery rib, chopped
2 garlic cloves, minced
2 tsp. herbes de Provence
1½ tsp. salt
1 tsp. pepper
1 carton (32 oz.) unsalted chicken stock
French bread

1. Rinse and sort dried beans; soak according to package directions. Drain and rinse beans, discarding liquid.

2. Transfer beans to a 6-qt. electric pressure cooker. Add tomatoes; crush with a wooden spoon until chunky. Stir in ham, vegetables, garlic, seasonings and stock. Lock lid; make sure vent is closed. Select manual setting; adjust pressure to high and set time for 10 minutes. When finished cooking, allow pressure to naturally release for 10 minutes, and then quick-release any remaining pressure according to manufacturer's directions. Serve with bread.

**1⅓ CUPS:** 212 cal., 2g fat (0 sat. fat), 17mg chol., 887mg sod., 33g carb. (5g sugars, 9g fiber), 17g pro.

## DO YOU HAVE TO SOAK BEANS WHEN USING A PRESSURE COOKER?

**Soaking beans overnight—or using the quick-soak technique—is so well ingrained in our minds that it's become a given. But do you really need to take this step when cooking with your pressure cooker?**

Almost any from-scratch bean recipe starts with the same instructions: soak beans in cold water overnight, or use the quicker method—soaking them in warm water for an hour.

But not all pressure cooker recipes call for soaking. What gives?

The high temperatures reached inside the pressure cooker dramatically decrease the cooking time of beans. They may cook as much as 75 percent faster! That's why

many recipes—such as a braised beef soup with dried beans—might skip the soaking step. The beans can fully cook from a dried state in the time it takes a tougher cut of meat to become tender.

If you want to speed things up, though, using presoaked beans gives you a fully cooked soup like this one with tender veggies in just 10 minutes. Here's another benefit: When you soak beans and drain the liquid, you're discarding some of the hard-to-digest carbs that can cause gas.

So the choice is yours. One thing to bear in mind: When deciding whether to soak beans for your pressure-cooker recipes, know that thin-skinned beans such as black-eyed peas, pintos and black beans yield the best results.

# MEXICAN BEEF SOUP

*My family loves this stew, and I'm happy to make it since it's so simple! You can serve it with cornbread instead of tortilla chips to make it an even more filling meal.*
—*Angela Lively, Conroe, TX*

**PREP:** 15 min. • **COOK:** 15 min. + releasing • **MAKES:** 8 servings (2 qt.)

1 lb. beef stew meat (1¼-in. pieces)
¾ lb. potatoes (about 2 medium), cut into ¾-in. cubes
2 cups frozen corn (about 10 oz.), thawed
2 medium carrots, cut into ½-in. slices
1 medium onion, chopped
2 garlic cloves, minced
1½ tsp. dried oregano
1 tsp. ground cumin
½ tsp. salt
¼ tsp. crushed red pepper flakes
2 cups beef stock
1 can (10 oz.) diced tomatoes and green chilies, undrained
Sour cream and tortilla chips, optional

**1.** In a 6-qt. electric pressure cooker, combine first 12 ingredients. Lock lid; make sure vent is closed. Select manual setting; adjust pressure to high and set time for 15 minutes. When finished cooking, allow pressure to naturally release for 10 minutes, and then quick-release any remaining pressure according to manufacturer's directions.

**2.** If desired, serve with sour cream and chips.

**1 CUP:** 172 cal., 4g fat (2g sat. fat), 35mg chol., 453mg sod., 20g carb. (3g sugars, 3g fiber), 14g pro. **DIABETIC EXCHANGES:** 1 starch, 1 lean meat.

**✳ STAFF HACK**

*"One thing to remember—the Instant Pot doesn't necessarily save you time, but it does free up time. You don't have to babysit a bunch of pots and pans on the stove. And it is quicker than a slow cooker.*

*"I always immediately turn mine to saute while I'm prepping for the meal. A hot Instant Pot comes to pressure faster than a cold one!"*

—JEN STOWELL, VOLUNTEER FIELD EDITOR

# CHICKEN MARBELLA

Here's a great summertime pressure cooker recipe! It's sweet, briny, savory and herbal, and it packs a big punch of garlic. The Mediterranean flavors make me think of dinner on the patio with family or friends.

—*Beth Jacobson, Milwaukee, WI*

**PREP:** 30 min. • **COOK:** 10 min. + releasing • **MAKES:** 6 servings

1 cup reduced-sodium chicken broth
1 cup pimiento-stuffed olives, divided
1 cup pitted dried plums, divided
2 Tbsp. dried oregano
2 Tbsp. packed brown sugar
2 Tbsp. capers, drained
2 Tbsp. olive oil
4 garlic cloves, minced
½ tsp. salt
½ tsp. pepper
6 bone-in chicken thighs, skin removed (about 2 lbs.)
1 Tbsp. minced fresh parsley
1 Tbsp. white wine
1 Tbsp. lemon juice
Hot cooked couscous

**1.** Place broth, ½ cup olives, ½ cup dried plums, oregano, brown sugar, capers, oil, garlic, salt and pepper in a food processor; process until smooth. Transfer mixture to a 6-qt. electric pressure cooker. Place chicken in pressure cooker. Lock lid; make sure vent is closed. Select manual setting; adjust pressure to high and set time for 10 minutes. When finished cooking, allow pressure to naturally release for 10 minutes, and then quick-release any remaining pressure according to the manufacturer's directions.

**2.** Chop remaining olives and dried plums. Remove chicken; keep warm. Stir parsley, wine, lemon juice and remaining olives and plums into olive mixture. Serve with chicken and cooked couscous.

**1 SERVING:** 352 cal., 17g fat (3g sat. fat), 77mg chol., 908mg sod., 26g carb. (13g sugars, 2g fiber), 23g pro.

# EASY CORNED BEEF & CABBAGE

I first tried this fuss-free way to cook traditional corned beef and cabbage for St. Patrick's Day a few years ago. Now it's a regular in my menu planning. This is fantastic with Dijon mustard and crusty bread.
—*Karen Waters, Laurel, MD*

**PREP:** 15 min. ● **COOK:** 70 min. + releasing ● **MAKES:** 8 servings

1 medium onion, cut into wedges
4 large red potatoes
1 lb. fresh baby carrots
3 cups water
3 garlic cloves, minced
1 bay leaf
2 Tbsp. sugar
2 Tbsp. cider vinegar
½ tsp. pepper
1 corned beef brisket with spice packet (2½ to 3 lbs.), cut in half
1 small head cabbage, cut into wedges

1. Place the onion, potatoes and carrots in a 6-qt. electric pressure cooker. Combine the water, garlic, bay leaf, sugar, vinegar, pepper and contents of spice packet; pour over vegetables. Top with brisket and cabbage. Lock lid; make sure vent is closed. Select manual setting; adjust pressure to high and set time for 70 minutes.

2. When finished cooking, allow pressure to naturally release for 10 minutes, and then quick-release any remaining pressure according to manufacturer's directions. Discard bay leaf before serving.

**1 SERVING:** 414 cal., 19g fat (6g sat. fat), 97mg chol., 1191mg sod., 38g carb. (11g sugars, 6g fiber), 23g pro.

# RISOTTO WITH CHICKEN & MUSHROOMS

Portobello mushrooms add an earthy flavor to this creamy classic, while rotisserie chicken makes it a snap to prepare.
—*Charlene Chambers, Ormond Beach, FL*

**TAKES:** 30 min. ● **MAKES:** 4 servings

4 Tbsp. unsalted butter, divided
2 Tbsp. olive oil
½ lb. sliced baby portobello mushrooms
1 small onion, finely chopped
1½ cups uncooked arborio rice
½ cup white wine or chicken broth
1 Tbsp. lemon juice
1 carton (32 oz.) chicken broth
2 cups shredded rotisserie chicken
3 Tbsp. grated Parmesan cheese
2 Tbsp. minced fresh parsley
½ tsp. salt
¼ tsp. pepper

1. Select saute setting and adjust for high heat on a 6-qt. electric pressure cooker. Heat 2 Tbsp. butter and oil. Add mushrooms and onion; cook and stir until tender, 6-8 minutes. Add the rice; cook and stir until rice is coated, 2-3 minutes.

2. Stir in wine and lemon juice; cook and stir until wine mixture is absorbed. Pour in chicken broth. Lock lid; make sure vent is closed. Select manual setting; adjust pressure to low and set time for 4 minutes. When finished cooking, quick-release pressure according to manufacturer's directions. Stir until combined; continue stirring until creamy.

3. Stir in remaining ingredients and remaining butter. Select saute setting; adjust for high heat and heat through. Serve immediately.

**1½ CUPS:** 636 cal., 26g fat (10g sat. fat), 101mg chol., 1411mg sod., 66g carb. (4g sugars, 2g fiber), 29g pro.

# CHICKEN BOG

Traditional South Carolina chicken bog has lots of variations (think herbs, spices and fresh veggies), but the standard ingredients remain: sausage, chicken and rice. This pressure-cooked rendition is a simple take on the classic.
—*Anna Hanson, Spanish Fork, UT*

**PREP:** 20 min. ● **COOK:** 10 min. + releasing ● **MAKES:** 8 servings

1 Tbsp. canola oil
1 medium onion, chopped
8 oz. smoked sausage, halved and sliced ½-in. thick
3 garlic cloves, minced
5 cups chicken broth, divided
2 cups uncooked converted rice
1 tsp. salt
1 tsp. pepper
1 rotisserie chicken (about 3 lbs.), meat removed and shredded
Thinly sliced green onions, optional
Hot sauce

**1.** Select saute setting and adjust for high heat on a 6-qt. electric pressure cooker. Heat oil. Add the onion and sausage; cook until the sausage is lightly browned. Add garlic; cook 1 minute more.

**2.** Stir in 4 cups broth, rice, salt and pepper. Lock lid; make sure vent is closed. Select manual setting; adjust pressure to low and set time for 3 minutes. When finished cooking, allow pressure to naturally release for 10 minutes, then quick-release any remaining pressure according to manufacturer's directions. Rice should be tender.

**3.** Select saute setting; adjust for high heat. Stir in chicken and remaining broth. Cook until chicken is heated through, about 5 minutes. If desired, sprinkle with green onions. Serve with hot sauce.

**1¼ CUPS:** 409 cal., 14g fat (5g sat. fat), 77mg chol., 1275mg sod., 40g carb. (2g sugars, 0 fiber), 27g pro.

# CREAMY EGG SALAD

I love this egg salad's versatility—serve it on a bed of mixed greens, tucked into a sandwich or with your favorite crackers.
—*Cynthia Kolberg, Syracuse, IN*

**TAKES:** 10 min. • **MAKES:** 3 cups

- 3 oz. cream cheese, softened
- ¼ cup mayonnaise
- ½ tsp. salt
- ⅛ tsp. pepper
- ¼ cup finely chopped green or sweet red pepper
- ¼ cup finely chopped celery
- ¼ cup sweet pickle relish
- 2 Tbsp. minced fresh parsley
- 8 hard-boiled large eggs, chopped

In a bowl, mix cream cheese, mayonnaise, salt and pepper until smooth. Stir in green pepper, celery, relish and parsley. Fold in eggs. Refrigerate, covered, until serving.

**½ CUP:** 234 cal., 19g fat (6g sat. fat), 268mg chol., 466mg sod., 5g carb. (4g sugars, 0 fiber), 9g pro.

## THIS IS THE EASIEST WAY TO HARD-BOIL EGGS

Once you use a pressure cooker to hard-boil eggs you'll never go back! We tried what's known as the "5-5-5 method." It's easy to remember off the top of your head: 5 minutes to pressure-cook, 5 minutes to release and 5 minutes to cool.

- Place 1 cup water in an Instant Pot. Place a steamer basket or trivet on top of the water and carefully place up to 12 eggs on top.

- Lock lid; set the pressure release to sealing. Select manual setting; adjust pressure to high (for large eggs), and set time for 5 minutes. Meanwhile, prepare an ice bath.

- When cooking is complete, allow pressure to naturally release for 5 minutes. Then move the pressure release to venting to release remaining steam. Open the pot and transfer the eggs to the ice bath to cool for 5 minutes. Peel when ready to use.

# FABULOUS FAJITAS

When friends call to ask for new recipes to try, suggest these flavorful fajitas.
It's wonderful to put the beef in the pressure cooker and quickly have a hot, delicious main dish.
—*Taste of Home Test Kitchen*

**PREP:** 20 min. ● **COOK:** 25 min. + releasing ● **MAKES:** 8 servings

1½ lbs. beef top sirloin steak, cut into
  thin strips
1½ tsp. ground cumin
½ tsp. seasoned salt
½ tsp. chili powder
¼ to ½ tsp. crushed red pepper flakes
2 Tbsp. canola oil
2 Tbsp. lemon juice
1 garlic clove, minced
1 large sweet red pepper, thinly sliced
1 large onion, thinly sliced
8 flour tortillas (8 in.), warmed
  Optional toppings: sliced avocado
    and jalapeno peppers, shredded
    cheddar cheese and chopped
    tomatoes

**1.** In a bowl, toss steak with cumin, salt, chili powder and red pepper flakes. Select saute setting and adjust for high heat on a 6-qt. electric pressure cooker. Heat oil; brown meat in batches. Add lemon juice and garlic to cooker; stir to loosen browned bits. Return beef to cooker. Lock lid; make sure vent is closed. Select manual setting; adjust pressure to high and set time for 20 minutes.

**2.** When finished cooking, allow pressure to naturally release for 10 minutes, then quick-release any remaining pressure according to the manufacturer's directions. Remove steak; keep warm.

**3.** Add red pepper and onion to cooker; lock lid. Select steam setting; cook for 5 minutes. When finished cooking, quick-release pressure according to manufacturer's directions. Serve vegetables and steak with tortillas and desired toppings.

**1 FAJITA:** 314 cal., 11g fat (2g sat. fat), 34mg chol., 374mg sod., 31g carb. (1g sugars, 2g fiber), 23g pro. **DIABETIC EXCHANGES:** 3 lean meat, 2 starch, 1 fat.

## THOSE HANDLES DOUBLE AS LID HOLDERS

Lid handles on newer models do double duty, holding the Instant Pot open with the lid out of the way. Not only is this great for the buffet line, it lets you store the appliance uncovered to ensure the inside fully dries.

# TURKEY WITH BERRY COMPOTE

This delicious dish is a terrific way to get all that yummy turkey flavor without heating up the house, and the berries make the perfect summer chutney. For a browner turkey, just broil for a few minutes before serving.
—*Margaret Bracher, Robertsdale, AL*

**PREP:** 15 min. + standing ● **COOK:** 45 min. + releasing ● **MAKES:** 12 servings (3¼ cups compote)

1 tsp. salt
½ tsp. garlic powder
½ tsp. dried thyme
½ tsp. pepper
2 boneless skinless turkey breast halves (2 lbs. each)
⅓ cup water

COMPOTE

2 medium apples, peeled and finely chopped
2 cups fresh raspberries
2 cups fresh blueberries
1 cup white grape juice
¼ tsp. crushed red pepper flakes
¼ tsp. ground ginger

**1.** Mix salt, garlic powder, thyme and pepper; rub over turkey breasts. Place in a 6-qt. electric pressure cooker. Pour water around turkey. Lock lid; make sure vent is closed. Select manual setting; adjust pressure to high and set time for 30 minutes. When finished cooking, allow pressure to naturally release for 10 minutes, then quick-release any remaining pressure according to manufacturer's directions. A thermometer inserted in the turkey breasts should read at least 165°.

**2.** Remove turkey and cooking juices from pressure cooker; tent with foil. Let stand before slicing.

**3.** Select saute setting on pressure cooker and adjust for high heat. Add the compote ingredients. Bring to a boil. Reduce heat; cook, uncovered, stirring occasionally, until mixture is slightly thickened and the apples are tender, 15-20 minutes. Serve turkey with compote.

**5 OZ. TURKEY WITH ¼ CUP COMPOTE:** 215 cal., 1g fat (0g sat. fat), 94mg chol., 272 mg sod., 12g carb. (8g sugars, 2g fiber), 38 g pro. **DIABETIC EXCHANGES:** 5 lean meat, 1 starch.

**✱ TEST KITCHEN TIP**

Use frozen fruit when fresh is out of season.

# MEDITERRANEAN CHICKEN ORZO

Orzo pasta with chicken, olives and herbes de Provence has the bright flavors
of Mediterranean cuisine. Here's a bonus: Leftovers reheat well.
—*Thomas Faglon, Somerset, NJ*

**PREP:** 15 min. ● **COOK:** 5 min. + standing ● **MAKES:** 6 servings

6 **boneless skinless chicken thighs (about 1½ lbs.), cut into 1-in. pieces**
2 **cups reduced-sodium chicken broth**
2 **medium tomatoes, chopped**
1 **cup sliced pitted green olives, drained**
1 **cup sliced pitted ripe olives, drained**
1 **large carrot, halved lengthwise and chopped**
1 **small red onion, finely chopped**
1 **Tbsp. grated lemon zest**
3 **Tbsp. lemon juice**
2 **Tbsp. butter**
1 **Tbsp. herbes de Provence**
1 **cup uncooked orzo pasta**

**1.** In a 6-qt. electric pressure cooker, combine the first 11 ingredients; stir to combine. Lock lid; make sure vent is closed. Select manual setting; adjust pressure to high and set time for 8 minutes. When finished cooking, quick-release pressure according to manufacturer's directions.

**2.** Add orzo. Lock lid; make sure vent is closed. Select manual setting; adjust pressure to low and set the time for 3 minutes. When finished cooking, allow pressure to naturally release for 4 minutes, then quick-release any remaining pressure according to manufacturer's directions. Let stand 8-10 minutes before serving.

**1 SERVING:** 415 cal., 19g fat (5g sat. fat), 86mg chol., 941mg sod., 33g carb. (4g sugars, 3g fiber), 27g pro.

### ✱ TEST KITCHEN TIP

Herbes de Provence is a mixture of dried spices associated with France's Provence region. It is available in the spice aisle. Use herbes de Provence to flavor mild main ingredients, like chicken, fish and vegetables.

# MELT-IN-YOUR-MOUTH CHUCK ROAST

My husband and I like well-seasoned foods, so this pressure-cooked recipe is terrific.
You'll also love how flavorful and tender this comforting roast turns out.
—*Bette McCumber, Schenectady, NY*

**PREP:** 20 min. ● **COOK:** 20 min. + releasing ● **MAKES:** 6 servings

1 can (14½ oz.) Italian stewed tomatoes, undrained
½ cup beef broth
½ cup ketchup
3 Tbsp. brown sugar
2 Tbsp. Worcestershire sauce
4 tsp. prepared mustard
3 garlic cloves, minced
1 Tbsp. soy sauce
2 tsp. pepper
¼ tsp. crushed red pepper flakes
1 large onion, halved and sliced
1 medium green pepper, halved and sliced
1 celery rib, chopped
1 boneless beef chuck roast (2 to 3 lbs.)
3 Tbsp. cornstarch
¼ cup cold water

**1.** In a bowl, mix first 10 ingredients. Place onion, green pepper and celery in a 6-qt. electric pressure cooker; place roast over top. Pour tomato mixture over roast. Lock lid; make sure vent is closed. Select manual setting; adjust pressure to high and set time for 35 minutes. When finished cooking, allow pressure to naturally release for 10 minutes and then quick-release any remaining pressure according to manufacturer's directions.

**2.** Remove roast. Strain cooking juices, reserving vegetables. Skim fat from juices. Return juices to the pressure cooker. Select saute setting and adjust for high heat; bring juices to a boil. In a small bowl, mix cornstarch and water until smooth; stir into cooking juices. Cook and stir until sauce is thickened, 1-2 minutes. Return beef mixture to pressure cooker. Stir. Serve roast and vegetables with gravy.

**1 SERVING:** 365 cal., 15g fat (6g sat. fat), 98mg chol., 792mg sod., 25g carb. (16g sugars, 2g fiber), 31g pro.

# MIXED FRUIT & PISTACHIO CAKE

This cake is easy to make on a lazy day and a guaranteed-delicious dessert for several days, if you can make it last that long. It's wonderful for fall and even the holidays.

*—Nancy Heishman, Las Vegas, NV*

**PREP:** 20 min. ● **COOK:** 50 min. + releasing ● **MAKES:** 8 servings

1 cup water
1½ cups all-purpose flour
1½ tsp. ground cinnamon
½ tsp. baking soda
½ tsp. baking powder
½ tsp. ground allspice
¼ tsp. salt
1 can (8 oz.) jellied cranberry sauce
⅓ cup packed brown sugar
⅓ cup buttermilk
¼ cup butter, melted
2 tsp. grated orange zest
½ tsp. orange extract
1 large egg
1 cup mixed dried fruit bits
1 cup pistachios, chopped
Whipped cream, optional

**1.** In a 6-qt. electric pressure cooker, add 1 cup of water.

**2.** In a bowl, whisk together the dry ingredients; In another bowl, combine next seven ingredients. Add cranberry mixture to the flour mixture; stir until smooth. Add dried fruit and pistachios.

**3.** Pour batter into a greased 1½-qt. baking dish. Place a piece of aluminum foil loosely on top of dish to prevent moisture from getting in; place on a trivet with handles. Lower dish into pressure cooker. Lock lid; make sure vent is closed. Select manual setting; adjust pressure to high and set time for 50 minutes.

**4.** When finished cooking, allow pressure to naturally release for 15 minutes, and then quick-release any remaining pressure according to manufacturer's directions. A toothpick inserted in center should come out clean. Remove baking dish from pressure cooker to a wire rack. Cool 30 minutes before inverting onto a serving platter.

**5.** Cut into wedges with a serrated knife; if desired, serve with sweetened whipped cream.

**1 SERVING:** 385 cal., 14g fat (5g sat. fat), 39mg chol., 364mg sod., 59g carb. (32g sugars, 4g fiber), 7g pro.

# CHERRY & SPICE RICE PUDDING

I live in Traverse City, which calls itself the cherry capital of the world. What better way to celebrate our wonderful fruit orchards than by using plump cherries in my favorite desserts? This pressure-cooked rice pudding recipe always turns out wonderfully.

—*Deb Perry, Traverse City, MI*

**PREP:** 15 min. ● **COOK:** 5 min. + releasing ● **MAKES:** 12 servings

4 cups cooked rice
1 can (12 oz.) evaporated milk
1 cup 2% milk
⅓ cup sugar
¼ cup water
¾ cup dried cherries
3 Tbsp. butter, softened
2 tsp. vanilla extract
½ tsp. ground cinnamon
¼ tsp. ground nutmeg

**1.** Generously grease a 6-qt. electric pressure cooker. Add rice, milks, sugar and water; stir to combine. Stir in the remaining ingredients.

**2.** Lock lid; make sure vent is closed. Select manual setting; adjust pressure to high and set time for 3 minutes. When finished cooking, allow pressure to naturally release for 5 minutes, then quick-release any remaining pressure according to the manufacturer's directions. Stir lightly. Serve warm or cold. Refrigerate leftovers.

**1 SERVING:** 202 cal., 6g fat (4g sat. fat), 19mg chol., 64mg sod., 33g carb. (16g sugars, 1g fiber), 4g pro.

**✱ TEST KITCHEN TIP**
Use any combination of dried fruits in this recipe. Top with whipped cream and a sprinkle of cinnamon.

# AIR FRYER

Fish and chips and fried chicken are just the beginning. You can also use the handy air fryer to roast a veggie side dish for a family dinner or bake up a little treat to cure a sweet craving anytime.

# AIR FRYER TIPS

**Get ready for crispy french fries, onion rings, chicken wings and more fun foods without the unpleasant mess or excess fat of deep-frying! Here's how to get started with the air fryer.**

- Some air fryers have digital screens with the setting options; others have simple timer and temperature dials. Choose the style you are most comfortable using.

- Some models can perform functions besides air-frying. These are often more expensive and can be larger; choose the model that best suits your needs.

- Many models are sized to cook for one or two people. Some have a larger capacity, allowing you to cook for up to four people at a time.

- With a smaller appliance, you may have to cook in batches, so be sure to account for that in your planning.

- Read the instruction manual before getting started.

- Ensure all packing material, tape, etc., has been removed from both outside and inside the appliance. Look up into the heating element as well (see photo on facing page), to make sure no stray material is lodged in the coil or fan. This can cause the appliance to smoke.

- Thoroughly wipe the heating coil before the first use to remove any residue.

## WHAT OUR TESTING REVEALED

Our Test Kitchen cooked recipes using six different air fryer models.

Cook times vary dramatically across the various brands of air fryers.

Our recipes have a wider than normal range of suggested cook times to accommodate that range.

Begin checking at the first time listed in the recipe and adjust as needed.

A. Heating coil
(shown bottom right)
B. Fan (inside unit)
C. Basket
D. Maximum fill line
E. Temp. setting
F. Time setting
G. Power
H. Basket release

## HERE'S HOW IT WORKS

The air fryer is basically a countertop convection oven. Because of its small size, this appliance heats up fast: The air fryer is ready to cook after about three minutes of heating.

The main unit holds a heating coil and a fan, and you put your food in the removable fryer basket below. Hot air rushes down and around the food in the basket. This rapid circulation makes the food crisp, much like deep-frying does, with little or no added cooking oil.

# COOK LIKE A PRO

**1. VERIFY THE TEMPERATURE.** Just like with ovens, temperatures may vary among air fryer models. Test your air fryer to see if it runs above or below the selected temperature setting.

**2. GIVE FOOD PLENTY OF AIR.** Cook food in a single layer, with room for air to circulate around the pieces. For crispy results, don't forget to flip, rotate or shake the basket's contents halfway through cooking.

**3. USE A THERMOMETER WHEN COOKING MEAT.** Because air-fried food can brown so nicely, it may look done before reaching an appropriate temperature on the inside. So check the temp with a thermometer for safety.

# CLEANING TIPS

**BASKET:** The basket, its holder and any dividing compartments that came with your air fryer are dishwasher-safe.

**GIVE IT A WIPE:** Unplug the appliance and gently wipe it clean with a damp cloth. That's it!

**CHECK THE COIL:** If there is oil or residue on the heating coil, let the unplugged machine cool, then wipe the coil with a damp cloth—just like the heating element on an electric stove.

# PEPPER POPPERS

These creamy stuffed jalapenos have some bite. They may be the most popular treats I make!
My husband is always hinting that I should make a batch.
—Lisa Byington, Johnson City, NY

**PREP:** 20 min. • **COOK:** 15 min./batch • **MAKES:** about 2 dozen

1 pkg. (8 oz.) cream cheese, softened
¾ cup shredded cheddar cheese
¾ cup shredded Monterey Jack cheese
6 bacon strips, cooked and crumbled
¼ tsp. salt
¼ tsp. garlic powder
¼ tsp. chili powder
¼ tsp. smoked paprika
1 lb. fresh jalapenos, halved lengthwise and seeded
½ cup dry bread crumbs
Sour cream, French onion dip, ranch salad dressing, optional

**1.** Preheat air fryer to 325°. In a large bowl, combine the cheeses, bacon and seasonings; mix well. Spoon 1½-2 tablespoonfuls into each pepper half. Roll in bread crumbs.

**2.** Spritz air fryer basket with cooking spray. Working in batches if needed, place poppers in a single layer in air fryer basket. Cook for 15 minutes for spicy flavor, 20 minutes for medium and 25 minutes for mild, being careful not to over overcook. If desired, serve with sour cream, dip or dressing.

**1 STUFFED PEPPER HALF:** 81 cal., 6g fat (4g sat. fat), 18mg chol., 145mg sod., 3g carb. (1g sugars, 1g fiber), 3g pro.

## HOW TO SEED A JALAPENO

Up to 80 percent of the capsaicin (the compound that gives peppers their heat) is in the seeds and the membranes. When handling hot peppers—especially if you have sensitive skin—wear rubber gloves and avoid touching your face. To reduce the heat in the dish, cut the peppers in half and use a spoon to scrape out the seeds and membranes. If you like very spicy foods, add a few of the seeds to the dish instead of discarding them.

# AIR-FRIED PICKLES

Like deep-fried pickles? You'll love this version even more. Dill pickle slices are coated with panko bread crumbs and spices, then air-fried until crispy. Dip them in ranch dressing for an appetizer you won't soon forget.
—*Nick Iverson, Denver, CO*

**PREP:** 20 min. + standing ● **COOK:** 15 min./batch ● **MAKES:** 32 slices

- 32 dill pickle slices
- ½ cup all-purpose flour
- ½ tsp. salt
- 3 large eggs, lightly beaten
- 2 Tbsp. dill pickle juice
- ½ tsp. cayenne pepper
- ½ tsp. garlic powder
- 2 cups panko (Japanese) bread crumbs
- 2 Tbsp. snipped fresh dill
  Cooking spray
  Ranch salad dressing, optional

**1.** Let pickles stand on a paper towel until liquid is almost absorbed, about 15 minutes. Preheat air fryer to 425°.

**2.** Meanwhile, in a shallow bowl, combine flour and salt. In another shallow bowl, whisk eggs, pickle juice, cayenne and garlic powder. Combine panko and dill in a third shallow bowl.

**3.** Dip pickles in flour mixture to coat both sides; shake off excess. Dip in egg mixture, then in crumb mixture, patting to help coating adhere. Spritz pickles and air fryer basket with cooking spray. Working in batches if needed, place pickles in a single layer in air fryer basket and cook until golden brown and crispy, 7-10 minutes. Turn pickles; spritz with additional cooking spray. Continue cooking until golden brown and crispy, 7-10 minutes. Serve immediately. If desired, serve with ranch dressing.

**1 PICKLE SLICE:** 26 cal., 1g fat (0 sat. fat), 13mg chol., 115mg sod., 4g carb. (0 sugars, 0 fiber), 1g pro.

# ROSEMARY SAUSAGE MEATBALLS

This recipe was created as an hors d'oeuvre for a friend's wedding and became an instant hit and family treasure. Enjoy!
—*Steve Hansen, Redmond, WA*

**PREP:** 20 min. • **COOK:** 10 min./batch • **MAKES:** about 2 dozen

2 Tbsp. olive oil
4 garlic cloves, minced
1 tsp. curry powder
1 large egg, lightly beaten
1 jar (4 oz.) diced pimientos, drained
¼ cup dry bread crumbs
¼ cup minced fresh parsley
1 Tbsp. minced fresh rosemary
2 lbs. bulk pork sausage
    Pretzel sticks or toothpicks,
        optional

**1.** Preheat air fryer to 400°. In a small skillet, heat oil over medium heat; saute garlic with curry powder until tender, 1-2 minutes. Cool slightly.

**2.** In a bowl, combine egg, pimientos, bread crumbs, parsley, rosemary and garlic mixture. Add sausage; mix lightly but thoroughly.

**3.** Shape into 1¼-in. balls. Place in a single layer in air fryer basket. Working in batches if needed, cook until lightly browned and cooked through, 7-10 minutes. Remove and keep warm; repeat with remaining meatballs. If desired, serve with pretzels.

**1 MEATBALL:** 96 cal., 8g fat (2g sat. fat), 24mg chol., 208mg sod., 2g carb. (0 sugars, 0 fiber), 4g pro.

**✳ TEST KITCHEN TIP**

To keep parsley fresh for up to a month, trim the stems and place the bunch in a tumbler with an inch of water. Be sure there are no leaves are in the water. Tie a produce bag around the tumbler to trap humidity; store in the refrigerator. Each time you use the parsley, change the water and turn the produce bag inside out so any moisture that has built up inside the bag can escape.

# QUENTIN'S PEACH-BOURBON WINGS

My father and husband love bourbon flavor, so I add it to tangy wings
air-fried in peach preserves. Stand back and watch these wings fly.
—*Christine Winston, Richmond, VA*

**PREP:** 35 min. ● **COOK:** 15 min./batch ● **MAKES:** about 1½ dozen pieces

½ cup peach preserves
1 Tbsp. brown sugar
1 garlic cloves, minced
¼ tsp. salt
2 Tbsp. white vinegar
2 Tbsp. bourbon
1 tsp. cornstarch
1½ tsp. water
2 lbs. chicken wings

**1.** Preheat air fryer to 400°. Place preserves, brown sugar, garlic and salt in a food processor; process until blended. Transfer to a small saucepan. Add vinegar and bourbon; bring to a boil. Reduce heat; simmer, uncovered, until slightly thickened, 4-6 minutes.

**2.** In a small bowl, mix cornstarch and water until smooth; stir into preserve mixture. Return to a boil, stirring constantly; cook and stir 1-2 minutes or until thickened. Reserve ¼ cup sauce for serving.

**3.** Using a sharp knife, cut through the two joints on each chicken wing; discard wing tips. Spray air fryer basket with cooking spray. Working in batches as needed, place wing pieces in a single layer in air fryer basket. Cook wings 6 minutes; turn and brush with the preserve mixture. Return to air fryer and cook until browned and juices run clear, 6-8 minutes longer. Remove and keep warm. Repeat with the remaining wing pieces. Serve wings immediately with reserved sauce.

**1 PIECE WITH ABOUT ½ TSP. SAUCE:** 79 cal., 3g fat (1g sat. fat), 15mg chol., 47mg sod., 7g carb. (6g sugars, 0 fiber), 5g pro.

# COCONUT SHRIMP & APRICOT SAUCE

Coconut and panko crumbs give this spicy shrimp its crunch. It's perfect for an appetizer or for your main meal.

—*Debi Mitchell, Flower Mound, TX*

**PREP:** 25 min. • **COOK:** 10 min./batch • **MAKES:** 6 servings

1½ lbs. uncooked large shrimp
1½ cups sweetened shredded coconut
½ cup panko (Japanese) bread crumbs
4 large egg whites
3 dashes Louisiana-style hot sauce
¼ tsp. salt
¼ tsp. pepper
½ cup all-purpose flour

**SAUCE**
1 cup apricot preserves
1 tsp. cider vinegar
¼ tsp. crushed red pepper flakes

**1.** Preheat air fryer to 375°. Peel and devein shrimp, leaving tails on.

**2.** In a shallow bowl, toss the coconut with bread crumbs. In another shallow bowl, whisk egg whites, hot sauce, salt and pepper. Place the flour in a third shallow bowl.

**3.** Dip shrimp in flour to coat lightly; shake off excess. Dip in egg white mixture, then in coconut mixture, patting to help coating adhere.

**4.** Spray air fryer basket with cooking spray. Working in batches as needed, place shrimp in a single layer in air fryer basket. Cook 4 minutes; turn shrimp and continue cooking until coconut is lightly browned and shrimp turn pink, about 4 minutes.

**5.** Meanwhile, combine the sauce ingredients in a small saucepan; cook and stir over medium-low heat until preserves are melted. Serve shrimp immediately with sauce.

**6 SHRIMP WITH 2 TBSP. SAUCE:** 410 cal., 10g fat (8g sat. fat), 138mg chol., 418mg sod., 58g carb. (34g sugars, 2g fiber), 24g pro.

## HOW TO PEEL & DEVEIN SHRIMP

Start on the underside by the head area to remove shell. Pull legs and first section of shell to one side. Continue pulling shell up and off. Leave tail on or remove if desired.

Remove the black vein running down the back of the shrimp by making a shallow slit with a paring knife along the back from head to tail.

Rinse shrimp under cold water to remove the vein.

# FISH & FRIES

Dine like you're in a traditional British pub. These moist fish fillets from the air fryer have a fuss-free coating that's healthier but just as crunchy and golden as the deep-fried kind. Simply seasoned, the crispy fries are perfect on the side.

—*Janice Mitchell, Aurora, CO*

**PREP:** 15 min. ● **COOK:** 25 min. ● **MAKES:** 4 servings

1 lb. potatoes (about 2 medium)
2 Tbsp. olive oil
¼ tsp. pepper
¼ tsp. salt
FISH
⅓ cup all-purpose flour
¼ tsp. pepper
1 large egg
2 Tbsp. water
⅔ cup crushed cornflakes
1 Tbsp. grated Parmesan cheese
⅛ tsp. cayenne pepper
¼ tsp. salt
1 lb. haddock or cod fillets
   Tartar sauce, optional

**1.** Preheat air fryer to 400°. Peel and cut potatoes lengthwise into ½-in.-thick slices; cut slices into ½-in.-thick sticks.

**2.** In a large bowl, toss the potatoes with oil, pepper and salt. Working in batches as needed, place potatoes in a single layer in air fryer basket; cook until just tender, 5-10 minutes. Toss potatoes in basket to redistribute; continue to cook until lightly browned and crisp, 5-10 minutes longer.

**3.** Meanwhile, in a shallow bowl, mix flour and pepper. In another shallow bowl, whisk egg with water. In a third bowl, toss cornflakes with cheese and cayenne. Sprinkle fish with salt; dip into flour mixture to coat both sides; shake off excess. Dip in egg mixture, then in cornflake mixture, patting to help coating adhere.

**4.** Remove fries from basket; keep warm. Place fish in a single layer in air fryer basket. Cook until fish is lightly browned and just beginning to flake easily with a fork, turning halfway through cooking, 8-10 minutes. Do not overcook them. Return fries to basket to heat through. Serve immediately. If desired, serve with tartar sauce.

**1 SERVING:** 312 cal., 9g fat (2g sat. fat), 85mg chol., 503mg sod., 35g carb. (3g sugars, 1g fiber), 23g pro. **DIABETIC EXCHANGES:** 3 lean meat, 2 starch, 2 fat.

**✱ STAFF HACK**

*"I love using my air fryer to cook frozen onion rings. They come out golden and crispy in a jiffy without frying them in oil. They're way better than oven-baked. No mess, no fuss, a perfect snack for just one or two...yum!"*

—MARK HAGEN, DEPUTY EDITOR

# GREEN TOMATO BLT

I have used this frying method on eggplant slices for years and decided to try it on my green tomatoes. It worked! Now my family loves them in BLTs.
—*Jolene Martinelli, Fremont, NH*

**PREP:** 20 min. ● **COOK:** 10 min./batch ● **MAKES:** 4 servings

2 medium green tomatoes (about 10 oz.)
½ tsp. salt
¼ tsp. pepper
1 large egg, beaten
¼ cup all-purpose flour
1 cup panko (Japanese) bread crumbs
 Cooking spray
½ cup reduced-fat mayonnaise
2 green onions, finely chopped
1 tsp. snipped fresh dill or ¼ tsp. dill weed
8 slices whole wheat bread, toasted
8 cooked center-cut bacon strips
4 Bibb or Boston lettuce leaves

**1.** Preheat air fryer to 350°. Spritz basket with cooking spray. Cut tomato into eight slices, about ¼ in. thick each. Sprinkle tomato slices with salt and pepper. Place egg, flour and bread crumbs in separate shallow bowls. Dip tomato slices in flour, shaking off excess, then dip into egg, and finally into bread crumb mixture, patting to help adhere.

**2.** Working in batches as needed, place tomato slices in a single layer in air fryer basket; spritz with cooking spray. Cook until slices are golden brown, 8-12 minutes, turning halfway and spritzing with additional cooking spray. Remove and keep warm; repeat with remaining tomato slices.

**3.** Meanwhile, mix mayonnaise, green onions and dill. Layer each of four slices of bread with two bacon strips, one lettuce leaf and two tomato slices. Spread mayonnaise mixture over remaining slices of bread; place over top. Serve immediately.

**1 SANDWICH:** 390 cal., 17g fat (3g sat. fat), 45mg chol., 1006mg sod., 45g carb. (7g sugars, 5g fiber), 16g pro.

# HERB & CHEESE-STUFFED BURGERS

Tired of the same old ground-beef burgers? This quick-fix alternative, with its creamy cheese filling, will wake up your taste buds.
—*Sherri Cox, Lucasville, OH*

**PREP:** 20 min. • **COOK:** 20 min./batch • **MAKES:** 4 servings

¼ cup cubed cheddar cheese
2 green onions, thinly sliced
2 Tbsp. minced fresh parsley
3 tsp. Dijon mustard, divided
3 Tbsp. dry bread crumbs
2 Tbsp. ketchup
½ tsp. salt
½ tsp. dried rosemary, crushed
¼ tsp. dried sage leaves
1 lb. lean ground beef (90% lean)
4 hamburger buns, split
Optional toppings: lettuce leaves and tomato slices

**1.** Preheat air fryer to 375°. In a small bowl, mix cheddar cheese, green onions, parsley and 1 tsp. mustard. In another bowl, mix bread crumbs, ketchup, seasonings and remaining mustard. Add beef to bread crumb mixture; mix lightly but thoroughly.

**2.** Shape meat mixture into eight thin patties. Spoon cheese mixture onto the center of four patties; top with remaining patties, pressing edges together firmly, taking care to seal completely.

**3.** Place burgers in a single layer in air fryer basket. Working in batches as needed, cook 10 minutes; flip and continue cooking until a thermometer reads 160°, 8-10 minutes longer.

**1 BURGER:** 369 cal., 14g fat (6g sat. fat), 79mg chol., 850mg sod., 29g carb. (6g sugars, 1g fiber), 29g pro.

# EVERYTHING BAGEL CHICKEN STRIPS

I love the flavor profile of everything bagels, so I recreated it with traditional breaded chicken fingers. Serve them with your favorite dipping sauce.
—*Cyndy Gerken, Naples, FL*

**PREP:** 15 min. ● **COOK:** 15 min./batch ● **MAKES:** 4 servings

1 day-old everything bagel, torn
½ cup panko (Japanese) bread crumbs
½ cup grated Parmesan cheese
¼ tsp. crushed red pepper flakes
¼ cup butter, cubed
1 lb. chicken tenderloins
½ tsp. salt

1. Preheat air fryer to 400°. Pulse torn bagel in a food processor until coarse crumbs form. Place ½ cup bagel crumbs in a shallow bowl; toss with panko, cheese and pepper flakes. (Discard or save remaining bagel crumbs for another use.)

2. In a microwave-safe shallow bowl, microwave the butter until melted. Sprinkle chicken tenderloins with salt. Dip in warm butter, then coat with crumb mixture, patting to help adhere. Spray air fryer basket with cooking spray. Place chicken in a single layer in air fryer basket.

3. Working in batches if needed, cook 7 minutes; turn chicken over. Continue cooking until coating is golden brown and chicken is no longer pink, 7-8 minutes. Serve immediately.

**1 SERVING:** 269 cal., 13g fat (7g sat. fat), 88mg chol., 663mg sod., 8g carb. (1g sugars, 0 fiber), 31g pro.

# RASPBERRY BALSAMIC SMOKED PORK CHOPS

*Smoked chops are so delicious and so easy to make. My husband loves them.*
*—Lynn Moretti, Oconomowoc, WI*

**PREP:** 15 min. ● **COOK:** 15 min./batch ● **MAKES:** 4 servings

2 large eggs
¼ cup 2% milk
1 cup panko (Japanese) bread crumbs
1 cup finely chopped pecans
4 smoked bone-in pork chops (7½ oz. each )
¼ cup all-purpose flour
  Cooking spray
⅓ cup balsamic vinegar
2 Tbsp. brown sugar
2 Tbsp. seedless raspberry jam
1 Tbsp. thawed frozen orange juice concentrate

1. Preheat air fryer to 400°. Spritz air fryer basket with cooking spray. In a shallow bowl, whisk together eggs and milk. In another shallow bowl, toss bread crumbs with pecans.

2. Coat pork chops with flour; shake off excess. Dip in egg mixture, then in crumb mixture, patting to help adhere. Working in batches as needed, place chops in single layer in air fryer basket; spritz with cooking spray.

3. Cook until chops are golden brown, 12-15 minutes, turning them halfway through cooking and spritzing with additional cooking spray. Remove and keep warm. Repeat with remaining chops. Meanwhile, place remaining ingredients in a small saucepan; bring to a boil. Cook and stir until slightly thickened, 6-8 minutes. Serve with pork chops.

**1 PORK CHOP WITH 1 TBSP. GLAZE:** 579 cal., 36g fat (10g sat. fat), 106mg chol., 1374mg sod., 36g carb. (22g sugars, 3g fiber), 32g pro.

# REUBEN CALZONES

I love a Reuben sandwich, so I tried the fillings in a pizza pocket instead of on rye bread. This hand-held dinner is a big-time winner at our house.
—*Nickie Frye, Evansville, IN*

**PREP:** 15 min. ● **COOK:** 10 min./batch ● **MAKES:** 4 servings

1 tube (13.8 oz.) refrigerated pizza crust
4 slices Swiss cheese
1 cup sauerkraut, rinsed and well drained
½ lb. sliced cooked corned beef
Thousand Island salad dressing

1. Preheat air fryer to 400°. Spritz air fryer basket with cooking spray. On a lightly floured surface, unroll pizza crust dough and pat into a 12-in. square. Cut into four squares. Layer one slice of cheese and a fourth of the sauerkraut and corned beef diagonally over half of each square to within ½ in. of edges. Fold one corner over filling to the opposite corner, forming a triangle; press edges with a fork to seal. Place two calzones in a single layer in a greased air fryer basket.

2. Cook until calzones are golden brown, 8-12 minutes, flipping halfway through cooking. Remove and keep warm; repeat with remaining calzones. Serve with salad dressing.

**1 CALZONE:** 430 cal., 17g fat (6g sat. fat), 66mg chol., 1471mg sod., 49g carb. (7g sugars, 2g fiber), 21g pro.

# SOUTHERN-STYLE CHICKEN

I call this America's best-loved chicken. The secret is in the breading, which
makes the chicken super moist and flavorful, herby and golden brown.
—*Elaina Morgan, Rickman, TN*

**PREP:** 15 min. • **COOK:** 20 min./batch • **MAKES:** 6 servings

2 cups crushed Ritz crackers
1 Tbsp. minced fresh parsley
1 tsp. garlic salt
1 tsp. paprika
½ tsp. pepper
¼ tsp. ground cumin
¼ tsp. rubbed sage
1 large egg, beaten
1 broiler/fryer chicken (3 to 4 lbs.),
   cut up
   Cooking spray

1. Preheat air fryer to 375°. Spritz the air fryer basket with cooking spray.

2. In a shallow bowl, combine the first seven ingredients. Place the egg in a separate shallow bowl. Dip chicken in egg, then in cracker mixture, patting to help coating adhere. Place a few pieces of chicken in a single layer in prepared basket; spritz with cooking spray.

3. Cook 10 minutes. Turn chicken and spritz with additional cooking spray; cook until chicken is golden brown and juices run clear, 10-20 minutes longer. Repeat with remaining chicken.

**5 OZ. COOKED CHICKEN:** 405 cal., 22g fat (6g sat. fat), 135mg chol., 460mg sod., 13g carb. (2g sugars, 1g fiber), 36g pro.

# WASABI CRAB CAKES

With wasabi in both the crab cakes and the dipping sauce, this festive appetizer brings its own heat to the holiday party.
—*Marie Rizzio, Interlochen, MI*

**PREP:** 20 min. • **COOK:** 10 min./batch • **MAKES:** 2 dozen (½ cup sauce)

1 medium sweet red pepper, finely
   chopped
1 celery rib, finely chopped
3 green onions, finely chopped
2 large egg whites
3 Tbsp. reduced-fat mayonnaise
¼ tsp. prepared wasabi
¼ tsp. salt
⅓ cup plus ½ cup dry bread crumbs,
   divided
1½ cups lump crabmeat, drained
   Cooking spray
**SAUCE**
1 celery rib, chopped
⅓ cup reduced-fat mayonnaise
1 green onion, chopped

1 Tbsp. sweet pickle relish
½ tsp. prepared wasabi
¼ tsp. celery salt

1. Preheat air fryer to 375°. Spritz the air fryer basket with cooking spray. Combine first seven ingredients; add ⅓ cup bread crumbs. Gently fold in crab.

2. Place remaining crumbs in a shallow bowl. Drop heaping tablespoonfuls of crab mixture into crumbs. Gently coat and shape into ¾-in.-thick patties. Working in batches as needed, place crab cakes in a single layer in air fryer basket. Spritz crab cakes with cooking spray. Cook cakes until golden brown, 8-12 minutes, carefully turning halfway through cooking and spritzing with additional cooking spray. Remove and keep warm. Repeat with remaining crab cakes.

3. Meanwhile, place sauce ingredients in food processor; pulse two to three times to blend or until the desired consistency is reached. Serve crab cakes immediately with dipping sauce.

**1 CRAB CAKE WITH 1 TSP. SAUCE:** 49 cal., 2g fat (0 sat. fat), 13mg chol., 179mg sod., 4g carb. (1g sugars, 0 fiber), 3g pro.

# EGGPLANT FRIES

My kids love this snack—and I like that it's healthy. Coated with Italian seasoning, Parmesan cheese and garlic salt, these are delicious and guilt-free.
—*Mary Murphy, Atwater, CA*

**PREP:** 15 min. • **COOK:** 10 min./batch • **MAKES:** 6 servings

2 large eggs
½ cup grated Parmesan cheese
½ cup toasted wheat germ
1 tsp. Italian seasoning
¾ tsp. garlic salt
1 medium eggplant (about 1¼ lbs.)
    Cooking spray
1 cup meatless pasta sauce, warmed

**1.** Preheat air fryer to 400°. In a shallow bowl, whisk eggs. In another shallow bowl, mix cheese, wheat germ and seasonings.

**2.** Trim ends of eggplant; cut eggplant lengthwise into ½-in.-thick slices. Cut slices lengthwise into ½-in. strips. Dip eggplant in eggs, then coat with the cheese mixture.

**3.** Spritz eggplant and air fryer basket with cooking spray. Working in batches if needed, place eggplant in a single layer in air fryer basket and cook until golden brown, 5-7 minutes. Turn the eggplant; spritz with additional cooking spray. Continue cooking until golden brown, 4-5 minutes. Serve immediately with pasta dipping sauce.

**1 SERVING:** 135 cal., 5g fat (2g sat. fat), 68mg chol., 577mg sod., 15g carb. (6g sugars, 4g fiber), 9g pro. **DIABETIC EXCHANGES:** 1 vegetable, 1 fat, ½ starch.

# GARLIC-ROSEMARY BRUSSELS SPROUTS

This is my go-to Thanksgiving side dish. It's healthy, easy and doesn't take very much time or effort to make. I usually season my turkey with rosemary, so this lets me use up some of the leftover herbs!

—*Elisabeth Larsen, Pleasant Grove, UT*

**TAKES:** 30 min. ● **MAKES:** 4 servings

3 Tbsp. olive oil
2 garlic cloves, minced
½ tsp. salt
¼ tsp. pepper
1 lb. Brussels sprouts, trimmed and halved
½ cup panko (Japanese) bread crumbs
1½ tsp. minced fresh rosemary

**1.** Preheat air fryer to 350°. Place first four ingredients in a small microwave-safe bowl; microwave on high for 30 seconds.

**2.** Toss the Brussels sprouts with 2 Tbsp. oil mixture. Place all the sprouts in air fryer basket and cook 4-5 minutes. Stir sprouts. Continue to cook, stirring every 4-5 minutes, until sprouts are nearing desired tenderness and are lightly browned, about 8 minutes longer.

**3.** Toss bread crumbs with rosemary and remaining oil mixture; sprinkle over sprouts. Continue cooking until the crumbs are browned and the sprouts are tender, 3-5 minutes. Serve immediately.

**¾ CUP:** 164 cal., 11g fat (1g sat. fat), 0 chol., 342mg sod., 15g carb. (3g sugars, 4g fiber), 5g pro. **DIABETIC EXCHANGES:** 2 fat, 1 vegetable, ½ starch.

# LEMON SLICE SUGAR COOKIES

Here's a refreshing variation of my grandmother's sugar cookie recipe.
Lemon pudding mix and icing add a subtle tartness that tingles your taste buds.
—Melissa Turkington, Camano Island, WA

**PREP:** 15 min. + chilling • **COOK:** 10 min./ batch + cooling • **MAKES:** about 2 dozen

- ½ cup unsalted butter, softened
- 1 pkg. (3.4 oz.) instant lemon pudding mix
- ½ cup sugar
- 1 large egg
- 2 Tbsp. 2% milk
- 1½ cups all-purpose flour
- 1 tsp. baking powder
- ¼ tsp. salt

ICING
- ⅔ cup confectioners' sugar
- 2 to 4 tsp. lemon juice

**1.** In a large bowl, cream the butter, pudding mix and sugar until light and fluffy. Beat in egg and milk. In another bowl, whisk flour, baking powder and salt; gradually beat into creamed mixture.

**2.** Divide dough in half. On a lightly floured surface, shape each into a 6-in.-long roll. Wrap and refrigerate 3 hours or until firm.

**3.** Preheat air fryer to 325°. Unwrap and cut dough crosswise into ½-in. slices. Place slices in a single layer in foil-lined air fryer basket. Cook until edges are light brown, 8-12 minutes. Cool in basket 2 minutes. Remove to wire racks to cool completely. Repeat with remaining dough.

**4.** In a small bowl, mix confectioners' sugar and enough lemon juice to reach a drizzling consistency. Drizzle over cookies. Let stand until set.

**FREEZE OPTION:** Place wrapped logs in a resealable container and freeze. To use, unwrap frozen logs and cut into slices. Cook as directed, increasing time by 1-2 minutes.

**1 COOKIE:** 110 cal., 4g fat (2g sat. fat), 18mg chol., 99mg sod., 17g carb. (11g sugars, 0 fiber), 1g pro.

### ✳ TEST KITCHEN TIP

Slice-and-bake cookies make a great last-minute treat. Just pull the dough out of the freezer, slice off as many cookies as you'd like, and pop the roll back in.

COFFEE KLATCH
**FRESH-BAKED ROLLS TO ORDER**

# BOURBON BACON CINNAMON ROLLS

This recipe is the perfect combination of savory and sweet. The bourbon-soaked bacon adds a smoky, savory, bold taste to cinnamon rolls. The ginger and pecan topping makes for a crunchy, spicy finish.
—*Shannen Casey, Berkeley, CA*

**PREP:** 25 min. + marinating ● **COOK:** 10 min./batch ● **MAKES:** 8 rolls

8 **bacon strips**
¾ **cup bourbon**
1 **tube (12.4 oz.) refrigerated cinnamon rolls with icing**
½ **cup chopped pecans**
2 **Tbsp. maple syrup**
1 **tsp. minced fresh gingerroot**

1. Place bacon in a shallow dish; add bourbon. Seal and refrigerate overnight. Remove bacon and pat dry; discard bourbon.

2. In a large skillet, cook the bacon in batches over medium heat until nearly crisp but still pliable. Remove to paper towels to drain. Discard all but 1 tsp. drippings.

3. Preheat air fryer to 350°. Separate dough into eight rolls, reserving icing packet. Unroll spiral rolls into long strips; pat dough to form 6x1-in. strips. Place one bacon strip on each strip of dough, trimming bacon as needed; reroll, forming a spiral. Pinch ends to seal. Repeat with remaining dough. Transfer four rolls to air fryer basket; cook 5 minutes. Turn rolls over and cook until rolls are golden brown, about 4 minutes.

4. Meanwhile, combine pecans and maple syrup. In another bowl, stir ginger together with contents of icing packet. In same skillet, heat remaining bacon drippings over medium heat. Add pecan mixture; cook, stirring frequently, until lightly toasted, 2-3 minutes.

5. Drizzle half of icing over warm cinnamon rolls; top with half of pecans. Repeat to make a second batch.

**1 ROLL:** 267 cal., 14g fat (3g sat. fat), 9mg chol., 490mg sod., 28g carb. (13g sugars, 1g fiber), 5g pro.

# SLOW COOKER

To our dear hardworking slow cookers, thank you for the many warm welcome-homes! Thanks for freeing up holiday oven space, for making us the most put-together party hosts on the block, and for being the all-around potluck star that you are. We love you!

*DON'T BE TEMPTED TO LIFT THE LID*

*BROWN YOUR MEAT IN A SKILLET*

*PREP INGREDIENTS THE NIGHT BEFORE*

# SLOW-COOK WITH CONFIDENCE

**Follow these tips for slow-cooking success every time.**

- **PLAN AHEAD TO PREP AND GO.** In most cases, you can prepare and load ingredients into the slow-cooker insert beforehand and store it in the refrigerator overnight. But an insert can crack if exposed to rapid temperature changes. Let the insert sit out just long enough to reach room temperature (20-30 minutes) before placing in the slow cooker.

- **USE THAWED INGREDIENTS.** Although throwing frozen chicken breasts into the slow cooker may seem easy, it's not a smart shortcut. Thawing foods in a slow cooker can create the ideal environment for bacteria to grow, so thaw frozen meat and veggies ahead of time. The exception is if you're using a prepackaged slow-cooker meal kit and follow the instructions as written.

- **TAKE THE TIME TO BROWN.** Give yourself a few extra minutes to brown the meat in a pan before placing in the slow cooker. Doing so adds rich color and flavor to the dish.

- **MAKE USE OF SMART LAYERING.** Dense foods like potatoes can take a long time to cook. They are often layered in the bottom of the slow cooker, where they can be closer to the heat than an item that is layered on top. For best results, always follow any layering instructions that a recipe provides.

- **ADJUST COOK TIME FOR HIGH ALTITUDE.** Slow-cooking will take longer at high altitude. Add about 30 minutes for each hour of cooking the recipe calls for; legumes will take about twice as long.

- **WANT YOUR FOOD READY SOONER?** Cooking 1 hour on high is roughly equal to 2 hours on low, so adjust the recipe to suit your schedule.

## HOW TO KEEP YOUR COOKER CLEAN

**ALLOW** the stoneware insert to cool before rinsing it. Wash it in the dishwasher or in the sink with warm, soapy water.

**DO NOT** use abrasive cleansers.

**USE** a damp sponge to clean the metal base. Do not soak the base in water.

**TO REMOVE** white mineral stains from the insert, fill the cooker with hot water mixed with 1 cup of white vinegar and heat on high for two hours. Empty the insert, let it cool, and wash as usual.

# TOP 10 TIPS FOR SLOW-COOKING

1. **READ THE RECIPE FIRST.** Not only will this ensure you have all the ingredients on hand, but reading the recipe allows you to consider and adjust time elements if necessary. If you live at a high altitude, for instance, you'll need to adjust the cooking time accordingly (see how to do that on facing page).

2. **CHOOSE THE RIGHT CUT OF MEAT.** Lower-cost cuts work better than higher-priced lean cuts. Trim excess fat from the outside, but look for good marbling on the inside. It will break down during cooking and make the meat tender.

3. **MAKE SURE THE LID FITS.** Be sure the lid is secure, not tilted or askew. Steam held in during cooking creates a seal.

4. **GO EASY ON THE ALCOHOL.** Alcohol won't evaporate from the slow cooker, so use sparingly. If you brown the meat, use wine to deglaze the pan, then pour the liquid into the slow cooker. This bit of cooking on the stovetop will burn off the alcohol but leave the flavor.

5. **DON'T OVERFILL OR UNDERFILL.** Fill the slow cooker between half and two–thirds full. Less than half full, the food may burn. More than two–thirds full, the food may not cook completely.

6. **DON'T LET IT GET COLD.** If you won't be home when the cooking time is up, be sure the cooker will switch itself to warm. Temperatures between 40° and 140° allow bacteria to thrive.

7. **HALVE THE TIME BY DOUBLING THE SETTING.** On most models, low is 170° and high is 280°. For many recipes, cranking up the heat will cut down the cook time.

8. **DON'T PEEK!** Each time you lift the lid, you'll need to add 15-30 minutes of cooking time. Open only when the recipes calls for it.

9. **AVOID TEMPERATURE SHOCKS.** If your cooker has a ceramic insert, put a dish towel on a cold work surface before setting the hot insert down. Do not preheat your cooker. A cold insert should always be put into a cold base.

10. **KEEP IT FRESH.** Don't use your slow cooker to reheat food. Instead, use the microwave, oven or stovetop.

## HOW TO CONVERT RECIPES FOR THE SLOW COOKER

Almost any recipe that bakes in the oven or simmers on the stovetop can be converted for the slow cooker. Here are some guidelines.

- Select recipes that simmer for at least 45 minutes. Good choices are soups, stews, pot roasts, chili and one-dish meals.
- Look for a slow-cooker recipe that's similar to the one you want to convert. Note the quantity and size of the meat and vegetables, heat setting and cooking time.
- There's no evaporation from a slow cooker, so if a recipe calls for liquid, you'll need to use less. If a recipe calls for 6 to 8 cups of water, start with 5 cups. But if the recipe doesn't call for any liquid, add about ½ cup of water, broth or juice—all slow cooker recipes should include some liquid.

## COOK TIMES

| Conventional Oven | Slow Cooker |
| --- | --- |
| 15 to 30 minutes | Low: 4 to 6 hours<br>High: 1½ to 2 hours |
| 35 to 45 minutes | Low: 6 to 8 hours<br>High: 3 to 4 hours |
| 50 minutes or more | Low: 8 to 10 hours<br>High: 4 to 6 hours |

# HOW TO LINE THE CROCK

**Some recipes may benefit from a foil sling or collar. Here's why:**

- A **sling** (pictured left and lower right) helps you lift foods out of the crock without much fuss. To make, fold one or more pieces of heavy-duty foil into strips. Place on bottom and up sides of the slow cooker; coat with cooking spray.

- A **foil collar** (not shown) prevents rich, saucy dishes from scorching near the slow cooker's heating element. To make a collar, fold two 18-in.-long pieces of foil into strips 4 in. wide. Line the crock's perimeter with the strips; coat with cooking spray.

# SWEET & TANGY CHICKEN WINGS

This slow cooker recipe is perfect for parties. Start the wings before you prepare
for the party, and in a few hours, you'll have wonderful appetizers!
—*Ida Tuey, South Lyon, MI*

**PREP:** 20 min. ● **COOK:** 3¼ hours ● **MAKES:** about 2½ dozen

- 3 lbs. chicken wingettes (about 30)
- ½ tsp. salt, divided
- Dash pepper
- 1½ cups ketchup
- ¼ cup packed brown sugar
- ¼ cup red wine vinegar
- 2 Tbsp. Worcestershire sauce
- 1 Tbsp. Dijon mustard
- 1 tsp. minced garlic
- 1 tsp. liquid smoke, optional
- Sliced jalapeno peppers, finely chopped red onion and sesame seeds, optional

**1.** Sprinkle chicken with a dash of salt and pepper. Broil 4-6 in. from the heat until golden brown, 6-8 minutes on each side. Transfer to a greased 5-qt. slow cooker.

**2.** Combine the ketchup, brown sugar, red wine vinegar, Worcestershire sauce, mustard, garlic, liquid smoke, if desired, and remaining salt; pour over wings. Toss to coat.

**3.** Cover and cook on low until chicken is tender, 2-3 hours. If desired, top with jalapenos, onion and sesame seeds to serve.

**FREEZE OPTION:** Freeze cooled fully cooked wings in freezer containers. To use, partially thaw in refrigerator overnight. Reheat wings in a foil-lined 15x10x1-in. baking pan in a preheated 325° oven until wings are heated through, covering if necessary to prevent browning. Serve as directed.

**1 SERVING:** 116 cal., 7g fat (2g sat. fat), 32mg chol., 225mg sod., 5g carb. (3g sugars, 0 fiber), 8g pro.

# PINEAPPLE-ORANGE SPICED TEA

My daughter served this for a holiday open house, and coffee drinkers were instantly converted.
—*Carole J. Drennan, Abilene, TX*

**PREP:** 15 min. ● **COOK:** 2 hours ● **MAKES:** 12 servings (3 qt.)

2 qt. boiling water
16 individual tea bags
2 cinnamon sticks (3 in.)
1 piece fresh gingerroot (½ in.), peeled and thinly sliced
4 whole cloves
1 cup sugar
1 can (12 oz.) frozen orange juice concentrate, thawed
1 can (12 oz.) frozen pineapple juice concentrate, thawed
1 cup pomegranate or cranberry juice
½ cup lemon juice
    Orange slices, optional

1. In a 5- or 6-qt. slow cooker, combine boiling water and tea bags. Cover and let stand 5 minutes.

2. Meanwhile, place the cinnamon sticks, ginger and cloves on a double thickness of cheesecloth. Gather the corners of cloth to enclose seasonings; tie securely with string. Discard the tea bags. Stir in remaining ingredients; add spice bag. Cook, covered, on low until heated through, 2-3 hours. Discard the spice bag. Stir before serving. If desired, serve with orange slices.

**1 CUP:** 173 cal., 0 fat (0 sat. fat), 0 chol., 10mg sod., 43g carb. (41g sugars, 1g fiber), 1g pro.

# SPINACH & ARTICHOKE DIP

With this creamy dip, I can get my daughters to eat spinach and artichokes. We serve it with chips, toasted pitas or veggies.
—*Jennifer Stowell, Deep River, IA*

**PREP:** 10 min. ● **COOK:** 2 hours ● **MAKES:** 8 cups

2 cans (14 oz. each) water-packed artichoke hearts, drained and chopped
2 pkg. (10 oz. each) frozen chopped spinach, thawed and squeezed dry
1 jar (15 oz.) Alfredo sauce
1 pkg. (8 oz.) cream cheese, cubed
2 cups shredded Italian cheese blend
1 cup shredded part-skim mozzarella cheese
1 cup shredded Parmesan cheese
1 cup 2% milk
2 garlic cloves, minced
    Assorted crackers and/or cucumber slices

In a greased 4-qt. slow cooker, combine the first nine ingredients. Cook, covered, on low until heated through, 2-3 hours. Serve with crackers and/or cucumber slices.

**¼ CUP:** 105 cal., 7g fat (4g sat. fat), 21mg chol., 276mg sod., 5g carb. (1g sugars, 1g fiber), 6g pro.

# MINI TERIYAKI TURKEY SANDWICHES

Preparing pulled turkey in a delicious teriyaki sauce for these snack-size sandwiches is a breeze using a slow cooker. Serve them on lightly toasted sweet dinner rolls for the finishing touch.
—Amanda Hoop, Seaman, OH

**PREP:** 20 min. ● **COOK:** 5½ hours ● **MAKES:** 20 sandwiches

2  boneless skinless turkey breast halves (2 lbs. each)
⅔  cup packed brown sugar
⅔  cup reduced-sodium soy sauce
¼  cup cider vinegar
3  garlic cloves, minced
1  Tbsp. minced fresh gingerroot
½  tsp. pepper
2  Tbsp. cornstarch
2  Tbsp. cold water
20  Hawaiian sweet rolls
2  Tbsp. butter, melted

1. Place turkey in a 5- or 6-qt. slow cooker. In a small bowl, combine the brown sugar, soy sauce, vinegar, garlic, ginger and pepper; pour over turkey. Cook, covered, on low until meat is tender, 5-6 hours.

2. Remove turkey from slow cooker. In a small bowl, mix cornstarch and cold water until smooth; gradually stir into cooking liquid. When cool enough to handle, shred meat with two forks and return meat to slow cooker. Cook, covered, on high until the sauce is thickened, 30-35 minutes.

3. Preheat oven to 325°. Split rolls and brush cut sides with butter; place on an ungreased baking sheet, cut side up. Bake 8-10 minutes or until toasted and golden brown. Spoon ⅓ cup turkey mixture on roll bottoms. Replace tops.

**1 SANDWICH:** 252 cal., 5g fat (2g sat. fat), 70mg chol., 501mg sod., 25g carb. (13g sugars, 1g fiber), 26g pro.

**✱ TEST KITCHEN TIP**
This recipe also works well with boneless skinless chicken breasts.

# EFFORTLESS BLACK BEAN CHILI

My mom found the inspiration for this chili in a slow-cooker cookbook. After a few updates, all of us love it (even those of us who usually steer clear of beans). We think it's even better served over rice.

—*Amelia Gormley, Ephrata, PA*

**PREP:** 25 min. • **COOK:** 6 hours • **MAKES:** 6 servings (1½ qt.)

1 lb. ground turkey
1 small onion, chopped
3 tsp. chili powder
2 tsp. minced fresh oregano or ¾ tsp. dried oregano
1 tsp. chicken bouillon granules
1 jar (16 oz.) mild salsa
1 can (15¼ oz.) whole kernel corn, drained
1 can (15 oz.) black beans, rinsed and drained
1 can (14½ oz.) diced tomatoes, undrained
½ cup water
  Optional toppings: sour cream, finely chopped red onion and corn chips

**1.** In a large skillet, cook and crumble turkey with onion over medium-high heat until no longer pink, 5-7 minutes. Transfer to a 4-qt. slow cooker.

**2.** Stir in all remaining ingredients except toppings. Cook, covered, on low until flavors are blended, 6-8 hours. Top as desired.

**1 CUP:** 242 cal., 6g fat (1g sat. fat), 50mg chol., 868mg sod., 26g carb. (9g sugars, 6g fiber), 20g pro.

**✱ TEST KITCHEN TIP**

If you prefer frozen corn, substitute about 1¾ cups of it for the can called for in the recipe.

# POTATO SOUP

I decided to add some character to a basic potato chowder by adding roasted red peppers. The extra flavor gives a deliciously unique twist to this otherwise classic soup.

—*Mary Shivers, Ada, OK*

**PREP:** 20 min. ● **COOK:** 5½ hours ● **MAKES:** 12 servings (3 qt.)

3 lbs. potatoes, peeled and cut into ½-in. cubes (8 cups)

1 large onion, chopped

1 jar (7 oz.) roasted sweet red peppers, drained and chopped

1 small celery rib, chopped

6 cups chicken broth

½ tsp. garlic powder

½ tsp. seasoned salt

½ tsp. pepper

⅛ tsp. rubbed sage

⅓ cup all-purpose flour

2 cups heavy whipping cream, divided

1 cup grated Parmesan cheese, divided

8 bacon strips, cooked and crumbled

2 Tbsp. minced fresh cilantro

**1.** Place the first nine ingredients in a 5- or 6-qt. slow cooker. Cook, covered, on low until the potatoes are tender, 5-6 hours.

**2.** Mix flour and ½ cup cream until smooth; stir into soup. Stir in ¾ cup cheese, bacon, cilantro and remaining cream. Cook, covered, on low until slightly thickened, about 30 minutes. Serve with remaining cheese.

**1 CUP:** 289 cal., 19g fat (11g sat. fat), 59mg chol., 848mg sod., 23g carb. (4g sugars, 1g fiber), 7g pro.

✱ **TEST KITCHEN TIP**

Any combination of potatoes will work in this recipe, but russet potatoes hold up best to the heat.

TACO TUESDAY
**MAKE IT QUICK WITH
DELI COLESLAW**

# BARBECUE PORK TACOS WITH APPLE SLAW

We celebrate taco Tuesdays, so I keep things interesting by switching up
the varieties. These pork tacos are super simple to make.
—*Jenn Tidwell, Fair Oaks, CA*

**PREP:** 15 min. ● **COOK:** 2¼ hours ● **MAKES:** 8 servings (16 tacos)

2 pork tenderloins (1 lb. each)
1 can (12 oz.) root beer
**SLAW**
6 cups shredded red cabbage (about 12 oz.)
2 medium Granny Smith apples, julienned
⅓ cup cider vinegar
¼ cup minced fresh cilantro
¼ cup lime juice
2 Tbsp. sugar
½ tsp. salt
½ tsp. pepper
**ASSEMBLY**
1 bottle (18 oz.) barbecue sauce
16 taco shells

**1.** Place pork in a 3-qt. slow cooker. Pour the root beer over top. Cook, covered, on low just until tender (a thermometer inserted in pork should read at least 145°), 2-2½ hours.

**2.** Meanwhile, in a large bowl, toss the slaw ingredients. Refrigerate, covered, until serving.

**3.** Remove tenderloins to a cutting board; let stand, covered, 5 minutes. Discard cooking juices.

**4.** Coarsely chop pork; return to slow cooker. Stir in barbecue sauce; heat through. Serve in taco shells; top with some of the slaw. Serve remaining slaw on the side.

**2 TACOS WITH 1 CUP SLAW:** 396 cal., 9g fat (2g sat. fat), 64mg chol., 954mg sod., 53g carb. (31g sugars, 3g fiber), 25g pro.

# CHEDDAR-TOPPED BARBECUE MEAT LOAF

My family loves the bold barbecue flavor of this tender meat loaf.
I love that it's such an easy recipe to prepare in the slow cooker.
—*David Snodgrass, Columbia, MO*

**PREP:** 20 min. • **COOK:** 3¼ hours • **MAKES:** 8 servings

3  large eggs, lightly beaten
¾  cup old-fashioned oats
1  large sweet red or green pepper, chopped (about 1½ cups)
1  small onion, finely chopped
1  envelope onion soup mix
3  garlic cloves, minced
½  tsp. salt
¼  tsp. pepper
2  lbs. lean ground beef (90% lean)
1  cup ketchup
2  Tbsp. brown sugar
1  Tbsp. barbecue seasoning
1  tsp. ground mustard
1  cup shredded cheddar cheese

**1.** Cut three 18x3-in. strips of heavy-duty foil; crisscross so they resemble spokes of a wheel. Place strips on bottom and up sides of a 3-qt. slow cooker. Coat strips with cooking spray.

**2.** In a large bowl, combine eggs, oats, chopped pepper, onion, soup mix, garlic, salt and pepper. Add beef; mix lightly but thoroughly. Shape into a 7-in. round loaf. Place loaf in center of strips in slow cooker. Cook, covered, on low until a thermometer reads at least 160°, 3-4 hours.

**3.** In a small bowl, mix the ketchup, brown sugar, barbecue seasoning and mustard; pour over the meat loaf and sprinkle with the cheese. Cook, covered, on low until cheese is melted, about 15 minutes longer. Let stand for 5 minutes. Using foil strips as handles, remove meat loaf to a platter.

**1 SLICE:** 356 cal., 17g fat (7g sat. fat), 154mg chol., 1358mg sod., 22g carb. (13g sugars, 2g fiber), 29g pro.

## HOW TO EASILY LIFT MEAT LOAF

After cooking, gather up the foil strips and gently lift the meat loaf out of the crock. This technique also works great with lasagna and other layered dishes.

# CABBAGE ROLL STEW

A head of cabbage seems like it never ends. Here's a delicious way to use it up. My husband is this stew's biggest fan.
—*Pamela Kennemer, Sand Springs, OK*

**PREP:** 25 min. • **COOK:** 5 hours • **MAKES:** 8 servings (3 qt.)

2 cans (14½ oz. each) petite diced tomatoes, drained
1 can (14½ oz.) reduced-sodium beef broth
1 can (8 oz.) tomato sauce
1 Tbsp. cider vinegar
1 Tbsp. Worcestershire sauce
1 tsp. garlic powder
1 tsp. Cajun seasoning
½ tsp. salt
½ tsp. pepper
1 medium head cabbage (about 2 lbs.), cut into 1½-in. pieces
1½ lbs. ground beef
½ lb. bulk Italian sausage
1 medium onion, chopped
3 garlic cloves, minced
Hot cooked rice and chopped fresh parsley, optional

1. Mix first nine ingredients. Place cabbage in a 5- or 6-qt. slow cooker.

2. In a large skillet, cook and crumble beef and sausage with onion and garlic over medium-high heat until no longer pink, 7-9 minutes; drain. Spoon over cabbage; top with tomato mixture.

3. Cook, covered, on low until cabbage is tender and flavors are blended, 5-6 hours. If desired, serve with rice and sprinkle with parsley.

**FREEZE OPTION:** Freeze cooled meat mixture in freezer containers. To use, partially thaw stew in the refrigerator overnight. Heat through in a saucepan, stirring occasionally.

**1½ CUPS CABBAGE MIXTURE:** 195 cal., 11g fat (4g sat. fat), 46mg chol., 564mg sod., 11g carb. (6g sugars, 4g fiber), 14g pro.

**✱ TEST KITCHEN TIP**

Using a combination of ground beef and Italian sausage gives this recipe a flavor boost (and it's a great idea for perking up most ground beef meals).

# PEPPER STEAK

Pepper steak is one of my favorite dishes, but sometimes the beef can be tough. This recipe solves that problem! The slow cooker keeps things simple and makes the meat very tender. I've stored leftovers in one big container and also in individual portions for quick lunches.
—*Julie Rhine, Zelienople, PA*

**PREP:** 30 min. ● **COOK:** 6¼ hours ● **MAKES:** 12 servings

- 1 beef top round roast (3 lbs.)
- 1 large onion, halved and sliced
- 1 large green pepper, cut into ½-in. strips
- 1 large sweet red pepper, cut into ½-in. strips
- 1 cup water
- 4 garlic cloves, minced
- ⅓ cup cornstarch
- ½ cup reduced-sodium soy sauce
- 2 tsp. sugar
- 2 tsp. ground ginger
- 8 cups hot cooked brown rice

1. Place roast, onion and peppers in a 5-qt. slow cooker. Add water and garlic. Cook, covered, on low until meat is tender, 6-8 hours.

2. Remove beef to a cutting board. Transfer vegetables and cooking juices to a large saucepan. Bring to a boil. In a small bowl, mix cornstarch, soy sauce, sugar and ginger until smooth; stir into vegetable mixture. Return to a boil, stirring constantly; cook and stir until thickened, 1-2 minutes.

3. Cut beef into slices. Stir gently into sauce; heat through. Serve with rice.

**FREEZE OPTION:** Freeze cooled beef mixture in freezer containers. To use, partially thaw in refrigerator overnight. Heat through in a saucepan, stirring occasionally and adding a little water if necessary.

**1 SERVING:** 322 cal., 5g fat (1g sat. fat), 64mg chol., 444mg sod., 38g carb. (3g sugars, 3g fiber), 30g pro. **DIABETIC EXCHANGES:** 3 lean meat, 2 starch.

# BUTTER & HERB TURKEY

My kids love turkey for dinner, and this easy recipe lets me make it whenever I want. No special occasion required! The meat is so tender it comes right off the bone.
—*Rochelle Popovic, South Bend, IN*

**PREP:** 10 min. ● **COOK:** 5 hours ● **MAKES:** 12 servings (3 cups gravy)

- 1 bone-in turkey breast (6 to 7 lbs.)
- 2 Tbsp. butter, softened
- ½ tsp. dried rosemary, crushed
- ½ tsp. dried thyme
- ¼ tsp. garlic powder
- ¼ tsp. pepper
- 1 can (14½ oz.) chicken broth
- 3 Tbsp. cornstarch
- 2 Tbsp. cold water

1. Rub turkey with butter. Combine the rosemary, thyme, garlic powder and pepper; sprinkle over the turkey. Place in a 6-qt. slow cooker. Pour broth over top. Cover and cook on low until tender, 5-6 hours.

2. Remove turkey to a serving platter; keep warm. Skim fat from cooking juices; transfer to a small saucepan. Bring to a boil. Combine cornstarch and water until smooth. Gradually stir into the pan. Bring to a boil; cook and stir until thickened, about 2 minutes. Serve with turkey.

**5 OZ. COOKED TURKEY WITH ¼ CUP GRAVY:** 339 cal., 14g fat (5g sat. fat), 128mg chol., 266mg sod., 2g carb. (0 sugars, 0 fiber), 48g pro.

# CRAZY DELICIOUS BABY BACK RIBS

*My husband craves baby back ribs, so we cook them multiple ways.*
*This low and slow method with a tangy sauce is the best we've found.*
*—Jan Whitworth, Roebuck, SC*

**PREP:** 15 min. • **COOK:** 5¼ hours • **MAKES:** 8 servings

2 Tbsp. smoked paprika
2 tsp. chili powder
2 tsp. garlic salt
1 tsp. onion powder
1 tsp. pepper
½ tsp. cayenne pepper
4 lbs. pork baby back ribs
**SAUCE**
½ cup Worcestershire sauce
½ cup mayonnaise
½ cup yellow mustard
¼ cup reduced-sodium soy sauce
3 Tbsp. hot pepper sauce

1. In a small bowl, combine the first six ingredients. Cut ribs into serving-size pieces; rub with seasoning mixture. Place ribs in a 6-qt. slow cooker. Cook, covered, on low until meat is tender, 5-6 hours.

2. Preheat oven to 375°. In a small bowl, whisk the sauce ingredients. Transfer ribs to a foil-lined 15x10x1-in. baking pan; brush with some of the sauce. Bake until browned, 15-20 minutes, turning once and brushing occasionally with sauce. Serve with remaining sauce.

**1 SERVING:** 420 cal., 33g fat (9g sat. fat), 86mg chol., 1082mg sod., 6g carb. (2g sugars, 2g fiber), 24g pro.

# HAWAIIAN KIELBASA SANDWICHES

*If you are looking for a different way to use kielbasa, the sweet and*
*mildly spicy flavor of these sandwiches is a nice change of pace.*
*—Judy Dames, Bridgeville, PA*

**PREP:** 15 min. • **COOK:** 3 hours • **MAKES:** 12 sandwiches

3 lbs. smoked kielbasa or Polish sausage, cut into 3-in. pieces
2 bottles (12 oz. each) chili sauce
1 can (20 oz.) pineapple tidbits, undrained
¼ cup packed brown sugar
12 hoagie buns, split
   Thinly sliced green onions, optional

Place kielbasa in a 3-qt. slow cooker. Combine the chili sauce, pineapple and brown sugar; pour over kielbasa. Cover and cook on low until heated through, 3-4 hours. Serve on buns. If desired, top with green onions.

**1 SANDWICH:** 663 cal., 35g fat (12g sat. fat), 76mg chol., 2532mg sod., 64g carb. (27g sugars, 1g fiber), 23g pro.

# GRANDMA SCHWARTZ'S ROULADEN

This was one of my Grandma Schwartz's best recipes. Grandpa Schwartz was a German butcher and this was one of his (and our) favorite meals. It's an extra-special beef entree when served with mashed potatoes made with butter and sour cream.
—*Lynda Sharai, Summer Lake, OR*

**PREP:** 35 min. ● **COOK:** 6 hours ● **MAKES:** 6 servings

3 bacon strips, chopped
1½ lbs. beef top round steak
2 Tbsp. Dijon mustard
3 medium carrots, quartered lengthwise
6 dill pickle spears
¼ cup finely chopped onion
1 cup sliced fresh mushrooms
1 small parsnip, peeled and chopped
1 celery rib, chopped
1 can (10¾ oz.) condensed golden cream of mushroom soup, undiluted
⅓ cup dry red wine
2 Tbsp. Worcestershire sauce
2 Tbsp. minced fresh parsley

**1.** In a large skillet, cook bacon over medium heat until crisp. Remove to paper towels with a slotted spoon; drain, reserving drippings.

**2.** Meanwhile, cut the steak into six serving-size pieces; pound with a meat mallet to ¼-in. thickness. Spread the tops with mustard. Top each with two carrot pieces and one pickle spear; sprinkle with onion. Roll up each from a short side; secure with toothpicks.

**3.** In a large skillet, brown roll-ups in bacon drippings over medium-high heat. Place roll-ups in a 4-qt. slow cooker. Top with mushrooms, parsnip, celery and cooked bacon.

**4.** In a small bowl, whisk the soup, wine and Worcestershire sauce. Pour over top. Cover and cook on low until beef is tender, 6-8 hours. Sprinkle with parsley before serving.

**1 SERVING:** 288 cal., 11g fat (3g sat. fat), 74mg chol., 1030mg sod., 14g carb. (4g sugars, 3g fiber), 28g pro.

**✱ DID YOU KNOW?**

This is a version of *rindsrouladen*, a traditional German dish that features sliced beef rolled around bacon, onions and pickles.

# SWEET & SOUR PORK WRAPS

We always make these wraps at our family's annual party, and they're a true favorite.
The cabbage and cilantro give them great texture and flavor.
—*Andrew DeVito, Hartford, CT*

**PREP:** 15 min. • **COOK:** 6 hours • **MAKES:** 8 servings (16 wraps)

1 boneless pork shoulder butt roast
   (3 to 4 lbs.)
1 medium onion, chopped
1 cup water
1 cup sweet-and-sour sauce
¼ cup sherry or chicken broth
¼ cup reduced-sodium soy sauce
1 envelope onion soup mix
1 Tbsp. minced fresh gingerroot
3 garlic cloves, minced
16 flour tortillas (6 in.), warmed
4 cups shredded cabbage
¼ cup minced fresh cilantro

**1.** Place roast and onion in a 6-qt. slow cooker. In a small bowl, whisk the water, sweet-and-sour sauce, sherry, soy sauce, soup mix, ginger and garlic until blended; pour over pork. Cook, covered, on low until meat is tender, 6-8 hours.

**2.** When cool enough to handle, shred pork with two forks. To serve, spoon about ⅓ cup pork mixture onto the center of each tortilla. Top with ¼ cup cabbage; sprinkle with cilantro. Fold bottom of tortilla over filling; fold both sides to close.

**2 WRAPS:** 523 cal., 23g fat (6g sat. fat), 101mg chol., 1357mg sod., 42g carb. (8g sugars, 1g fiber), 36g pro.

## HOW TO SLOW-COOK PORK SHOULDER

Pat roast with paper towels to dry; liquid on the surface will prevent it from browning.

Brown the roast in a skillet over medium-high heat, turning to brown all sides. Browning provides added flavor to the finished dish.

Pour liquid over the roast in the slow cooker. Liquid in a slow cooker won't evaporate, so less is needed than with traditional cooking methods.

After cooking, the meat should shred easily with two forks.

# SAUSAGE, ARTICHOKE & SUN-DRIED TOMATO RAGU

This is a thick and hearty spaghetti sauce that's simple to prepare. Like all good spaghetti sauces, this one tastes even better the next day. If you prefer a little celery or bell pepper in your sauce, go ahead and throw them in. The results will still taste great.

*—Aysha Schurman, Ammon, ID*

**PREP:** 20 min. • **COOK:** 6 hours • **MAKES:** 2 qt.

1 lb. bulk Italian sausage
½ lb. lean ground beef (90% lean)
1 medium onion, finely chopped
3 cans (14½ oz. each) diced tomatoes, undrained
1 cup oil-packed sun-dried tomatoes, chopped
2 cans (6 oz. each) Italian tomato paste
1 jar (7½ oz.) marinated quartered artichoke hearts, drained and chopped
3 garlic cloves, minced
2 tsp. minced fresh rosemary
1 tsp. pepper
½ tsp. salt
1 bay leaf
3 Tbsp. minced fresh parsley
Hot cooked spaghetti
Grated Parmesan cheese, optional

**1.** In a large skillet, cook sausage, beef and onion over medium-high heat until meat is no longer pink, 4-6 minutes, breaking meat into crumbles; drain. Transfer to a 5- or 6-qt. slow cooker. Stir in the tomatoes, tomato paste, artichokes, garlic, rosemary, pepper, salt and bay leaf.

**2.** Cook, covered, on low until heated through, 6-8 hours. Remove bay leaf. Stir in parsley. Serve with spaghetti. If desired, top with grated Parmesan.

**FREEZE OPTION:** Freeze cooled sauce in freezer containers. To use, partially thaw in refrigerator overnight. Heat through in a saucepan, stirring the sauce occasionally.

**¾ CUP:** 259 cal., 17g fat (5g sat. fat), 39mg chol., 1535mg sod., 17g carb. (9g sugars, 3g fiber), 11g pro.

# JALAPENO MAC & CHEESE

A friend brought me a big casserole of mac and cheese along with the recipe many years ago when I was recuperating from knee surgery. Over the years, I fiddled with the recipe. Most recently, I added jalapenos at the request of my son. What an awesome spicy twist!
—*Teresa Gustafson, Elkton, MD*

**PREP:** 25 min. • **COOK:** 3 hours • **MAKES:** 15 servings

1 pkg. (16 oz.) uncooked elbow macaroni
6 Tbsp. butter, divided
4 jalapeno peppers, seeded and finely chopped
3 cups shredded cheddar cheese
2 cups shredded Colby-Monterey Jack cheese
2 cups whole milk
1 can (10¾ oz.) condensed cream of onion soup, undiluted
1 can (10¾ oz.) condensed cheddar cheese soup, undiluted
½ cup mayonnaise
¼ tsp. pepper
1 cup crushed Ritz crackers (about 25 crackers)
  Additional sliced jalapeno peppers, optional

1. Cook the macaroni according to package directions for al dente; drain. Transfer to a greased 5-qt. slow cooker.

2. Melt 2 Tbsp. butter in a large skillet over medium-high heat. Add jalapenos; cook and stir until crisp-tender, about 5 minutes. Add to slow cooker. Stir in the cheeses, milk, soups, mayonnaise and pepper.

3. Cook, covered, on low until the cheese is melted and the mixture is heated through, about 3 hours. Melt the remaining butter; stir in crackers. Sprinkle over macaroni mixture. If desired, top with jalapeno slices.

¾ **CUP:** 428 cal., 27g fat (13g sat. fat), 53mg chol., 654mg sod., 33g carb. (5g sugars, 2g fiber), 14g pro.

**❋ TEST KITCHEN TIP**
Be sure to cook the pasta just short of tender. It will continue to cook in the slow cooker.

# BROWN SUGAR-GLAZED BABY CARROTS

When things get busy on a special holiday, such as Thanksgiving or Christmas, these delicious glazed carrots are my "rescue-me" side dish because they cook while I'm preparing other parts of the meal. Also, I'm able to use my oven for other dishes, like the turkey!
—*Anndrea Bailey, Huntington Beach, CA*

**PREP:** 10 min. ● **COOK:** 6 hours ● **MAKES:** 6 servings

2 lbs. fresh baby carrots
1 celery rib, finely chopped
1 small onion, finely chopped
¼ cup packed brown sugar
3 Tbsp. butter, cubed
½ tsp. salt
½ tsp. pepper

In a 3-qt. slow cooker, combine all ingredients. Cover and cook on low until carrots are tender, 6-8 hours.

**¾ CUP:** 144 cal., 6g fat (4g sat. fat), 15mg chol., 364mg sod., 23g carb. (17g sugars, 3g fiber), 1g pro.

# "EVERYTHING" STUFFING

My husband and father both go crazy for this stuffing!
It also freezes well so we can enjoy it long after Thanksgiving has passed.
—*Bette Votral, Bethlehem, PA*

**PREP:** 30 min. ● **COOK:** 3 hours ● **MAKES:** 9 servings

½ lb. bulk Italian sausage
4 cups seasoned stuffing cubes
1½ cups crushed cornbread stuffing
½ cup chopped toasted chestnuts or pecans
½ cup minced fresh parsley
1 Tbsp. minced fresh sage or 1 tsp. rubbed sage
⅛ tsp. salt
⅛ tsp. pepper
1¾ cups sliced baby portobello mushrooms
1 pkg. (5 oz.) sliced fresh shiitake mushrooms
1 large onion, chopped
1 medium apple, peeled and chopped
1 celery rib, chopped
3 Tbsp. butter
1 can (14½ oz.) chicken broth

1. In a large skillet, cook sausage over medium heat until no longer pink; drain. Transfer to a large bowl. Stir in the stuffing cubes, cornbread stuffing, chestnuts, parsley, sage, salt and pepper.

2. In the same skillet, saute the mushrooms, onion, apple and celery in butter until tender. Stir into stuffing mixture. Add enough broth to reach desired moistness. Transfer to a 4-qt. slow cooker. Cover and cook on low for 3 hours, stirring once.

**¾ CUP:** 267 cal., 13g fat (4g sat. fat), 21mg chol., 796mg sod., 30g carb. (5g sugars, 3g fiber), 8g pro.

**✳ READER RAVE**

*"Excellent recipe! It did not, however, contain 'everything!' After tossing in a handful of dried cranberries, I decided it had 'everything.' Easy recipe, remarkably delicious, and our new favorite."*

—BLODYN, TASTEOFHOME.COM

# SLOW-COOKED STUFFED PEPPERS

*My favorite appliance is the slow cooker, and I use mine more than anyone else I know. Here's a tasty good-for-you dish.*
—Michelle Gurnsey, Lincoln, NE

**PREP:** 15 min. ● **COOK:** 3 hours ● **MAKES:** 4 servings

4 medium sweet red peppers
1 can (15 oz.) black beans, rinsed and drained
1 cup shredded pepper jack cheese
¾ cup salsa
1 small onion, chopped
½ cup frozen corn
⅓ cup uncooked converted long grain rice
1¼ tsp. chili powder
½ tsp. ground cumin
   Reduced-fat sour cream, optional

1. Cut and discard tops from peppers; remove seeds. In a large bowl, mix beans, cheese, salsa, onion, corn, rice, chili powder and cumin; spoon into peppers. Place in a 5-qt. slow cooker coated with cooking spray.

2. Cook, covered, on low until the peppers are tender and the filling is heated through, 3-4 hours. If desired, serve with sour cream.

**1 STUFFED PEPPER:** 317 cal., 10g fat (5g sat. fat), 30mg chol., 565mg sod., 43g carb. (6g sugars, 8g fiber), 15g pro. **DIABETIC EXCHANGES:** 2 starch, 2 vegetable, 2 lean meat, 1 fat.

# CALICO BEANS

*My sister-in-law gave me the recipe for these hearty beans that make an appearance at all of our family functions. The ingredients slowly cook to perfection for a mouthwatering sweet-and-smoky flavor. Everyone will be going back for seconds!*
—Donna Adam, Perth, ON

**PREP:** 30 min. ● **COOK:** 6 hours ● **MAKES:** 10 servings

1 lb. ground beef
2 cans (16 oz. each) baked beans
1 can (16 oz.) kidney beans, rinsed and drained
1 can (15 oz.) cannellini beans, rinsed and drained
1 can (20 oz.) unsweetened crushed pineapple, drained
1 medium onion, finely chopped
½ cup packed brown sugar
½ cup ketchup
2 Tbsp. cider vinegar
1 Tbsp. Dijon mustard
½ lb. bacon strips, cooked and crumbled

1. In a large skillet, cook the beef over medium heat until no longer pink; drain. Transfer to a 4-qt. slow cooker. Add the beans, pineapple, onion, brown sugar, ketchup, cider vinegar and mustard.

2. Cover and cook mixture on low until heated through, 6-8 hours. Just before serving, stir in bacon.

**¾ CUP:** 385 cal., 10g fat (4g sat. fat), 43mg chol., 863mg sod., 55g carb. (23g sugars, 9g fiber), 20g pro.

# APPLE PIE OATMEAL DESSERT

This warm and comforting dessert brings back memories of time spent with my family around the kitchen table. I serve the dish with sweetened whipped cream or vanilla ice cream as a topper.

—*Carol Greer, Earlville, IL*

**PREP:** 15 min. ● **COOK:** 4 hours ● **MAKES:** 6 servings

1 cup quick-cooking oats
½ cup all-purpose flour
⅓ cup packed brown sugar
2 tsp. baking powder
1½ tsp. apple pie spice
¼ tsp. salt
3 large eggs
1⅔ cups 2% milk, divided
1½ tsp. vanilla extract
3 medium apples, peeled and finely chopped
Vanilla ice cream, optional

**1.** In a large bowl, whisk the oats, flour, brown sugar, baking powder, pie spice and salt. In a small bowl, whisk eggs, 1 cup milk and vanilla until blended. Add to oat mixture, stirring just until moistened. Fold in apples.

**2.** Transfer to a greased 3-qt. slow cooker. Cook, covered, on low until the apples are tender and top is set, 4-5 hours.

**3.** Stir in remaining milk. Serve warm or cold, with ice cream if desired.

**¾ CUP:** 238 cal., 5g fat (2g sat. fat), 111mg chol., 306mg sod., 41g carb. (22g sugars, 3g fiber), 8g pro.

### ✱ STAFF HACK

*"I love to keep my oatmeal warm in the slow cooker so it doesn't solidify. I keep the cooked oats in the crock and put out bowls of fixin's like brown sugar, nuts, coconut, seeds, milk, agave or maple syrup, fresh berries and bananas. The oatmeal will stay soft and warm—and not turn to rubber—until each person is ready to eat."*

—LAURA BEDNARSKI, FOOD STYLIST

# FUDGY PEANUT BUTTER CAKE

*I clipped this cake recipe from a newspaper years ago. The house smells great while it's cooking. My husband and son enjoy this slow-cooked dessert with vanilla ice cream and nuts on top.*
*—Bonnie Evans, Norcross, GA*

**PREP:** 10 min. ● **COOK:** 1½ hours ● **MAKES:** 4 servings

⅓ cup whole milk
¼ cup peanut butter
1 Tbsp. canola oil
½ tsp. vanilla extract
¾ cup sugar, divided
½ cup all-purpose flour
¾ tsp. baking powder
2 Tbsp. baking cocoa
1 cup boiling water
   Vanilla ice cream

1. In a large bowl, beat the milk, peanut butter, oil and vanilla until well blended. In a small bowl, combine ¼ cup sugar, flour and baking powder; gradually beat into milk mixture until blended. Spread into a 1½-qt. slow cooker coated with cooking spray.

2. In a small bowl, combine cocoa and remaining sugar; stir in boiling water. Pour into slow cooker (do not stir).

3. Cover and cook on high until a toothpick inserted in center comes out clean, about 1½-2 hours. Serve warm with ice cream.

**NOTE:** Reduced-fat peanut butter is not recommended for this recipe.

**1 PIECE:** 348 cal., 13g fat (3g sat. fat), 3mg chol., 160mg sod., 55g carb. (39g sugars, 2g fiber), 7g pro.

# WAFFLE IRON

Turns out that handy waffle iron can make a lot more than crisp and fluffy morning treats. Turn here for savory biscuit breakfasts, hash browns, sandwiches, pizzas and even desserts.

*DON'T OVERFILL*

*LIGHTLY BUTTER IRON OR COAT WITH SPRAY*

*GENTLY LIFT*

# THINK OUT OF THE BRUNCH BOX FOR WAFFLE CREATIONS THAT WOW

**Ready to move beyond the standard butter-and-syrup routine? Here are some savory and sweet ideas to give you wow-worthy waffles any time of day.**

**Healthy kickstarts.** Freeze your favorite whole grain waffles (see how on facing page). Toast and add power-breakfast toppings, like:

- Greek yogurt with honey and blueberries
- Almond butter, sliced apples and honey
- Vanilla yogurt, granola and raspberries
- Fried egg, avocado and pico de gallo
- Sliced kiwi, pineapple segments and toasted coconut
- Applesauce, cinnamon and chopped walnuts

**Savory suppers.** Sandwich hearty ingredients between waffles for a satisfying lunch, or pile on some savory toppers:

- Pork chops, pears and maple syrup
- Sliced deli chicken, cheddar, mayo and sliced apple
- Pulled barbecue pork and tangy coleslaw
- Chili, sour cream and cheddar atop cornbread waffles

**Quirky pick-me-ups.** In place of plain waffle batter, try unique ingredients like brownie batter, cake batter or even cookie dough.

- Red velvet cake batter with coconut syrup
- Chocolate brownie waffle sundaes

- Sugar cookie waffles, sprinkled with powdered sugar
- Birthday-cake waffle ice cream sandwiches

**POP-UP BREAKFAST:** To freeze, layer cooled waffles in waxed paper and store in an airtight container. When you're ready to eat, simply pop a waffle or two in the toaster to reheat. You'll never go back to store-bought.

# HOW TO MAKE WAFFLES

**WHISK DRY AND WET INGREDIENTS.** First, separate the eggs and place whites in a clean, dry bowl. Combine yolks with melted butter, oil or other wet ingredients in a second bowl; whisk the dry ingredients together in a third.

**WHIP EGG WHITES UNTIL STIFF PEAKS FORM.** Not all waffle recipes call for this step. It's a bit fussy, but it gives waffles an unbeatable light texture. Some recipes may call for adding sugar, salt or cream of tartar to the beaten egg whites.

**MIX WET INGREDIENTS INTO DRY.** Add club soda, juice, milk and/or the egg yolk mixture to the dry ingredients. Be careful not to overmix or the waffles will be tough.

**GENTLY FOLD IN WHITES.** Work with a light hand so as not to deflate the egg whites. And don't overmix; a few streaks of egg white left in the waffle batter is just fine.

**BAKE IN A PREHEATED WAFFLE IRON.** Coat the grates lightly with cooking spray before the first batch. Letting the waffle iron's heat recover between batches will help prevent sticking. Avoid overfilling—that gets messy.

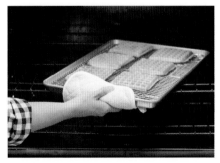

**KEEP 'EM HOT.** If baking waffles for a crowd, keep the first ones warm on a rack in a low (about 200°) oven as you finish up the rest. To prevent them from drying out, put a damp dish cloth in a heatproof bowl and place it in the oven, too.

# HAWAIIAN WAFFLES

I created this waffle recipe to recapture the memorable tropical tastes we enjoyed while visiting Hawaii.
—*Darlene Brenden, Salem, OR*

**TAKES:** 30 min. • **MAKES:** 16 (4-in.) waffles

1 can (20 oz.) crushed pineapple, undrained
½ cup sugar
½ cup sweetened shredded coconut
½ cup light corn syrup
¼ cup pineapple juice
**WAFFLES**
2 cups all-purpose flour
4 tsp. baking powder
1 Tbsp. sugar
½ tsp. salt
2 large eggs, separated
1 cup whole milk
¼ cup butter, melted
1 can (8 oz.) crushed pineapple, well drained
¼ cup sweetened shredded coconut
¼ cup chopped macadamia nuts
Additional chopped macadamia nuts, toasted, optional

**1.** In a large saucepan, combine the first five ingredients. Bring to a boil. Reduce heat. Simmer, uncovered, until the sauce begins to thicken, 12-15 minutes; set aside.

**2.** In a large bowl, combine the flour, baking powder, sugar and salt. In a second bowl, combine egg yolks, milk and butter; stir into dry ingredients just until combined. Stir in the pineapple, coconut and nuts. Beat egg whites until stiff peaks form; fold into batter (batter will be thick).

**3.** Preheat waffle iron. Fill and bake according to manufacturer's directions. Serve with pineapple sauce and additional nuts if desired.

**2 WAFFLES:** 446 cal., 14g fat (8g sat. fat), 73mg chol., 495mg sod., 76g carb. (43g sugars, 2g fiber), 7g pro.

**PIZZA CRUST TOTS**

• Press thawed Tater Tots into a waffle iron and cook until crispy.

• Use the Tot waffle as a pizza crust; spread with pizza sauce or pesto and add your favorite pizza toppings.

• Sausage, fried egg and veggies make a delicious breakfast pizza.

# CORN FRITTER WAFFLES WITH SPICY MAPLE SYRUP

My family used to vacation at a resort in Vermont that served corn fritters with maple syrup. Now when I serve these waffles for breakfast or supper, I'm transported back to those simple days of childhood.
—*Jennifer Beckman, Falls Church, VA*

**PREP:** 15 min. ● **BAKE:** 5 min./batch ● **MAKES:** 6 round waffles (1 cup syrup)

2 cups all-purpose flour
2 Tbsp. sugar
3 tsp. baking powder
½ tsp. salt
2 large eggs
2 cups 2% milk
½ cup canola oil
1½ cups fresh whole kernel corn or frozen corn
1 cup maple syrup
¼ tsp. cayenne pepper
Cooked whole kernel corn, optional

**1.** In a large bowl, combine the flour, sugar, baking powder and salt. In a second bowl, whisk the eggs, milk and oil. Stir into dry ingredients just until moistened. Stir in corn.

**2.** Bake batter in a preheated round Belgian waffle iron according to the manufacturer's directions until golden brown. Meanwhile, combine syrup and cayenne. Serve with waffles and, if desired, cooked corn.

**1 WAFFLE WITH 2 TBSP. SYRUP:** 574 cal., 23g fat (3g sat. fat), 69mg chol., 507mg sod., 84g carb. (44g sugars, 2g fiber), 10g pro.

**✱ DID YOU KNOW?**

American Indians taught the colonists how to make maple syrup.

# EGG-TOPPED BISCUIT WAFFLES

Breakfast for dinner is always a hit at our house. As a mom, I like transforming an ordinary breakfast sandwich into something magical and kid-friendly.

*—Amy Lents, Grand Forks, ND*

**TAKES:** 25 min. • **MAKES:** 4 waffles

1½ cups biscuit/baking mix
¾ cup shredded Swiss cheese
⅛ tsp. pepper
½ cup 2% milk
4 large eggs
4 bacon strips, cooked and crumbled
   Cubed avocado and pico de gallo, optional

**1.** Preheat a four-square waffle iron. Place baking mix, cheese and pepper in a bowl. Add milk and stir just until moistened. Transfer to a lightly floured surface; knead gently four to six times. Pat or roll dough into an 8-in. square; cut into four 4-in. squares.

**2.** Generously grease top and bottom grids of waffle iron. Place one portion of dough on each section of waffle iron, pressing an indentation in each for the eggs.

**3.** Break an egg over each biscuit; sprinkle with bacon. Close lid carefully over eggs and bake according to the manufacturer's directions until biscuits are golden brown. If desired, top with avocado and pico de gallo.

**1 WAFFLE:** 386 cal., 20g fat (8g sat. fat), 215mg chol., 802mg sod., 33g carb. (3g sugars, 1g fiber), 19g pro.

**✱ TEST KITCHEN TIP**

Recipe may also be baked in a round waffle iron. Divide biscuit dough into four equal portions; pat each into a 4½-in. circle. Assemble and bake one serving at a time.

# FAMILY-FAVORITE OATMEAL WAFFLES

These healthful, tasty waffles are a tried-and-true family favorite—even with our two children. My husband and I have a small herd of beef cattle and some pigs. A hearty breakfast really gets us going!
—*Marna Heitz, Farley, IA*

**TAKES:** 30 min. ● **MAKES:** 6 waffles

1½ cups all-purpose flour
1 cup quick-cooking oats
3 tsp. baking powder
½ tsp. ground cinnamon
¼ tsp. salt
2 large eggs, lightly beaten
1½ cups whole milk
6 Tbsp. butter, melted
2 Tbsp. brown sugar
Assorted fresh fruit and yogurt of your choice

**1.** In a large bowl, combine flour, oats, baking powder, cinnamon and salt; set aside. In a small bowl, whisk eggs, milk, butter and brown sugar. Add to flour mixture; stir until blended.

**2.** Pour batter into a lightly greased waffle iron (amount will vary with size of waffle iron). Close lid quickly. Bake according to the manufacturer's directions; do not open during baking. Use fork to remove baked waffle. Top with fresh fruit and yogurt.

**1 WAFFLE:** 344 cal., 16g fat (9g sat. fat), 99mg chol., 482mg sod., 41g carb. (8g sugars, 2g fiber), 9g pro.

**✳ READER RAVE**

*"Just made these and added blueberries to the mix. All I can say is yummy."*
— MSUMMER29, TASTEOFHOME.COM

# HASH BROWN WAFFLES WITH FRIED EGGS

Refrigerated hash brown potatoes help you make quick work of these crunchy waffles.
Put out lots of toppings so everyone can design his or her own.
—*Nancy Judd, Alpine, UT*

**TAKES:** 30 min. ● **MAKES:** 4 servings

5 **large eggs**
½ **tsp. salt**
½ **tsp. ground cumin**
½ **tsp. pepper**
¼ **tsp. chili powder**
1¾ **cups refrigerated shredded hash brown potatoes**
1 **small onion, finely chopped**
¼ **cup canned chopped green chilies**
2 **Tbsp. salsa**
2 **Tbsp. canola oil**
½ **cup shredded cheddar-Monterey Jack cheese**
**Optional toppings: salsa, guacamole, sour cream and minced fresh cilantro**

**1.** In a large bowl, whisk one egg, salt, cumin, pepper and chili powder. Stir in potatoes, onion, green chilies and salsa. Bake in a preheated waffle iron coated with cooking spray until golden brown and potatoes are tender, 8-12 minutes.

**2.** In a large skillet, heat the oil over medium-high heat. Break remaining eggs, one at a time, into pan. Reduce heat to low. Cook to desired doneness, turning after whites are set if desired. Remove from heat. Sprinkle with the cheese; cover and let stand 3 minutes or until melted.

**3.** Serve eggs with waffles and any desired toppings.

**1 WAFFLE WITH 1 FRIED EGG:** 273 cal., 17g fat (5g sat. fat), 245mg chol., 570mg sod., 17g carb. (2g sugars, 2g fiber), 12g pro.

### ✳ STAFF HACK

*"I make potato pancakes in my waffle iron with shredded raw sweet potatoes or a mix of sweet and regular potatoes. I mix in a few eggs or egg whites, olive oil or butter, depending upon how healthy I am being. I mostly go savory with my seasonings: salt, pepper, cumin, dried chives. Or try nutmeg and cinnamon or apple pie spice for sweet potatoes. Coat the waffle iron well with cooking spray so the potatoes don't stick."*
–HOLLI FLETCHER, EXECUTIVE ASSISTANT

# WAFFLED PIZZA BITES

The whole family will love this playful twist on waffles. Mozzarella and Parmesan cheeses are sandwiched between two layers of dough and cooked up in the waffle iron. It's like a pizza grilled cheese waffle!
—*Deirdre Cox, Kansas City, MO*

**TAKES:** 20 min. ● **MAKES:** 8 appetizers

1¼ cups shredded part-skim
     mozzarella cheese
¼ cup shredded Parmesan cheese
½ tsp. dried basil
½ tsp. dried oregano
2 tubes (8 oz. each) refrigerated
     crescent rolls
32 slices pepperoni (about 2 oz.)
1 jar (14 oz.) pizza sauce, warmed
     Optional toppings: sliced
     pepperoni, shredded mozzarella
     cheese and basil

**1.** In a small bowl, combine the cheeses, basil and oregano. Separate each roll of crescent dough into two 7x6-in. rectangles; seal perforations.

**2.** Place one rectangle on a preheated greased 8-in. square waffle iron (the dough will not cover entire surface). Layer with half the cheese mixture and half the pepperoni to ½ in. of edges; top with another rectangle. Bake until golden brown, 4-5 minutes. Repeat with rest of ingredients.

**3.** Remove to a cutting board and cool slightly. Cut each rectangle into four triangles; serve warm with pizza sauce and, if desired, toppings.

**1 TRIANGLE WITH ABOUT ¼ CUP SAUCE:**
329 cal., 19g fat (4g sat. fat), 21mg chol., 909mg sod., 29g carb. (9g sugars, 1g fiber), 12g pro.

# TURKEY WAFFLEWICHES

Who knew a sandwich could be so fun? You'll see smiles around the table when you serve this cute and simple recipe.

—*Taste of Home Test Kitchen*

**TAKES:** 15 min. ● **MAKES:** 4 servings

3  oz. cream cheese, softened
¼  cup whole-berry cranberry sauce
1  Tbsp. maple pancake syrup
¼  tsp. pepper
8  slices white bread
¾  lb. sliced deli turkey
2  Tbsp. butter, softened

**1.** In a small bowl, beat the cream cheese, cranberry sauce, syrup and pepper until combined. Spread over four slices of bread; top with turkey and remaining bread. Spread butter over both sides of sandwiches.

**2.** Bake in a preheated waffle iron or an indoor grill according to the manufacturer's directions until golden brown, 2-3 minutes.

**1 SANDWICH:** 407 cal., 17g fat (8g sat. fat), 67mg chol., 1179mg sod., 41g carb. (10g sugars, 2g fiber), 23g pro.

**✱ TEST KITCHEN TIP**

We find a cotton swab works well to clean up any nooks and crannies in your waffle iron!

# TEX-MEX CHICKEN & WAFFLES

While visiting Texas I bought a small bottle of jalapeno pepper jelly, which inspired me to try this spiced-up version of a southern classic. The syrup can be used as a dipping sauce for the chicken.
—*Debra Goforth, Newport, TN*

**PREP:** 30 min. + marinating • **COOK:** 20 min. • **MAKES:** 4 servings (¾ cup syrup)

4 boneless skinless chicken breast halves (4 oz. each)
½ cup buttermilk
¼ tsp. hot pepper sauce

**JALAPENO SYRUP**
1 cup sugar
½ cup coarsely chopped green pepper
2 jalapeno peppers, seeded and quartered
3 Tbsp. cider vinegar

**COATING**
⅓ cup all-purpose flour
⅓ cup yellow cornmeal
2 tsp. salt
½ tsp. pepper
¼ tsp. cayenne pepper
¼ tsp. ground cumin
1 tsp. paprika
¼ cup canola oil

**WAFFLES**
¾ cup all-purpose flour
¼ cup cornstarch
¼ cup yellow cornmeal
½ tsp. baking powder
¼ tsp. baking soda
¼ tsp. salt
¾ cup buttermilk
¼ cup canola oil
1 large egg
¼ cup shredded pepper jack cheese
Optional toppings: salsa, sliced avocados and fresh cilantro

1. Flatten each chicken breast to ¼-in. thickness. Place in a shallow bowl or dish. Add buttermilk and hot pepper sauce; turn chicken to coat. Cover and refrigerate for 2 hours or overnight.

2. In a small saucepan, combine all syrup ingredients; bring to a boil, stirring to dissolve sugar. Reduce heat; simmer for 5 minutes, stirring occasionally. Remove from the heat; steep for 1 hour. Strain and discard peppers. Cover and refrigerate syrup until serving.

3. In a large shallow dish, mix the flour, cornmeal and seasonings. Drain chicken, discarding marinade. Add chicken to flour mixture, one piece at a time, and turn to coat. In a large skillet, heat oil over medium heat. Add chicken; cook until no longer pink, 3-4 minutes on each side. Drain; keep warm.

4. In a large bowl, combine the first six waffle ingredients. In another bowl, whisk the buttermilk, oil and egg until blended. Add to flour mixture; stir just until moistened. Stir in cheese.

5. Bake in a preheated waffle iron according to manufacturer's directions until golden brown. Serve with the chicken breasts, warmed syrup and, if desired, toppings.

**1 WAFFLE WITH 1 CHICKEN BREAST AND 3 TBSP. SYRUP:** 845 cal., 35g fat (5g sat. fat), 119mg chol., 1246mg sod., 98g carb. (54g sugars, 2g fiber), 33g pro.

# WAFFLE-IRON PIZZAS

These little pizza pockets are a fun mashup using the waffle iron.
Try your favorite toppings or even breakfast fillings like ham and eggs.
—*Amy Lents, Grand Forks, ND*

**TAKES:** 30 min. • **MAKES:** 4 servings

1 pkg. (16.3 oz.) large refrigerated buttermilk biscuits
1 cup shredded part-skim mozzarella cheese
24 slices turkey pepperoni (about 1½ oz.)
2 ready-to-serve fully cooked bacon strips, chopped
Pizza sauce, warmed

**1.** Roll or press biscuits into 6-in. circles. On one biscuit, place ¼ cup cheese, six slices pepperoni and a scant tablespoon chopped bacon to within ½ in. of the edges. Top with a second biscuit; fold bottom edge over the top edge and press to seal completely.

**2.** Bake in a preheated waffle iron according to the manufacturer's directions until golden brown, 4-5 minutes. Repeat with remaining ingredients. Serve with pizza sauce.

**1 PIZZA:** 461 cal., 21g fat (8g sat. fat), 28mg chol., 1650mg sod., 50g carb. (5g sugars, 2g fiber), 19g pro.

# WAFFLED MONTE CRISTOS

My husband and I enjoy Monte Cristos so much that I created this non-fried version to cut down on fat. The addition of orange zest and pecans makes these beautiful sandwiches absolutely delicious!
—*Mary Shivers, Ada, OK*

**TAKES:** 25 min. • **MAKES:** 2 sandwiches

1 large egg
¼ cup 2% milk
1 tsp. sugar
1 tsp. grated orange zest
4 slices white bread
2 Tbsp. finely chopped pecans
4 slices process American cheese (⅔ oz. each)
2 thin slices deli turkey (½ oz. each)
2 slices Swiss cheese (¾ oz. each)
2 thin slices deli ham (½ oz. each)
2 tsp. butter
2 tsp. confectioners' sugar
¼ cup seedless raspberry jam

**1.** In a shallow bowl, combine the egg, milk, sugar and orange zest. Dip the bread into egg mixture. Place bread on a preheated waffle iron; sprinkle each slice of bread with pecans. Bake bread according to manufacturer's directions until golden brown.

**2.** Place an American cheese slice on two bread slices; layer with turkey, Swiss cheese, ham and remaining American cheese. Top with remaining bread; butter outsides of sandwiches.

**3.** Toast sandwiches in a skillet for 1-2 minutes on each side or until cheese is melted. Dust with confectioners' sugar; serve with jam.

**1 SANDWICH:** 611 cal., 28g fat (14g sat. fat), 177mg chol., 1241mg sod., 64g carb. (35g sugars, 2g fiber), 27g pro.

CHILD'S PLAY
**THESE ARE FUN TO DIP & SHARE**

# PEACHES & CREAM WAFFLE DIPPERS

*I've made these for many brunches using strawberries and blueberries,
but peaches are my favorite. People of all ages enjoy dipping the crispy waffle strips.*
—*Bonnie Geavaras-Bootz, Scottsdale, AZ*

**PREP:** 30 min. • **BAKE:** 5 min./batch • **MAKES:** 6 servings (2 cups sauce)

1 cup all-purpose flour
1 Tbsp. sugar
1 tsp. baking powder
¼ tsp. salt
2 large eggs, separated
1 cup 2% milk
2 Tbsp. butter, melted
¼ tsp. vanilla extract
1¼ cups chopped frozen peaches, thawed, divided
2 cups sweetened whipped cream or whipped topping
¾ cup peach yogurt
   Toasted pecans and ground cinnamon, optional

**1.** In a large bowl, whisk flour, sugar, baking powder and salt. In another bowl, whisk egg yolks, milk, butter and vanilla until blended. Add to dry ingredients; stir just until moistened. Stir in 1 cup peaches.

**2.** In a small bowl, beat egg whites until stiff but not dry. Fold into batter. Bake in a preheated waffle iron according to manufacturer's directions until golden brown. Cut waffles into 1-in. strips.

**3.** In a small bowl, fold whipped cream into yogurt. Serve with the waffles. Sprinkle with remaining peaches and, if desired, pecans and cinnamon.

**8 WAFFLE STRIPS WITH ⅓ CUP SAUCE:** 341 cal., 21g fat (13g sat. fat), 122mg chol., 279mg sod., 30g carb. (14g sugars, 1g fiber), 8g pro.

# BLT WAFFLE SLIDERS

(Pictured on page 108.)

*My BLTs are deliciously different. Make and freeze the waffles, then reheat them in the toaster.*
—*Stacy Joura, Stoneboro, PA*

**TAKES:** 30 min. • **MAKES:** 12 servings

¾ cup all-purpose flour
¾ cup cornmeal
3 tsp. baking powder
1 Tbsp. sugar
1 tsp. salt
2 large eggs, separated
1 cup 2% milk
3 Tbsp. butter, melted
½ cup shredded cheddar cheese
6 Tbsp. mayonnaise
12 bacon strips, cooked and drained
2 small tomatoes, sliced
6 lettuce leaves

**1.** Preheat waffle maker. Whisk together first five ingredients. In another bowl, whisk egg yolks, milk and butter. Stir into dry ingredients just until moistened. Stir in cheese.

**2.** In a separate bowl, beat the egg whites until stiff but not dry. Fold into batter. Drop 1 heaping Tbsp. of batter in the center of each waffle iron quadrant; bake according to manufacturer's directions until golden brown, about 5 minutes. Cool on wire rack. Repeat with the remaining batter.

**3.** Spread mayonnaise evenly over half of the waffle pieces; top with bacon, tomatoes, lettuce, seasonings and remaining waffle pieces to make sliders. Serve immediately.

**1 SLIDER:** 224 cal., 14g fat (5g sat. fat), 54mg chol., 574mg sod., 17g carb. (3g sugars, 1g fiber), 7g pro.

# CHOCOLATE BROWNIE WAFFLE SUNDAES

One of my best friends loves chocolate as much as I do, so I like to make this over-the-top treat when we're together playing board games in the winter.
—*Vicki DuBois, Milltown, IN*

**TAKES:** 30 min. ● **MAKES:** 8 waffles

2 oz. unsweetened chocolate, chopped
1¼ cups all-purpose flour
1 cup packed brown sugar
½ tsp. salt
½ tsp. baking soda
¼ tsp. ground cinnamon
2 large eggs
½ cup 2% milk
¼ cup canola oil
1 tsp. vanilla extract
¼ cup chopped pecans
4 scoops vanilla ice cream
¼ cup chopped pecans, toasted
  Hot caramel and/or fudge ice cream toppings

1. In a microwave, melt chocolate; stir until smooth. Cool slightly.

2. In a large bowl, combine the flour, brown sugar, salt, baking soda and cinnamon. In another bowl, whisk the eggs, milk, oil and vanilla; stir into dry ingredients until smooth. Stir in the pecans and melted chocolate (batter will be thick).

3. Bake in a preheated waffle iron according to manufacturer's directions until golden brown. Serve with the ice cream, toasted pecans and desired ice cream toppings.

**2 WAFFLES:** 852 cal., 42g fat (12g sat. fat), 125mg chol., 575mg sod., 107g carb. (70g sugars, 5g fiber), 14g pro.

# DUTCH WAFFLE COOKIES

*My mom taught me how to make these waffle iron cookies. Now I have my friends bring their waffle irons to my house and we make big batches.*
—*Rachel Setala, Surrey, BC*

**PREP:** 40 min. • **COOK:** 5 min./batch • **MAKES:** about 6 dozen

1 cup butter, softened
1 cup sugar
2 large eggs
½ cup 2% milk
1 Tbsp. vanilla extract
4 cups all-purpose flour
1¾ tsp. baking powder
¾ tsp. baking soda
Confectioners' sugar, optional

**1.** In large bowl, beat butter and sugar until blended. Beat in eggs, milk and vanilla. In a second bowl, whisk the flour, baking powder and baking soda; gradually beat into butter mixture.

**2.** Shape level tablespoons of dough into balls and place 2 in. apart on a preheated waffle iron coated with cooking spray. Bake on medium heat until the cookies are golden brown, 3-4 minutes. Remove cookies to wire racks to cool. If desired, dust with confectioners' sugar.

**FREEZE OPTION:** Freeze cookies, layered between waxed paper, in freezer containers. To use, thaw in covered containers. If desired, dust with additional confectioners' sugar.

**1 COOKIE:** 62 cal., 3g fat (2g sat. fat), 12mg chol., 46mg sod., 8g carb. (3g sugars, 0 fiber), 1g pro.

## SWEET TREATS ON THE GRILL

For a three-ingredient dessert, sandwich mini marshmallows and chocolate chips between waffles; wrap in foil and grill.

# BLENDER

For decades, the old-fashioned blender has given us wholesome eye-opening smoothies in the morning and elegant pureed soups at night. But this classic time-saver—and its modern cousin, the immersion blender—can be used to create gorgeous breads, sauces, sides and treats, too.

# CHOOSING A BLENDER

There are two main types of blenders, the traditional countertop blender and the immersion, or stick, blender. Here's what you need to know.

The **countertop blender** has a pitcher with spinning blades in the bottom that mounts onto a motorized base. More powerful and with more settings than immersion blenders, they can blend, mix, puree, grind, chop and even crush ice. If you cook often with vegetable purees or you love blender drinks and shakes, you'll definitely want a countertop blender.

The **immersion blender** is also called a handheld or stick blender. Some celebrity chefs affectionately call the gadget a boat motor, which it does resemble in some ways! Compact and portable, the immersion blender is ready to blend right in the soup pot, measuring cup or other food vessel. The tool is easy to clean, too, with a wand attachment that detaches from the motor with the push of a button for easy cleaning.

Immersion blenders work best with thin liquids and soft ingredients, such as salad dressings and sauces. While they can't blend up frozen fruit for a smoothie or carrots for a puree, immersion blenders are quite useful. Their small

size means they can be tucked into a drawer when not in use. You can use them to blend up hot foods, like soups and gravies, right in the pan, rather than messily having to transfer a hot liquid into a countertop blender.

Which blender you choose depends on your kitchen needs. If you find that you don't work with frozen or hard ingredients often, the immersion blender is a space-saving gadget that can work in ways a countertop blender can't. Likewise, if you would rather have a larger appliance that can do more, you might prefer to get just a countertop blender.

If you have space and room in the budget, both blenders are nice to have. Think about your cooking style before making your purchase.

---

## BLENDING TIPS

**LIQUIDS IN FIRST.** Placing liquids in the blender first helps get things moving. This technique gives you faster blending results.

**START SLOW.** While it's tempting to go full speed ahead with a high power setting when you blend, this could result in an uneven blend of ingredients. Instead, start at the lowest setting and work your way up.

**GET UNSTUCK.** If the blades get hung up on an item, hit the pulse button a couple of times to help dislodge it, then blend away.

**WHEN USING AN IMMERSION BLENDER,** it works best if there's enough liquid in the container to immerse its entire blade. When blending, move the immersion blender up and down if using a small container, or in circles for large containers.

BE SURE THE LID IS ON TIGHT

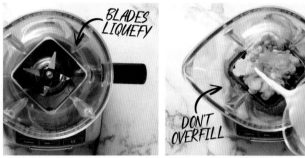

BLADES LIQUEFY

DON'T OVERFILL

# CLEANING TIPS

**Here's how to clean a countertop blender fast.** Cleaning a blender isn't easy. Unlike pots and pans, blenders have tons of nooks and crannies, plus sharp blades. You could pop the washable pieces in the dishwasher, but if you forget to remove the blades, they could get dull or rust over time. You also could take it apart, cleaning everything by hand. But between the preparation and taking a few minutes to enjoy your blended treat, who has time for that?

Start by filling half of your dirty blender with warm water, then add a few drops of dish soap. Fasten the lid onto the blender and turn it on for a few seconds. The soapy water swishing around the blender will help remove remnants of your pina colada. Remove the hot water, give your blender a quick rinse, and—voila—a clean blender.

**Here's how to clean an immersion blender.** The blender's wand attachment detaches from the motor with the push of a button. Hand-wash the wand or give it a quick rinse and pop it in the dishwasher.

| ADVANTAGES BY TYPE | |
|---|---|
| **Countertop Blender** | **Immersion Blender** |
| Powerful | Portable |
| Yields smoother, more finely blended results | Can puree a larger volume than a countertop blender in a single batch |
| Lid makes for more splash-free blending | Fewer components to wash |
| Ideal for frozen drinks, fruit and veggie purees, and emulsions | Ideal for large-batch cooking (blends right in the pot) and for small jobs |
| Versatile | Inexpensive |

# SOUTHWESTERN EGGS BENEDICT WITH AVOCADO SAUCE

I frequently make this spicy spinoff of classic eggs Benedict for my husband, who loves breakfast.
I like the heat from the jalapenos and that the avocado sauce is a healthier substitute for the typical hollandaise.
—Kara Scow, McKinney, TX

**TAKES:** 30 min. ● **MAKES:** 6 servings

- 1 medium ripe avocado, peeled and cubed
- ½ cup water
- ½ cup reduced-fat sour cream
- ¼ cup fresh cilantro leaves
- 2 Tbsp. ranch salad dressing mix
- 2 Tbsp. lime juice
- 2 Tbsp. pickled jalapeno slices
- 1 garlic clove, chopped
- ¼ tsp. salt
- ⅛ tsp. pepper
- 6 slices whole wheat bread, toasted
- 12 slices deli ham
- 6 slices Monterey Jack cheese
- 2 tsp. white vinegar
- 6 large eggs

**1.** Preheat oven to 425°. Place first 10 ingredients in a blender; cover and process until smooth.

**2.** Place toast on a baking sheet. Top each with two slices ham and one slice cheese. Bake until cheese is melted, 6-8 minutes.

**3.** Meanwhile, place 2-3 in. of water in a large saucepan or skillet with high sides; add the vinegar. Bring to a boil; adjust the heat to maintain a gentle simmer. Break cold eggs, one at a time, into a small bowl; holding bowl close to surface of water, slip egg into pan.

**4.** Cook, uncovered, until the whites are completely set and yolks begin to thicken but are not hard, 3-5 minutes. Using a slotted spoon, lift the eggs out of water. Serve eggs immediately with ham and cheese toasts and the avocado mixture.

**1 SERVING:** 345 cal., 19g fat (8g sat. fat), 232mg chol., 1069mg sod., 19g carb. (4g sugars, 3g fiber), 25g pro.

**✱ TEST KITCHEN TIP**
For perfect poached eggs, use the freshest eggs possible. Vinegar in the water keeps the eggs nice and compact, instead of spreading.

# CRANBERRY-BANANA SMOOTHIES

When the big meal is over, I make a smoothie using leftover cranberry sauce.
Don't have a frozen banana? Use a regular banana and add more ice.
—*Gina Fensler, Cincinnati, OH*

**TAKES:** 5 min. ● **MAKES:** 2 servings

1 large banana, peeled, quartered
  and frozen
⅔ cup whole-berry cranberry sauce
½ cup fat-free vanilla yogurt
½ cup ice cubes

Place all ingredients in a blender;
cover and process until smooth.
Serve immediately.

**1 CUP:** 230 cal., 0 fat (0 sat. fat), 2mg chol.,
21mg sod., 56g carb. (35g sugars, 3g fiber),
3g pro.

# CUCUMBER-MELON SMOOTHIES

My cool honeydew and cucumber smoothie has only five ingredients.
I sometimes add a small avocado to make it extra creamy.
—*Crystal Schlueter, Babbitt, MN*

**TAKES:** 15 min. ● **MAKES:** 6 servings

2 cups reduced-fat plain Greek
  yogurt
⅓ cup honey
3 cups chopped honeydew melon
2 medium cucumbers, peeled,
  seeded and chopped
1 to 2 Tbsp. fresh mint leaves,
  optional
2 cups crushed ice cubes

Place half of each of the following
ingredients in a blender: yogurt,
honey, melon, cucumber and, if
desired, mint. Cover; process until
blended. Add 1 cup ice; cover and
process until smooth. Pour smoothie
into three glasses; repeat with
remaining ingredients.

**1 CUP:** 155 cal., 2g fat (1g sat. fat), 4mg chol.,
48mg sod., 28g carb. (26g sugars, 2g fiber),
9g pro.

# BAKED OMELET ROLL

This hands-off omelet bakes in the oven, so you don't have to keep a constant eye on it like eggs you cook on the stovetop.
—*Susan Hudon, Fort Wayne, IN*

**TAKES:** 30 min. • **MAKES:** 6 servings

6 large eggs
1 cup whole milk
½ cup all-purpose flour
½ tsp. salt
¼ tsp. pepper
1 cup shredded cheddar cheese
Thinly sliced green onions, optional

1. Place eggs and milk in a blender. Add the flour, salt and pepper; cover and process until smooth. Pour into a greased 13x9-in. baking pan. Bake at 375° until eggs are set, 20-25 minutes.

2. Sprinkle with cheese. Roll up omelet in pan, starting with a short side. Place roll with seam side down on a serving platter. Cut into ¾-in. slices. If desired, sprinkle with green onions.

**2 SLICES:** 204 cal., 12g fat (6g sat. fat), 238mg chol., 393mg sod., 11g carb. (3g sugars, 0 fiber), 13g pro.

# HAM & CHEESE CREPES

These thin pancakes are easy to freeze and thaw, so you can cook up a batch, prepare just enough for two and save the rest for another time.
—*Marion Lowery, Medford, OR*

**PREP:** 20 min. + chilling • **BAKE:** 10 min. • **MAKES:** 4 filled crepes plus 4 unfilled crepes

⅓ cup cold water
⅓ cup plus 2 to 3 Tbsp. 2% milk, divided
½ cup all-purpose flour
1 large egg
2 Tbsp. butter, melted
⅛ tsp. salt
**ADDITIONAL INGREDIENTS (FOR 4 FILLED CREPES)**
1 Tbsp. Dijon mustard
4 thin slices deli ham
½ cup shredded cheddar cheese

1. Place the water, ⅓ cup milk, flour, egg, butter and salt in a blender; cover and process until smooth. Refrigerate for at least 30 minutes; stir. Add the remaining 2 to 3 Tbsp. milk if batter is too thick.

2. Heat a lightly greased 8-in. skillet; add about 3 Tbsp. batter. Lift and tilt pan to evenly coat bottom. Cook until top appears dry; turn and cook 15-20 seconds longer. Repeat with remaining batter, greasing skillet as needed. Stack four of the crepes with waxed paper in between; cover and freeze for up to 3 months.

3. Spread mustard over remaining four crepes; top each with ham and cheese. Roll up tightly. Place in an 8-in. square baking dish coated with cooking spray. Bake the filed crepes, uncovered, at 375° until heated through, 10-14 minutes.

4. To use frozen crepes, thaw in the refrigerator for about 2 hours. Fill and bake as directed.

**2 FILLED CREPES:** 423 cal., 24g fat (11g sat. fat), 159mg chol., 2540mg sod., 17g carb. (2g sugars, 0 fiber), 37g pro.

# APPLE PAN GOODY

I found the recipe for this unique casserole years ago and adapted it to my family's taste. Dotted with dried cranberries, the tender apple bake is sweetened with brown sugar and a little cinnamon. We enjoy it on breakfast buffets, but it also makes a lovely side dish, particularly with a pork entree.
—*Jeanne Bredemeyer, Orient, NY*

**PREP:** 20 min. ● **BAKE:** 20 min. ● **MAKES:** 8 servings

4 to 5 medium tart apples, peeled and sliced
¾ cup dried cranberries
6 Tbsp. brown sugar
1 tsp. ground cinnamon, divided
3 Tbsp. butter
6 large eggs
1½ cups orange juice
1½ cups all-purpose flour
¾ tsp. salt
2 Tbsp. sugar
Maple syrup, optional

**1.** In a large skillet, saute the apples, cranberries, brown sugar and ¾ tsp. cinnamon in butter until apples begin to soften, about 6 minutes. Transfer to a greased 13x9-in. baking dish.

**2.** Place eggs, orange juice, flour and salt in a blender; cover and process until smooth. Pour over the apple-cranberry mixture. Sprinkle with sugar and remaining cinnamon.

**3.** Bake, uncovered, at 425° until a knife inserted in the center comes out clean, 20-25 minutes. Serve with syrup if desired.

**1 CUP:** 316 cal., 8g fat (4g sat. fat), 171mg chol., 316mg sod., 54g carb. (32g sugars, 2g fiber), 7g pro.

**✳ STAFF HACK**

*"I use an immersion blender or regular blender when making a large batch of scrambled eggs. It makes them super fluffy."*
—SHANNON ROUM, SENIOR FOOD STYLIST

# MIXED FRUIT WITH LEMON-BASIL DRESSING

A slightly savory dressing really compliments the sweet fruit in this recipe. I also use the dressing on salad greens.
—*Dixie Terry, Goreville, IL*

**TAKES:** 15 min. ● **MAKES:** 8 servings

2  Tbsp. lemon juice
½  tsp. sugar
¼  tsp. salt
¼  tsp. ground mustard
⅛  tsp. onion powder
   Dash pepper
6  Tbsp. olive oil
4½  tsp. minced fresh basil
1  cup cubed fresh pineapple
1  cup sliced fresh strawberries
1  cup sliced peeled kiwifruit
1  cup seedless watermelon balls
1  cup fresh blueberries
1  cup fresh raspberries

**1.** Place the lemon juice, sugar, salt, mustard, onion powder and pepper in a blender; cover and process for 5 seconds. Continue processing while gradually add oil in a steady stream. Stir in basil.

**2.** In a large bowl, combine the fruit. Drizzle with dressing and toss to coat. Refrigerate until serving.

**¾ CUP:** 145 cal., 11g fat (1g sat. fat), 0 chol., 76mg sod., 14g carb. (9g sugars, 3g fiber), 1g pro. **DIABETIC EXCHANGES:** 2 fat, 1 fruit.

## HOW TO PREP A KIWI

● Cut both ends from fruit. Using a vegetable peeler, peel off fuzzy brown skin.

● Cut into slices, wedges or chunks with a sharp knife.

# BANANAS FOSTER BAKED FRENCH TOAST

This yummy baked French toast serves up all the taste of the spectacular dessert in fine fashion.

—*Laurence Nasson, Hingham, MA*

**PREP:** 20 min. + chilling ● **BAKE:** 35 min. ● **MAKES:** 6 servings

½ cup butter, cubed
⅔ cup packed brown sugar
½ cup heavy whipping cream
½ tsp. ground cinnamon
½ tsp. ground allspice
¼ cup chopped pecans, optional
3 large bananas, sliced
12 slices egg bread or challah
   (about ¾ lb.)
1½ cups 2% milk
3 large eggs
1 Tbsp. sugar
1 tsp. vanilla extract

**1.** Place butter in a microwave-safe bowl; microwave, covered, until it is melted, 30-45 seconds. Stir in brown sugar, cream, cinnamon, allspice and, if desired, pecans. Add bananas; toss gently to coat.

**2.** Transfer to a greased 13x9-in. baking dish. Arrange bread over top, trimming to fit as necessary.

**3.** Place remaining ingredients in a blender; process just until blended. Pour over bread. Refrigerate, covered, 8 hours or overnight.

**4.** Preheat oven to 375°. Remove French toast from refrigerator while oven heats. Bake, uncovered, until a knife inserted in the center comes out clean, 35-40 minutes. Let stand 5-10 minutes. Invert to serve.

**1 PIECE:** 658 cal., 31g fat (17g sat. fat), 218mg chol., 584mg sod., 84g carb. (39g sugars, 4g fiber), 14g pro.

# BLUE CHEESE CHEESECAKE

*Whenever I set out this savory cheese spread, guests can't seem to stop eating it!*
—*Niki Trapp, Cudahy, WI*

**PREP:** 20 min. ● **BAKE:** 50 min. + chilling ● **MAKES:** 20 servings

1 cup crushed Ritz crackers
3 Tbsp. butter, melted
12 oz. cream cheese, softened
2 pkg. (4.4 oz. each) crumbled blue cheese
1 pkg. (6½ oz.) garlic-herb spreadable cheese
1 cup sour cream
3 large eggs, lightly beaten
⅓ cup whole milk
¼ cup sherry
¼ tsp. coarsely ground pepper
Assorted crackers

**1.** In a small bowl, combine cracker crumbs and butter; press mixture onto the bottom of an ungreased 9-in. springform pan. Bake at 350° until lightly browned, about 5 minutes.

**2.** Place cream cheese, blue cheese, spreadable cheese, sour cream, eggs, milk, sherry and pepper in a blender; cover and process until blended. Pour over crust. Place springform pan in a large baking pan; add 1 in. of hot water to larger pan.

**3.** Bake until center is almost set, 50-55 minutes. Remove springform pan from water bath. Cool on a wire rack for 10 minutes. Carefully run a knife around edge of pan to loosen cheesecake. Refrigerate overnight. Serve with crackers.

**1 SERVING:** 219 cal., 19g fat (12g sat. fat), 84mg chol., 352mg sod., 5g carb. (2g sugars, 0 fiber), 6g pro.

## FREEZE SOME CHEESE

If you're hosting a smaller gathering, you may want to cut the Blue Cheese Cheesecake into four wedges after refrigerating overnight. Set aside one wedge for serving. Wrap the remaining pieces individually and freeze in a freezer container for future use. To use, thaw completely in the refrigerator.

# SWEET PEA PESTO CROSTINI

I made a healthier spin on my favorite celebrity chef's recipe by subbing in vegetable broth for some of the oil and going easy on the cheese. To top crostini, use less broth for a pastelike pesto. For use on pasta, add more broth for a saucelike consistency.
—*Amber Massey, Argyle, TX*

**TAKES:** 25 min. ● **MAKES:** 1½ dozen

12 oz. fresh or frozen peas, thawed
4 garlic cloves, halved
1 tsp. rice vinegar
½ tsp. salt
⅛ tsp. lemon-pepper seasoning
3 Tbsp. olive oil
¼ cup shredded Parmesan cheese
⅓ cup vegetable broth
1 whole wheat French bread demi-baguette (about 6 oz. and 12 in. long)
2 cups cherry tomatoes (about 10 oz.), halved or quartered

1. Preheat broiler. Place peas, garlic, vinegar, salt and lemon pepper in a blender or food processor; pulse until well blended. Continue processing while gradually adding oil in a steady stream. Add cheese; pulse just until blended. Add broth; pulse until mixture reaches desired consistency.

2. Cut baguette into 20 slices, each ½ in. thick. Place on ungreased baking sheet. Broil 4-5 in. from the heat until golden brown, 45-60 seconds per side. Remove to wire rack to cool.

3. To assemble crostini, spread each slice with about 1 Tbsp. pesto mixture; top with tomato pieces.

**1 CROSTINI:** 77 cal., 2g fat (trace sat. fat), 1mg chol., 190mg sod., 11g carb. (2g sugars, 1g fiber), 3g pro. **DIABETIC EXCHANGES:** ½ starch, ½ fat.

# CURRY CARROT DIP

The flavors of sweet carrots, mustard and curry blend deliciously in this appetizing dip. It's perfect with an assortment of vegetables.
—*Louise Weyer, Marietta, GA*

**TAKES:** 30 min. ● **MAKES:** 1 cup

1 **small onion, chopped**
2 **tsp. canola oil**
4 **medium carrots, sliced**
⅓ **cup water**
¼ **tsp. salt**
¼ **tsp. pepper**
¼ **tsp. curry powder**
2 **Tbsp. reduced-fat mayonnaise**
2 **tsp. prepared mustard**
**Assorted raw vegetables**

**1.** In a nonstick skillet, saute onion in oil. Add the carrots, water, salt, pepper and curry. Bring to a boil. Reduce heat; cover and simmer until vegetables are tender, about 6 minutes. Uncover; cook until liquid has evaporated, about 8 minutes. Cool.

**2.** Transfer to a blender or food processor; cover and process until smooth. Add the mayonnaise and mustard; mix well. Serve dip with raw vegetables.

**2 TBSP.:** 40 cal., 3g fat (0 sat. fat), 1mg chol., 133mg sod., 4g carb. (2g sugars, 1g fiber), 0 pro.

# PEACH-BASIL COOLER

Mix this with club soda for a cool and refreshing mocktail!
*—Dana Hinck, Pensacola, FL*

**PREP:** 25 min. + chilling ● **MAKES:** 12 servings

2 cups sugar
4 cups chopped peeled fresh peaches or 1 lb. frozen unsweetened sliced peaches
1 pkg. (¾ oz.) fresh basil leaves
2 cups cold water
1½ cups fresh lemon juice
   Additional cold water
   Ice cubes
   Club soda or champagne
   Additional fresh basil leaves

1. In a large saucepan, combine sugar, peaches, basil and water; bring to a boil. Reduce heat; simmer, uncovered, 5 minutes. Remove from the heat; let stand 30 minutes. Discard the basil; stir in the lemon juice. Refrigerate until cooled completely.

2. Place peach mixture in a blender; cover and process until blended. Strain into a pitcher; add more cold water to reach desired consistency. To serve, fill glasses with ice. Pour peach mixture halfway up glass; top with club soda or, if desired, champagne. Serve with additional basil.

**1 CUP:** 157 cal., 0 fat (0 sat. fat), 0 chol., 1mg sod., 41g carb. (38g sugars, 1g fiber), 1g pro.

# PEACHY KEEN DAIQUIRIS

You won't mind breaking out the blender for these frosty fruit drinks—they're a breeze to whip up with frozen peaches. A dash of grenadine lends a splash of contrasting color.
*—Joan Antonen, Arlington, SD*

**TAKES:** 10 min. ● **MAKES:** 3 servings

2½ cups ice cubes
3 medium peaches, peeled and sliced
¾ cup thawed frozen limeade concentrate
¼ cup orange juice
2 Tbsp. confectioners' sugar
½ cup rum, optional
   Grenadine syrup, optional

Place the ice cubes, sliced peaches, limeade concentrate, orange juice, confectioners' sugar and, if desired, rum in a blender; cover and process for 30 seconds or until smooth. Pour into chilled glasses; add grenadine syrup, if desired. Serve immediately.

**1 CUP:** 247 cal., 0 fat (0 sat. fat), 0 chol., 2mg sod., 62g carb. (58g sugars, 1g fiber), 1g pro.

# RED, WHITE & BLUE FROZEN LEMONADE

This patriotic drink is as pretty as it is delicious. With raspberries, blueberries and lemon juice, we created a striped lemonade that is perfect for your Fourth of July celebrations.
—*Shawn Carleton, San Diego, CA*

**TAKES:** 10 min. • **MAKES:** 4 servings

1 cup lemon juice
1 cup sugar
4 cups ice cubes
1 cup fresh or frozen blueberries
  Maraschino cherries

Place lemon juice, sugar and ice in a blender; cover and process until slushy. Divide blueberries among four chilled glasses; muddle slightly. Add lemon slush; top with cherries.

**¾ CUP:** 229 cal., 0 fat (0 sat. fat), 0 chol., 1mg sod., 60g carb. (55g sugars, 1g fiber), 0 pro.

### ✱ READER RAVE

*"We had this treat for the first time on a cold day and it was still really good! The kids all had seconds. The tartness from the blueberries and lemon juice goes well with the sweetness of the sugar. I like that it has only a few ingredients and comes together quickly. I can't wait to make this on a hot summer day to enjoy."*
—TAMMYCOOKBLOGSBOOKS, TASTEOFHOME.COM

# WATERMELON-LIME COOLER

When temps are heating up, chill some glasses and cool down with a slushy blend of watermelon, lime and ginger ale. Slurp and repeat.
—*Taste of Home Test Kitchen*

**TAKES:** 10 min. ● **MAKES:** 12 servings

12 **cups cubed seedless watermelon, frozen, divided**
¾ **tsp. grated lime zest, divided**
6 **cups chilled ginger ale, divided**

Place 4 cups frozen watermelon, ¼ tsp. grated lime zest and 2 cups ginger ale in a blender; cover and process until slushy. Serve beverage immediately. Repeat twice.

**1 CUP:** 82 cal., 0 fat (0 sat. fat), 0 chol., 14mg sod., 24g carb. (23g sugars, 1g fiber), 1g pro.

# CHEDDAR PEAR SOUP

Pears and sharp cheddar have always been one of my favorite flavor combos. This recipe brings the two together in a creamy, delicious soup. I like to serve it with a warm baguette and fresh fruit for lunch or a light supper.
—*Trisha Kruse, Eagle, ID*

**PREP:** 15 min. • **COOK:** 35 min. • **MAKES:** 8 servings (2 qt.)

¼ cup butter, cubed
1 large onion, chopped
2 garlic cloves, minced
⅓ cup all-purpose flour
2 tsp. smoked paprika
5 cups chicken broth
3 medium ripe pears, peeled and chopped
3 cups sharp cheddar cheese, shredded
¼ tsp. freshly ground pepper
   Fresh pear slices, optional

1. In a Dutch oven, heat butter over medium-high heat; saute onion and garlic until tender, 7-9 minutes. Stir in flour and paprika until blended; cook and stir 2 minutes. Gradually stir in broth. Add chopped pears; bring to a boil. Reduce the heat; simmer, covered, until pears are tender, about 15 minutes, stirring occasionally.

2. Puree soup using an immersion blender or cool slightly and puree the soup in batches in a blender; return to pan. Add cheese and pepper; cook and stir over low heat until the cheese is melted, 3-5 minutes. If desired, top with pear slices.

**1 CUP:** 299 cal., 20g fat (12g sat. fat), 60mg chol., 938mg sod., 18g carb. (8g sugars, 3g fiber), 12g pro.

# CREAMY MUSHROOM-THYME SOUP

I pick the mushrooms for this soup in the beautiful forests of the Pacific Northwest. There is nothing like harvesting fresh ingredients all by yourself, surrounded by nature. It's a spiritual thing!
—*Kristy Arnett, Stevenson, WA*

**PREP:** 15 min. ● **COOK:** 40 min. ● **MAKES:** 8 servings

¼ cup butter, cubed
1 shallot, finely chopped
1 lb. fresh chanterelle mushrooms or other wild mushrooms, coarsely chopped
1 tsp. minced fresh thyme
¼ cup all-purpose flour
½ tsp. salt
¼ tsp. pepper
6 cups chicken stock
1 cup heavy whipping cream
½ cup cream sherry

**1.** In a 6-qt. stockpot, melt the butter over medium-high heat. Add shallot; cook and stir until tender, 1-2 minutes. Add the mushrooms and thyme; cook 5 minutes longer.

**2.** Stir in flour, salt and pepper until blended; gradually whisk in the stock. Bring to a boil. Reduce heat; simmer, uncovered, 15-20 minutes to allow flavors to blend.

**3.** Puree soup using an immersion blender or cool soup slightly and puree in batches in a blender; return to pan. Add cream and sherry; heat through.

**1 CUP:** 231 cal., 17g fat (11g sat. fat), 49mg chol., 685mg sod., 11g carb. (4g sugars, 2g fiber), 6g pro.

# HAZELNUT ASPARAGUS SOUP

My heart is happy when bundles of tender local asparagus start to appear at my grocery store in spring. No one would ever guess this restaurant-quality vegetarian soup can be prepared in about 30 minutes.
—*Cindy Beberman, Orland Park, IL*

**PREP:** 20 min. • **COOK:** 15 min. • **MAKES:** 4 servings (3 cups)

1 Tbsp. olive oil
½ cup chopped sweet onion
3 garlic cloves, sliced
  Dash crushed red pepper flakes
2½ cups cut fresh asparagus
  (about 1½ lbs.), trimmed
2 cups vegetable broth
⅓ cup whole hazelnuts, toasted
2 Tbsp. chopped fresh basil
2 Tbsp. lemon juice
½ cup unsweetened almond milk
2 tsp. gluten-free reduced-sodium
  tamari soy sauce
¼ tsp. salt
  Shaved asparagus, optional

**1.** In a large saucepan, heat oil over medium heat. Add onion, garlic and pepper flakes; cook and stir until onion is softened, 4-5 minutes. Add the asparagus and broth; bring to a boil. Reduce heat; simmer, covered, until asparagus is tender, 6-8 minutes. Remove from heat; cool slightly.

**2.** Place nuts, basil and lemon juice in a blender. Add asparagus mixture. Process until smooth and creamy. Return to saucepan. Stir in almond milk, tamari sauce and salt. Heat through, taking care not to boil soup. If desired, top with shaved asparagus.

**NOTE:** To toast nuts, bake in a shallow pan in a 350° oven for 5-10 minutes or cook in a skillet over low heat until lightly browned, stirring occasionally.

¾ **CUP:** 164 cal., 13g fat (1g sat. fat), 0 chol., 623mg sod., 11g carb. (4g sugars, 4g fiber), 5g pro. **DIABETIC EXCHANGES:** 2½ fat, ½ starch.

# SWEET POTATO & CRAB SOUP

This sweet and savory soup is so easy to prepare. You can substitute butternut squash or pumpkin for the sweet potatoes, depending on what you have on hand.

—*Judy Armstrong, Prairieville, LA*

**PREP:** 15 min. ● **COOK:** 35 min. ● **MAKES:** 8 servings (2 qt.)

4 Tbsp. butter, divided
2 medium leeks (white portion only), finely chopped
3 garlic cloves, minced
4 cups cubed peeled sweet potatoes (about 1½ lbs.)
1 tsp. salt, divided
½ tsp. ground cinnamon
½ tsp. cayenne pepper
5 cups vegetable stock
2 cups heavy whipping cream
4 tsp. fresh thyme leaves, divided
12 oz. lump crabmeat, drained
Croutons, optional

**1.** In a Dutch oven, heat 2 Tbsp. butter over medium heat; saute the leeks and garlic until leeks are tender, 4-6 minutes.

**2.** Stir in sweet potatoes, ¾ tsp. salt, cinnamon, cayenne and stock; bring to a boil. Reduce the heat; simmer, covered, until the sweet potatoes are tender, 15-20 minutes.

**3.** Puree soup using an immersion blender or cool slightly and puree the soup in batches in a blender; return to pan. Stir in cream and 2 tsp. thyme; bring to a boil. Reduce heat; simmer, uncovered, 5 minutes.

**4.** Meanwhile, in a large skillet, melt remaining butter over medium heat. Add crab and the remaining salt and thyme; cook 5 minutes, stirring gently to combine. Top servings with crab mixture and, if desired, croutons.

**1 CUP:** 370 cal., 28g fat (18g sat. fat), 124mg chol., 994mg sod., 20g carb. (5g sugars, 3g fiber), 11g pro.

DINNER PARTY

**VEGETARIAN?**
**SKIP THE CRAB**

# HONEY-MINT LAMB SKEWERS

My hearty lamb bites are delicious and convenient. Assemble them the day before,
then pop them under the broiler when the party starts.
—*Trisha Kruse, Eagle, ID*

**PREP:** 15 min. + marinating • **BROIL:** 10 min./batch • **MAKES:** 3 dozen (2 cups dip)

½ cup olive oil
5 Tbsp. lemon juice
¼ cup minced fresh mint
2 Tbsp. honey
5 garlic cloves, minced
Dash salt
Dash pepper
3 lbs. lamb stew meat
**LEMON FETA DIP**
1 cup sour cream
2 Tbsp. lemon juice
2 cups (8 oz.) crumbled feta cheese
2 pepperoncini, minced

1. Mix the first seven ingredients in a shallow dish. Add lamb; turn to coat. Cover and refrigerate 4-6 hours.

2. Preheat broiler. For dip, place sour cream, lemon juice, feta cheese and pepperoncini in a blender; cover and process until smooth. Cover and refrigerate until serving.

3. Drain lamb and discard marinade. Thread two pieces of lamb on each of 36 soaked wooden skewers; place in two 15x10-in. pans. Broil 6-8 in. from heat until lamb reaches desired doneness, 10-12 minutes, turning occasionally. Serve with dip.

**1 SKEWER WITH 2½ TSP. DIP:** 105 cal., 7g fat (2g sat. fat), 29mg chol., 135mg sod., 2g carb. (1g sugars, 0 fiber), 9g pro.

# RED EYE BARBECUE SAUCE

I made this recipe for an assignment in culinary school—my first time making barbecue sauce. I have to say, it was the best
barbecue sauce I had in a long time! The hint of coffee livens up the sweet barbecue sauce perfectly.
—*Evan Haut, Canton, OH*

**PREP:** 30 min. • **COOK:** 1 hour • **MAKES:** 4 cups

¼ cup butter
4 garlic cloves, minced
1 shallot, finely chopped
1½ cups packed brown sugar
12 plum tomatoes, peeled, chopped and drained
½ cup cider vinegar
3 Tbsp. instant coffee granules
1 Tbsp. salt
1 tsp. pepper
1 tsp. adobo seasoning
1 tsp. harissa chili paste
1 tsp. cayenne pepper

1. In a Dutch oven, heat butter over medium heat. Add the garlic and shallot; cook and stir until softened, 5-7 minutes. Add brown sugar. Reduce heat to medium-low; cook, stirring occasionally, until deep golden brown, 15-17 minutes.

2. Add remaining ingredients; simmer 10 minutes. Remove from heat. Puree sauce using an immersion blender or cool slightly and puree in batches in a blender. Strain through a fine-mesh strainer. Return to pan; cook and stir until liquid is reduced by a third, 30-40 minutes.

3. Refrigerate, covered, until serving. Serve with grilled meats.

**2 TBSP.:** 60 cal., 2g fat (1g sat. fat), 4mg chol., 281mg sod., 12g carb. (11g sugars, 0 fiber), 0 pro.

# PASTA WITH CREAMY FENNEL SAUCE

*When pureeing fennel one day, I realized its velvety texture would make for a creamy, delicious and guilt-free pasta sauce. My experiment worked, and now I enjoy this good-for-you pasta sauce all the time.*
*—Deb Schwab, Moraga, CA*

**PREP:** 20 min. ● **COOK:** 40 min. ● **MAKES:** 6 servings

- 2 **large fennel bulbs**
- 1 **medium potato**
- 1 **shallot**
- 2 **garlic cloves**
- 2 **cups 2% milk**
- 1 **cup chicken broth**
- 3 **Tbsp. cream cheese, softened**
- 2 **Tbsp. grated Parmesan cheese**
- ½ **tsp. salt**
- ¼ **tsp. pepper**
- 1 **Tbsp. minced fresh parsley**
- 2 **pkg. (10 oz. each) fresh butternut squash ravioli**
  **Additional grated Parmesan cheese, optional**

1. Chop enough fennel fronds to measure 1 Tbsp. Set aside. Discard the rest of the tops or save for another use. Core and slice fennel bulbs. Peel and cube potato. Slice shallot; smash garlic cloves and peel.

2. Place vegetables, milk and chicken broth in a Dutch oven. Bring to a boil. Reduce heat; simmer, covered, until tender, 25-30 minutes. Drain, reserving ¼ cup cooking liquid; cool slightly. Stir in reserved cooking liquid, the cream cheese, Parmesan, salt and pepper.

3. Process in a blender or food processor until pureed. Return to Dutch oven. Stir in the parsley and reserved fennel fronds; keep warm.

4. Cook ravioli according to package directions. Drain. Toss with sauce. If desired, top with additional Parmesan.

**1 SERVING:** 309 cal., 7g fat (3g sat. fat), 19mg chol., 690mg sod., 51g carb. (11g sugars, 5g fiber), 12g pro.

**✳ TEST KITCHEN TIP**

To quickly prep garlic, smash each clove with the flat side of a chef's knife. The skin will peel right off, and the smashed cloves will be ready to use.

# PRONTO POTATO PANCAKES

*Pancakes aren't just for breakfast! Serve these as a side dish with any meat or eat them alone with applesauce on top.*
—*Darlene Brenden, Salem, OR*

**TAKES:** 30 min. • **MAKES:** 8 pancakes

2 large eggs
1 small onion, halved
2 medium potatoes, peeled and cut into 1-in. cubes
2 to 4 Tbsp. all-purpose flour
½ tsp. salt
⅛ tsp. cayenne pepper
4 to 6 Tbsp. canola oil
Applesauce, optional

**1.** Place eggs and onion in a blender; cover and process until blended. Add potatoes; cover and process until finely chopped. Transfer to a small bowl. Stir in the flour, salt and cayenne.

**2.** Heat 2 Tbsp. oil in a large nonstick skillet over medium heat. Drop batter by ¼ cupfuls into oil. Fry in batches until golden brown on both sides, using remaining oil as needed. Drain pancakes on paper towels. Serve with applesauce if desired.

**2 PANCAKES:** 263 cal., 17g fat (2g sat. fat), 93mg chol., 338mg sod., 23g carb. (2g sugars, 3g fiber), 6g pro.

# YUMMY CORN CHIP SALAD

Corn chips give a special crunch and unexpected flavor to this potluck-favorite salad. Bacon adds a hint of smokiness, while the cranberries bring a touch of sweetness. This is the perfect picnic companion!

—*Nora Friesen, Aberdeen, MS*

**TAKES:** 25 min. • **MAKES:** 12 servings

¾ cup canola oil
¼ cup cider vinegar
¼ cup mayonnaise
2 Tbsp. yellow mustard
½ tsp. salt
¾ cup sugar
½ small onion
¾ tsp. poppy seeds
**SALAD**
2 bunches leaf lettuce, chopped (about 20 cups)
1 pkg. (9¼ oz.) corn chips
8 bacon strips, cooked and crumbled
1 cup shredded part-skim mozzarella cheese
1 cup dried cranberries

**1.** For dressing, place first seven ingredients in a blender. Cover; process until smooth. Stir in the poppy seeds.

**2.** Place salad ingredients in a large bowl and toss with the dressing. Serve immediately.

**1⅓ CUPS:** 436 cal., 30g fat (4g sat. fat), 12mg chol., 456mg sod., 38g carb. (24g sugars, 2g fiber), 7g pro.

# PASSOVER POPOVERS

Popovers have an important role at the table, substituting for bread. When puffed and golden brown, they're ready to share.
—*Gloria Mezikofsky, Wakefield, MA*

**PREP:** 25 min. • **BAKE:** 20 min. + standing • **MAKES:** 1 dozen

1 cup water
½ cup safflower oil
⅛ to ¼ tsp. salt
1 cup matzo cake meal
7 large eggs

**✱ TEST KITCHEN TIP**

This recipe was tested with Manischewitz cake meal. Look for it in the baking aisle or kosher foods section.

**1.** Preheat oven to 450°. Generously grease 12 muffin cups. In a large saucepan, bring water, oil and salt to a rolling boil. Add cake meal all at once and beat until blended. Remove from heat; let stand 5 minutes.

**2.** Transfer mixture to a blender. Add two eggs and process, covered, until blended. Continue adding eggs, one at a time, and process until incorporated. Process 2 minutes longer or until mixture is smooth.

**3.** Fill prepared muffin cups three-fourths full. Bake until popovers are puffed, very firm and golden brown, 18-22 minutes. Turn off oven (do not open oven door); leave popovers in oven for 10 minutes. Immediately remove popovers from pan to a wire rack. Serve hot.

**1 POPOVER:** 174 cal., 12g fat (2g sat. fat), 109mg chol., 66mg sod., 11g carb. (0 sugars, 0 fiber), 5g pro.

# BLENDER YEAST ROLLS

Use your blender to combine the wet ingredients and stir into the flour—no kneading required!
—*Regena Newton, Oktaha, OK*

**PREP:** 20 min. + rising • **BAKE:** 20 min. • **MAKES:** about 1 dozen

1 cup warm 2% milk (110° to 115°)
1 pkg. (¼ oz.) active dry yeast
¼ cup sugar
2 large eggs
¼ cup canola oil
3¼ cups all-purpose flour
1 tsp. salt

**1.** Place the warm milk, yeast, sugar, eggs and oil in a blender; cover and process on low speed 30 seconds or until blended.

**2.** In a large bowl, combine the flour and salt. Add yeast mixture; stir with a spoon until combined (do not knead). Cover and let rise in a warm place until doubled, about 30 minutes.

**3.** Stir down dough. Fill greased muffin cups half full. Cover and let rise until doubled, about 30 minutes.

**4.** Bake at 350° until golden brown, 18-20 minutes. Remove from pans to wire racks. Serve warm.

**1 ROLL:** 206 cal., 6g fat (1g sat. fat), 38mg chol., 218mg sod., 31g carb. (6g sugars, 1g fiber), 5g pro.

# EASY IRISH CREAM

Blend up this fast and easy recipe for a holiday treat.
There's plenty of coffee flavor in every cozy cup.
—*Anna Hansen, Park City, UT*

**TAKES:** 15 min. • **MAKES:** 5 cups

2 cups half-and-half cream
1 can (13.4 oz.) dulce de leche or sweetened condensed milk
1¼ cups Irish whiskey
¼ cup chocolate syrup
2 Tbsp. instant coffee granules
2 tsp. vanilla extract
Hot brewed coffee or ice cubes

Pulse all ingredients in a blender until smooth. Stir 1-2 Tbsp. into a mug of hot coffee, or pour coffee and cream over ice.

½ **CUP:** 415 cal., 21g fat (13g sat. fat), 79mg chol., 116mg sod., 35g carb. (34g sugars, 0 fiber), 4g pro.

**TOASTED HAZELNUT:** Pulse 2 cups half-and-half cream, 1 can dulce de leche or sweetened condensed milk, 1¼ cups hazelnut liqueur and 2 Tbsp. instant coffee granules in a blender until smooth.

**BUTTER MINT:** Pulse 2 cups half-and-half cream, 1 can dulce de leche or sweetened condensed milk, 1¼ cups peppermint schnapps and 2 Tbsp. butter extract in a blender until smooth.

**SALTED CARAMEL:** Pulse 2 cups half-and-half cream, 1 can dulce de leche or sweetened condensed milk, 1¼ cups butterscotch schnapps and ¼ tsp. salt in a blender until smooth.

**CHOCOLATE-COVERED CHERRY:** Pulse 2 cups half-and-half cream, 1 can dulce de leche or sweetened condensed milk, 1¼ cups amaretto and ½ cup chocolate syrup in a blender until smooth.

# TOASTED COCONUT MILK SHAKES

I created this recipe as a reminder of my oldest brother, Brad, who was a picky eater who loved any dessert with coconut. It has a short list of ingredients, but it's certainly tall on coconut flavor!
—*Laurie Hudson, Westville, FL*

**TAKES:** 15 min. ● **MAKES:** 4 servings

½ cup flaked coconut
⅔ cup coconut milk, stirred before measuring then chilled
½ cup cream of coconut, stirred before measuring then chilled
4 cups vanilla ice cream
  Sweetened whipped cream

1. In a small skillet, cook and stir coconut over medium-low heat until toasted, 6-8 minutes. Cool completely.

2. Place the coconut milk, cream of coconut, ¼ cup toasted coconut and ice cream in a blender; cover and process until blended.

3. Pour into four glasses. Top with whipped cream; sprinkle shakes with remaining coconut. Serve immediately.

**1 CUP:** 502 cal., 30g fat (23g sat. fat), 58mg chol., 161mg sod., 54g carb. (51g sugars, 1g fiber), 6g pro.

**✱ STAFF HACK**

*"I reach for the immersion blender when I need to whip up some cream. I like how I can make small amounts in a measuring cup."*
**—SARAH FARMER, CULINARY DIRECTOR**

# SHEET PAN

Hearty, nutritious sheet-pan dinners are more popular than ever—and for good reason. Prep work is simple, the flavors are fresh and cleanup is a breeze. Oh—and these meals make us feel warm and cozy, too!

# SELECTING A SHEET PAN

Sheet pans are among the most versatile tools you can find in the kitchen. Here are some tips to help you select sheet pans and to get the most from them. Then turn the page to start cooking up simple sheet-pan dinners.

- Know the terminology. A sheet pan (called a 15x10x1-in. baking pan in our recipes) is a rimmed baking sheet. A baking (or cookie) sheet, on the other hand, does not have a rim. This gives you more surface area to fit on a few extra cookies, plus easy access to all parts of the baking sheet with a spatula.

- Sheet pans can stand in for cookie sheets, but it doesn't always work the other way around. The rolled edges of a sheet pan give you versatility because they catch juices, prevent spills and corral things like vegetables or meats for roasting

- To find a sheet pan that will cook your food evenly and stand up to the abuse of a high-temperature oven, look for heavy-duty, warp-resistant pans.

- Heavy-gauge aluminum is a great option. It's one of our favorites for great heat conductivity, which helps produce nice browning. Tri-ply pans (so called because they're made of three fused layers of metal, often with an aluminum core) are another great option.

- It pays to spend a little more for quality. An inexpensive pan won't lay flat and has a tendency to warp in the oven. Not only that, but its thin, flimsy material can easily cause the undersides of your food to burn.

- Nonstick pans are wonderful in the kitchen. But for roasting sheet-pan dinners (and making well-browned cookies), we recommend an uncoated metal surface. Nonstick can wear down and become scratched over time. It's also not safe for the broiler or other extreme temperatures, and you might want this versatility when roasting your dinner.

- Once you find sheet pans you like, buy two at a time. That way you know they will cook ingredients and perform the same. And they'll nest together for easy storage.

ELEVATE INGREDIENTS FOR CRISPY RESULTS

THE RIM STOPS SPILLS

DON'T OVERCROWD

# THESE SHEET-PAN IDEAS MAKE COOKING EASIER

**Freezer Tray.** A sheet pan makes it easy to freeze fresh fruit. Slice fruit if needed and place in a single layer on a sheet pan. Place the pan in the freezer and allow the fruit to freeze until solid. Remove, place in a freezer container, then return to the freezer until ready to use.

**Oven Protector.** There's nothing better than hot blueberry pie—unless it's bubbling all over the bottom of the oven because the juices overflowed. Slip a sheet pan on the bottom rack each time you bake a pie, lasagna or other dish that might bubble over, and you'll save yourself a messy chore. It's much easier to wash a pan than the floor of the oven.

**Cutting Companion.** If your cutting board doesn't have a rim, slicing juicy foods like pineapple or watermelon for fruit salad recipes can be tricky. To avoid juice dripping down the front of your cupboards, place a cutting board in a sheet pan before slicing. The sheet pan catches the excess juice and contains the mess. This also works when cutting the kernels off an ear of corn.

**Pizza Pan.** Cooking pizza on a preheated pizza stone makes it nice and crispy, but how do you get the pizza into and out of the oven? Flip a sheet pan over and use the back side to transfer the pizza without losing the toppings. If you don't have a pizza stone, preheat an oiled sheet pan in the oven. Place pizza dough in the sheet pan and top with your favorite sauce and toppings. Cook until done, cool slightly, cut and serve.

**Dish Carrier.** A sheet pan is the perfect tool for loading and unloading individual ramekins into and out of the oven. It's also handy for transporting hot food or dishes that might spill on their way to a potluck. And how many times have you sloshed water out of the ice cube trays when carrying them from the sink to the freezer? Load them onto a sheet pan and then simply dump any excess water off once you get the trays in the freezer.

## HOW TO REVIVE A GRIMY SHEET PAN

**GOT BAKED-ON GUNK?** Here's how to make a sheet pan look brand-new. Whether you're whipping up a sheet-pan supper for the family or carefully crafting a gorgeous slab pie, a chef's sheet pan is likely to see plenty of wear and tear. Before you throw away a favorite pan because of baked-on grime, try this easy way to clean and refresh it.

**YOU'LL NEED:**
• Hydrogen peroxide
• Baking soda
• Washcloth or scrubbing sponge

**STEP 1:** Apply the cleaning agents. Sprinkle some baking soda on the baking pan. Follow that with hydrogen peroxide and another sprinkling of baking soda. Let this mixture sit for at least two hours.

**NOTE:** Because this combination of soda and peroxide could be too harsh for some pans' material or coating, do a test run before cleaning the entire baking sheet, especially if it is made of a specialized material or has a coating of any kind.

**STEP 2:** Scrub away. Use a cloth or sponge to wipe away the homemade cleaner. Hard scrubbing usually isn't required. If stains remain, switch to a nonscratch scrubbing pad, try a second application of baking soda and hydrogen peroxide—or both. You just need a little patience!

**STEP 3:** Keep it clean. Now that your sheet pan is looking brand-new, consider lining it with parchment paper or aluminum foil before each use to keep it that way.

# SPINACH-EGG BREAKFAST PIZZAS

I like my food pretty, and this breakfast pizza is eye-popping.
Bring it to the table with a bowl of berries or grapes and cafe au lait.
—Lily Julow, Lawrenceville, GA

**PREP:** 20 min. ● **BAKE:** 15 min. ● **MAKES:** 4 pizzas

Cornmeal
1 loaf (1 lb.) frozen pizza dough, thawed
1 Tbsp. plus additional extra virgin olive oil, divided
5 to 6 oz. fresh baby spinach
⅓ cup plus additional grated Parmesan cheese, divided
3 Tbsp. sour cream
1 small garlic clove, minced
¼ tsp. sea salt
⅛ tsp. plus additional coarsely ground pepper, divided
4 large eggs

1. Preheat the oven to 500°. Line two 15x10x1-in. baking pans with parchment paper; sprinkle lightly with cornmeal. Cut dough into four pieces; stretch and shape the dough into 6- to 7-in. circles; place in pans.

2. Meanwhile, in a large skillet, heat 1 Tbsp. olive oil over medium-high heat. Add the spinach; cook and stir until just starting to wilt, 1-2 minutes. Combine the spinach with next five ingredients; spread spinach mixture over each pizza. Leave a slight border of raised dough along edge. Bake on a lower oven rack about 5 minutes.

3. Remove from oven; break an egg into center of each pizza. Return to lower oven rack, baking until the egg whites are set but yolks are still runny, 6-10 minutes. Drizzle olive oil over pizzas; top with additional Parmesan and pepper. Serve immediately.

**1 PIZZA:** 433 cal., 14g fat (4g sat. fat), 199mg chol., 865mg sod., 55g carb. (3g sugars, 1g fiber), 16g pro.

## ✱ STAFF HACK

*"My son, who's a restaurant cook, taught me how to use a big sheet pan to make French toast. Pour the egg mixture into the sheet pan. It lets you soak a lot of bread at the same time with a lot less fuss than a bowl or smaller dishes.*

*"I also use sheet pans for patting meat dry, cleaning shrimp, seasoning and dredging chicken—that kind of thing. It confines the mess, and cleanup is easy."*
—AMY SILVERS, COPY EDITOR

# AVOCADO CRAB BOATS

These boats are great with tortilla chips, beans or rice. You can also cover them, pack them on ice, and take them to a picnic or potluck. Straight from the oven or cold, they're always delicious.
—*Frances Benthin, Scio, OR*

**TAKES:** 20 min. ● **MAKES:** 8 servings

- 5 medium ripe avocados, peeled and halved
- ½ cup mayonnaise
- 2 Tbsp. lemon juice
- 2 cans (6 oz. each) lump crabmeat, drained
- ¼ cup chopped fresh cilantro, divided
- 2 Tbsp. minced chives
- 1 serrano pepper, seeded and minced
- 1 Tbsp. capers, drained
- ¼ tsp. pepper
- 1 cup shredded pepper jack cheese
- ½ tsp. paprika
  Lemon wedges

**1.** Preheat broiler. Place two avocado halves in a large bowl; mash lightly with a fork. Add the mayonnaise and lemon juice; mix until well blended. Stir in the crab, 3 Tbsp. cilantro, chives, serrano pepper, capers and pepper. Spoon into remaining avocado halves.

**2.** Transfer to a 15x10x1-in. baking pan. Sprinkle with cheese and paprika. Broil 4-5 in. from heat 3-5 minutes or until the cheese is melted. Sprinkle with remaining cilantro; serve with lemon wedges.

**NOTE:** Wear disposable gloves when cutting hot peppers; the oils can burn skin. Avoid touching your face.

**1 FILLED AVOCADO HALF:** 325 cal., 28g fat (6g sat. fat), 57mg chol., 427mg sod., 8g carb. (0 sugars, 6g fiber), 13g pro.

# CITRUS SALMON EN PAPILLOTE

This salmon dish is so simple, nutritious and easy to
make yet so delicious, elegant and impressive.
—*Dahlia Abrams, Detroit, MI*

**PREP:** 20 min. ● **BAKE:** 15 min. ● **MAKES:** 6 servings

6 orange slices
6 lime slices
6 salmon fillets (4 oz. each)
1 lb. fresh asparagus, trimmed and
    halved
    Olive oil-flavored cooking spray
½ tsp. salt
¼ tsp. pepper
2 Tbsp. minced fresh parsley
3 Tbsp. lemon juice

1. Preheat the oven to 425°. Cut parchment paper or heavy-duty foil into six 15x10-in. pieces; fold in half. Arrange citrus slices on one side of each piece. Top with the fish and asparagus. Spritz with cooking spray. Sprinkle with salt, pepper and parsley. Drizzle with lemon juice.

2. Fold parchment paper over fish; draw edges together and crimp with fingers to form tightly sealed packets. Place in baking pans.

3. Bake until fish flakes easily with a fork, 12-15 minutes. Open packets carefully to allow steam to escape.

**1 PACKET:** 224 cal., 13g fat (2g sat. fat), 57mg chol., 261mg sod., 6g carb. (3g sugars, 1g fiber), 20g pro. **DIABETIC EXCHANGES:** 3 lean meat, 1 vegetable.

# EASY MEMPHIS-STYLE BBQ RIBS

A friend of mine who loves barbecue gave me her recipe for ribs. Use just enough of the spice mixture to rub over them before baking and sprinkle on the rest later.
—*Jennifer Ross, Arlington, TN*

**PREP:** 20 min. ● **BAKE:** 3½ hours ● **MAKES:** 6 servings

¼ cup packed brown sugar
¼ cup paprika
2 Tbsp. kosher salt
2 Tbsp. onion powder
2 Tbsp. garlic powder
2 Tbsp. coarsely ground pepper
3 racks (1½ to 2 lbs. each) pork baby back ribs
   Barbecue sauce, optional

**1.** Preheat oven to 350°. In a small bowl, mix the first six ingredients; rub ¾ cup over ribs. Wrap rib racks in large pieces of heavy-duty foil; seal tightly. Place in a 15x10x1-in. baking pan. Bake 1½ hours. Reduce oven setting to 250°. Bake until tender, about 1½ hours longer.

**2.** Carefully remove ribs from foil; return to baking pan. Sprinkle ribs with remaining spice mixture. Bake 30 minutes longer or until lightly browned, brushing with barbecue sauce, if desired.

**1 SERVING (WITHOUT BARBECUE SAUCE):**
497 cal., 32g fat (11g sat. fat), 122mg chol., 2066mg sod., 17g carb. (10g sugars, 3g fiber), 35g pro.

# COD & ASPARAGUS BAKE

The lemon pulls this flavorful and healthy dish together.
You can also use grated Parmesan cheese instead of Romano.
—*Thomas Faglon, Somerset, NJ*

**TAKES:** 30 min. • **MAKES:** 4 servings

4 cod fillets (4 oz. each)
1 lb. fresh thin asparagus, trimmed
1 pint cherry tomatoes, halved
2 Tbsp. lemon juice
1½ tsp. grated lemon zest
¼ cup grated Romano cheese

1. Preheat oven to 375°. Place the cod and asparagus in a 15x10x1-in. baking pan brushed with oil. Add tomatoes, cut side down. Brush fish with lemon juice; sprinkle with lemon zest. Sprinkle the fish and vegetables with Romano cheese. Bake until the fish just begins to flake easily with a fork, about 12 minutes.

2. Remove pan from oven; preheat broiler. Broil the cod mixture 3-4 in. from heat until vegetables are lightly browned, 2-3 minutes.

**1 SERVING:** 141 cal., 3g fat (2g sat. fat), 45mg chol., 184mg sod., 6g carb. (3g sugars, 2g fiber), 23g pro. **DIABETIC EXCHANGES:** 3 lean meat, 1 vegetable.

**✳ TEST KITCHEN TIP**

We tested this recipe with cod fillets that were about ¾ in. thick. You'll need to adjust the bake time up or down if your fillets are thicker or thinner.

# HERB-BRINED CORNISH GAME HENS

Instead of a turkey or a big roast, why not serve individual Cornish game hens for the holidays?
They cook in a fraction of the time and they're guaranteed to impress all of your guests.
—*Shannon Roum, Cudahy, WI*

**PREP:** 35 min. + chilling ● **BAKE:** 35 min. + standing ● **MAKES:** 8 servings

⅔ cup kosher salt
¼ cup packed brown sugar
12 whole peppercorns
5 fresh sage leaves
2 garlic cloves
1 fresh thyme sprig
1 fresh rosemary sprig
1 qt. water
1½ qt. cold water
2 large turkey-size oven roasting bags
4 Cornish game hens (20 oz. each)

**HERB BUTTER**

14 whole peppercorns
2 garlic cloves
¾ cup butter, softened
3 Tbsp. plus 1 tsp. olive oil, divided
⅓ cup packed fresh parsley sprigs
3 Tbsp. fresh sage leaves
1 Tbsp. fresh rosemary leaves
2 Tbsp. fresh thyme leaves
2 lbs. fresh Brussels sprouts, trimmed and halved
2 small red onions, cut into wedges
½ tsp. kosher salt
½ tsp. coarsely ground pepper

**1.** In a saucepan, combine the salt, brown sugar, peppercorns, sage, garlic, thyme, rosemary and 1 qt. water. Bring to a boil. Cook and stir until salt and sugar are dissolved. Remove from the heat. Add the cold water to cool the brine to room temperature.

**2.** Place a turkey-size oven roasting bag inside a second roasting bag; add hens. Carefully pour cooled brine into the bag. Squeeze out as much air as possible; seal bags and turn to coat. Place in a roasting pan. Refrigerate for 1-2 hours, turning occasionally. Drain and discard brine; pat hens dry.

**3.** Meanwhile, place the peppercorns and garlic in a food processor; cover and pulse until coarsely chopped. Add the butter, 3 Tbsp. olive oil and herbs; cover and process until smooth. With fingers, carefully loosen skin from hens; rub half of the butter mixture under skin. Secure skin to underside of breast with toothpicks; tie drumsticks together. Rub the remaining butter mixture over skin.

**4.** In a 15x10x1-in. baking pan, toss the Brussels sprouts and onions with remaining olive oil, salt and pepper. Arrange in a single layer. Place the hens, breast side up, on top of the vegetables. Bake at 450° until a thermometer inserted in breast reads 165°, 35-40 minutes. Cover loosely with foil if hens brown too quickly.

**5.** Remove hens and vegetables to a serving platter; cover and let stand for 10 minutes before carving. If desired, garnish with additional herbs.

**1 SERVING:** 592 cal., 39g fat (16g sat. fat), 199mg chol., 474mg sod., 12g carb. (3g sugars, 4g fiber), 49g pro.

## HOW TO CUT POULTRY IN HALF

Halved chicken, game hens and duckling make a pretty presentation. Using a large knife or kitchen shears, carefully cut out and remove the backbone.

Resting the area near the tip of the knife on the cutting board, cut through the breastbone in a firm motion. Or use kitchen shears to carefully cut through the breastbone.

Rearrange the skin to neatly cover the breast meat. Season as desired and bake until a thermometer reads 165°, adjusting the bake time as needed.

# HOISIN SRIRACHA SHEET-PAN CHICKEN

The convenience and simplicity of this chicken dinner make it extra awesome. Change up the veggies throughout the year—the sticky-spicy-sweet sauce is delicious on all of them!
—*Julie Peterson, Crofton, MD*

**PREP:** 20 min. ● **BAKE:** 40 min. ● **MAKES:** 4 servings

⅓ cup hoisin sauce
⅓ cup reduced-sodium soy sauce
2 Tbsp. maple syrup
2 Tbsp. Sriracha Asian hot chili sauce
1 Tbsp. rice vinegar
2 tsp. sesame oil
2 garlic cloves, minced
½ tsp. minced fresh gingerroot
4 bone-in chicken thighs (6 oz. each)
¼ tsp. salt
¼ tsp. pepper
1 medium sweet potato, cut into ¾-in. cubes
2 Tbsp. olive oil, divided
4 cups fresh cauliflowerets
1 medium sweet red pepper, cut into ¾-in. pieces
  Sesame seeds, optional

**1.** Preheat oven to 400°. Whisk together the first eight ingredients. Set aside.

**2.** Sprinkle both sides of the chicken with salt and pepper. Place the chicken and the sweet potato in a single layer in a foil-lined 15x10x1-in. baking pan. Drizzle with 1 Tbsp. olive oil and a third of the hoisin mixture; toss to coat.

**3.** Bake 15 minutes; turn chicken and potatoes. Add cauliflower and red pepper; drizzle with another third of hoisin mixture and remaining olive oil. Bake until a thermometer inserted in chicken reads 170°-175°, about 25 minutes longer. Drizzle with the remaining sauce. If desired, sprinkle with sesame seeds.

**1 SERVING:** 490 cal., 24g fat (5g sat. fat), 81mg chol., 1665mg sod., 40g carb. (23g sugars, 5g fiber), 28g pro.

**✱ TEST KITCHEN TIP**

Hoisin sauce is a thick, sweet and somewhat spicy condiment popular in Chinese cooking. It's often made with fermented soybeans (miso), garlic, spices and sweet ingredients such as plums or sweet potatoes.

# LEMON-DIJON PORK SHEET-PAN SUPPER

Most nights, I need something that requires minimal effort and yields delicious results. Sheet-pan suppers like this one have become an all-time favorite, not only because of their bright flavors, but their speedy cleanup time, too!
—*Elisabeth Larsen, Pleasant Grove, UT*

**TAKES:** 30 min. • **MAKES:** 4 servings

4 tsp. Dijon mustard
2 tsp. grated lemon zest
1 garlic clove, minced
½ tsp. salt
2 Tbsp. canola oil
1½ lbs. sweet potatoes (about 3 medium), cut into ½-in. cubes
1 lb. fresh Brussels sprouts (about 4 cups), quartered
4 boneless pork loin chops (6 oz. each)
Coarsely ground pepper, optional

**1.** Preheat oven to 425°. In a large bowl, mix the first four ingredients; gradually whisk in oil. Remove 1 Tbsp. mixture for brushing pork. Add the vegetables to remaining mixture; toss to coat.

**2.** Place pork chops and vegetables in a 15x10x1-in. pan coated with cooking spray. Brush the chops with reserved mustard mixture. Roast 10 minutes.

**3.** Turn the chops and stir vegetables; roast until a thermometer inserted in pork reads 145° and vegetables are tender, 10-15 minutes. If desired, sprinkle with pepper. Let stand for 5 minutes before serving.

**1 PORK CHOP WITH 1¼ CUPS VEGETABLES:** 516 cal., 17g fat (4g sat. fat), 82mg chol., 505mg sod., 51g carb. (19g sugars, 9g fiber), 39g pro.
**DIABETIC EXCHANGES:** 5 lean meat, 3 starch, 1½ fat, 1 vegetable.

**✳ DID YOU KNOW?**
The bright colors in this dish ensure you're getting a variety of nutrients. Sweet potatoes are an excellent source of vitamin A, and Brussels sprouts are loaded with vitamin K.

PIZZA NIGHT

**WHOLESOME ZUCCHINI IS IN THE CRUST**

# MOZZARELLA CORNBREAD PIZZA

My sons like pizza but not takeout, so I pull out my trusty baking pan to make
a cornbread pizza with veggies in the crust. Adjust the toppings to your liking.
—Mary Leverette, Columbia, SC

**PREP:** 25 min. + standing ● **BAKE:** 20 min. ● **MAKES:** 10 servings

3 cups shredded zucchini
1 tsp. salt, divided
2 pkg. (8½ oz. each) cornbread/
    muffin mix
3 large eggs, lightly beaten
¼ tsp. pepper
**TOPPINGS**
1 jar (14 oz.) pizza sauce
¾ cup chopped sweet red or green
    pepper
1 can (2¼ oz.) sliced ripe olives,
    drained
4 green onions, chopped
⅓ cup coarsely chopped fresh basil
1 Tbsp. minced fresh oregano or 1
    tsp. dried oregano
3 cups shredded part-skim
    mozzarella cheese

**1.** Preheat oven to 450°. Place the zucchini in a colander over a bowl; sprinkle with ¾ tsp. salt and toss. Let stand 15 minutes.

**2.** Press zucchini and blot dry with paper towels; transfer to a large bowl. Add the muffin mixes, eggs, pepper and remaining salt; stir until blended. Spread mixture evenly into a greased 15x10x1-in. baking pan. Bake until lightly browned, 8-10 minutes. Reduce oven setting to 350°.

**3.** Spread pizza sauce over crust. Top with red pepper, olives and green onions. Sprinkle with herbs and cheese. Bake until cheese is melted, 12-15 minutes.

**1 PIECE:** 366 cal., 15g fat (6g sat. fat), 79mg chol., 912mg sod., 42g carb. (14g sugars, 5g fiber), 15g pro.

## ✳ READER RAVE

*"This is a great recipe! We added toppings to fit our family's tastes (like fresh baby spinach and pepperoni). I never would have thought of making pizza this way, but it's very good! I'll be making this again!"*
—DIANEC23, TASTEOFHOME.COM

# MAMA MIA MEATBALL TAQUITOS

We love lasagna, but it takes too long on weeknights. My solution: meatball taquitos. My kids get the flavors they want and I get it on the table in a hurry.
—*Lauren Wyler, Dripping Springs, TX*

**TAKES:** 30 min. ● **MAKES:** 1 dozen

12 **frozen fully cooked Italian turkey meatballs, thawed**
2 **cups shredded part-skim mozzarella cheese**
1 **cup whole-milk ricotta cheese**
1 **tsp. Italian seasoning**
12 **flour tortillas (8 in.)**
   **Cooking spray**
   **Warm marinara sauce**

**1.** Preheat oven to 425°. Place the meatballs in a food processor; pulse until finely chopped. Transfer to a large bowl; stir in cheeses and Italian seasoning.

**2.** Spread about ¼ cup meatball mixture down center of each tortilla. Roll up tightly. Place in a greased 15x10x1-in. baking pan, seam side down; spritz with cooking spray.

**3.** Bake until taquitos are golden brown, 16-20 minutes. Serve with marinara sauce.

**2 TAQUITOS:** 617 cal., 28g fat (11g sat. fat), 94mg chol., 1069mg sod., 60g carb. (3g sugars, 3g fiber), 33g pro.

# MEDITERRANEAN TILAPIA

I recently became a fan of tilapia. Its mild taste makes it easy to top with my favorite ingredients. Plus, it's low in calories and fat. What's not to love?
—*Robin Brenneman, Hilliard, OH*

**TAKES:** 20 min. ● **MAKES:** 6 servings

- 6 **tilapia fillets (6 oz. each)**
- 1 **cup canned Italian diced tomatoes**
- ½ **cup water-packed artichoke hearts, chopped**
- ½ **cup sliced ripe olives**
- ½ **cup crumbled feta cheese**

Preheat oven to 400°. Place fillets in a 15x10x1-in. baking pan coated with cooking spray. Top with tomatoes, artichoke hearts, olives and cheese. Bake, uncovered, until fish flakes easily with a fork, 15-20 minutes.

**1 FILLET:** 197 cal., 4g fat (2g sat. fat), 88mg chol., 446mg sod., 5g carb. (2g sugars, 1g fiber), 34g pro. **DIABETIC EXCHANGES:** 5 lean meat, ½ fat.

**ITALIAN TILAPIA:** Follow method as directed, but top fillets with 1 cup canned diced tomatoes with roasted garlic, ½ cup each julienned roasted sweet red pepper, sliced fresh mushrooms and diced fresh mozzarella cheese, and ½ tsp. dried basil.

**SOUTHWEST TILAPIA:** Follow method as directed, but top fillets with 1 cup canned diced tomatoes with mild green chilies, ½ cup each cubed avocado, frozen corn (thawed), cubed cheddar cheese, and ½ tsp. dried cilantro.

# PORK & ASPARAGUS SHEET-PAN DINNER

When time is of the essence, it's nice to have a quick and easy meal idea in your back pocket. Not only is it delicious, but you can clean it up in a flash.
—Joan Hallford, North Richland Hills, TX

**PREP:** 20 min. ● **BAKE:** 20 min. ● **MAKES:** 4 servings

¼ cup olive oil, divided
3 cups diced new potatoes
3 cups cut fresh asparagus
   (1-in. pieces)
¼ tsp. salt
¼ tsp. pepper
1 large Gala or Honeycrisp apple, peeled and cut into ½-in. slices
2 tsp. brown sugar
1 tsp. ground cinnamon
¼ tsp. ground ginger
4 boneless pork loin chops (1 in. thick and about 6 oz. each)
2 tsp. southwest seasoning

**❋ TEST KITCHEN TIP**

Lining the pan with foil not only means an easier cleanup—you can also get by with using a bit less olive oil.

**1.** Preheat the oven to 425°. Line a 15x10x1-in. baking pan with foil; brush with 2 tsp. olive oil.

**2.** In a large bowl, toss potatoes with 1 Tbsp. olive oil. Place in one section of the prepared baking pan. In the same bowl, toss the asparagus with 1 Tbsp. olive oil and place in another section of pan. Sprinkle the vegetables with salt and pepper.

**3.** In same bowl, toss apple with 1 tsp. olive oil. In a small bowl, mix brown sugar, cinnamon and ginger; sprinkle over apples and toss to coat. Transfer to a different section of pan.

**4.** Brush pork chops with remaining olive oil; sprinkle both sides with the southwest seasoning. Place chops in remaining section of pan. Bake until a thermometer inserted in pork reads 145° and potatoes and apples are tender, 20-25 minutes. Let stand 5 minutes before serving.

**1 SERVING:** 486 cal., 23g fat (5g sat. fat), 82mg chol., 447mg sod., 32g carb. (10g sugars, 5g fiber), 37g pro.

# PARMESAN CHICKEN WITH ARTICHOKE HEARTS

*I've liked the chicken and artichoke combo for a long time. Here's my own lemony twist. With all the praise it gets, this dinner is so much fun to serve.*
—*Carly Giles, Hoquiam, WA*

**PREP:** 20 min. ● **BAKE:** 20 min. ● **MAKES:** 4 servings

4 boneless skinless chicken breast halves (6 oz. each)
3 tsp. olive oil, divided
1 tsp. dried rosemary, crushed
½ tsp. dried thyme
½ tsp. pepper
2 cans (14 oz. each) water-packed artichoke hearts, drained and quartered
1 medium onion, coarsely chopped
½ cup white wine or reduced-sodium chicken broth
2 garlic cloves, chopped
¼ cup shredded Parmesan cheese
1 lemon, cut into 8 slices
2 green onions, thinly sliced

**1.** Preheat oven to 375°. Place the chicken in a 15x10x1-in. baking pan coated with cooking spray; drizzle with 1½ tsp. oil. In a small bowl, mix the rosemary, thyme and pepper; sprinkle half over chicken.

**2.** In a large bowl, combine artichoke hearts, onion, wine, garlic, remaining oil and remaining herb mixture; toss to coat. Arrange around chicken. Sprinkle the chicken with cheese; top with the lemon slices.

**3.** Roast until a thermometer inserted in chicken reads 165°, 20-25 minutes. Sprinkle with green onions.

**1 CHICKEN BREAST HALF WITH ¾ CUP ARTICHOKE MIXTURE:** 339 cal., 9g fat (3g sat. fat), 98mg chol., 667mg sod., 18g carb. (2g sugars, 1g fiber), 42g pro. **DIABETIC EXCHANGES:** 5 lean meat, 1 vegetable, 1 fat, ½ starch.

## HOW TO QUICKLY SEPARATE AND PEEL GARLIC CLOVES

Place the head of garlic in one bowl and smash with the bottom of a similar-sized bowl. You can also smash between two cutting boards.

Put the whole crushed bulb in a hard-sided bowl with a similar-sized bowl over the top. Metal is best, but you can use glass or even a firm plastic food storage container with a lid. A jar works, too, but it takes longer to shake. Shake vigorously for 10-15 seconds to separate the papery outer layer from the garlic clove.

The cloves are peeled and the skin can be easily discarded.

# ORANGE-GLAZED PORK WITH SWEET POTATOES

When it's chilly outside, I like to roast pork tenderloin with sweet potatoes, apples and an orange. The sweetness and spices make any evening cozy.
—*Danielle Lee Boyles, Weston, WI*

**PREP:** 20 min. • **BAKE:** 55 min. + standing • **MAKES:** 6 servings

1 lb. sweet potatoes
   (about 2 medium)
2 medium apples
1 medium orange
1 tsp. salt
½ tsp. pepper
1 cup orange juice
2 Tbsp. brown sugar
2 tsp. cornstarch
1 tsp. ground cinnamon
1 tsp. ground ginger
2 pork tenderloins (about 1 lb. each)

**1.** Preheat oven to 350°. Peel sweet potatoes; core apples. Cut potatoes, apples and orange crosswise into ¼-in.-thick slices. Arrange in a foil-lined 15x10x1-in. baking pan coated with cooking spray; sprinkle with salt and pepper. Roast 10 minutes.

**2.** Meanwhile, in a microwave-safe bowl, mix orange juice, brown sugar, cornstarch, cinnamon and ginger. Microwave, covered, on high, stirring every 30 seconds until thickened, 1-2 minutes. Stir until smooth.

**3.** Place pork over the sweet potato mixture; drizzle with the orange juice mixture. Roast until a thermometer inserted in the pork reads 145° and sweet potatoes and apples are tender, 45-55 minutes longer. Remove from oven and tent with foil. Let stand for 10 minutes before slicing.

**4 OZ. COOKED PORK WITH ABOUT 1 CUP SWEET POTATO MIXTURE:** 325 cal., 5g fat (2g sat. fat), 85mg chol., 467mg sod., 36g carb. (21g sugars, 3g fiber), 32g pro. **DIABETIC EXCHANGES:** 4 lean meat, 2 starch.

# OVEN-FRIED FISH & CHIPS

My baked fish is a shoo-in when you want fish and chips without the frying mess. Dare I say, they're a little upgrade from the English pub classic.
—*Reeni Pisano, Wappingers Falls, NY*

**PREP:** 15 min. • **BAKE:** 55 min. • **MAKES:** 4 servings

⅓ cup mayonnaise
2 Tbsp. dill pickle relish or chopped dill pickle
2 tsp. grated lemon zest
**FISH AND POTATOES**
1½ lbs. baking potatoes (about 3 medium)
2 tsp. olive oil
¾ tsp. kosher salt, divided
½ tsp. coarsely ground pepper, divided
½ cup panko (Japanese) bread crumbs
¼ cup seasoned bread crumbs
4 cod fillets (4 oz. each)
2 Tbsp. mayonnaise
2 Tbsp. grated Parmesan cheese
2 tsp. chopped fresh parsley
Malt vinegar, optional

1. For tartar sauce, in a small bowl, mix mayonnaise, relish and lemon zest. Refrigerate until serving.

2. Preheat oven to 400°. Cut potatoes lengthwise into 1-in.-thick wedges; toss with the oil, ½ tsp. salt and ¼ tsp. pepper. Spread evenly in a greased 15x10x1-in. baking pan. Roast until golden brown, stirring occasionally, 40-45 minutes.

3. Meanwhile, in a small skillet, toast the panko bread crumbs over medium-low heat until lightly browned, stirring occasionally, 5-7 minutes. Transfer to a shallow bowl; stir in the seasoned bread crumbs.

4. Sprinkle cod with the remaining salt and pepper; spread top and sides of fish with mayonnaise. Dip cod in crumb mixture to cover mayonnaise, pressing firmly to help adhere. Place in a greased 15x10x1-in. baking pan, crumb side up. Sprinkle with any remaining crumb mixture. Bake until fish just begins to flake easily with a fork, 12-15 minutes.

5. Toss potatoes with cheese and parsley. Serve fish and potatoes with tartar sauce and, if desired, vinegar.

**1 SERVING:** 475 cal., 24g fat (4g sat. fat), 54mg chol., 789mg sod., 40g carb. (2g sugars, 5g fiber), 23g pro.

**✱ DID YOU KNOW?**

Mild-tasting malt vinegar is a classic British accompaniment to fish and chips. It's made from sprouted, dried and ground barley, the same product used to make malted milk powder.

# SASSY SALSA MEAT LOAVES

Here's a twist on classic meat loaf that can be made ahead and will last for a few days afterward. Leftovers reheat easily in the microwave. Make meat loaf sandwiches with the leftovers, buns and a little Monterey Jack cheese.

—*Tasha Tully, Owings Mills, MD*

**PREP:** 25 min. ● **BAKE:** 65 min. + standing ● **MAKES:** 2 loaves (6 servings each)

¾ cup uncooked instant brown rice
1 can (8 oz.) tomato sauce
1½ cups salsa, divided
1 large onion, chopped
1 large egg, lightly beaten
1 celery rib, finely chopped
¼ cup minced fresh parsley
2 Tbsp. minced fresh cilantro
2 garlic cloves, minced
1 Tbsp. chili powder
1½ tsp. salt
½ tsp. pepper
2 lbs. lean ground beef (90% lean)
1 lb. ground turkey
½ cup shredded reduced-fat Monterey Jack cheese or Mexican cheese blend

1. Preheat oven to 350°. Cook rice according to package directions; cool slightly. In a large bowl, combine the tomato sauce, ½ cup salsa, onion, egg, celery, parsley, cilantro, garlic and seasonings; stir in rice. Add beef and turkey; mix lightly but thoroughly.

2. Shape into two 8x4-in. loaves in a greased 15x10x1-in. baking pan. Bake until a thermometer inserted in center reads 165°, 1-1¼ hours.

3. Spread with remaining salsa and sprinkle with cheese; bake until cheese is melted, about 5 minutes. Let stand 10 minutes before slicing.

**FREEZE OPTION:** Bake meat loaves without topping. Cool; securely wrap in plastic, then foil. To use, partially thaw in refrigerator overnight. Unwrap meat loaves; place in a greased 15x10x1-in. baking pan. Reheat in a preheated 350° oven or until a thermometer inserted in the center reads 165°, 40-45 minutes; top as directed.

**1 SLICE:** 237 cal., 11g fat (4g sat. fat), 91mg chol., 634mg sod., 9g carb. (2g sugars, 1g fiber), 25g pro. **DIABETIC EXCHANGES:** 3 lean meat, ½ starch, ½ fat.

# ROASTED BUTTERNUT SQUASH TACOS

Spicy butternut squash makes a great base for these vegetarian tacos.
I'm always looking for quick and nutritious weeknight dinners
for my family, and these are delicious, too!
—*Elisabeth Larsen, Pleasant Grove, UT*

**PREP:** 10 min. ● **BAKE:** 30 min. ● **MAKES:** 6 servings

2  Tbsp. canola oil
1  Tbsp. chili powder
½  tsp. ground cumin
½  tsp. ground coriander
½  tsp. salt
¼  tsp. cayenne pepper
1  medium butternut squash
   (3 to 4 lbs.), peeled and cut
   into ½-in. pieces
12  corn tortillas (6 in.), warmed
1  cup crumbled queso fresco or feta
   cheese
1  medium ripe avocado, peeled and
   sliced thin
¼  cup diced red onion
   Pico de gallo, optional

1. Preheat oven to 425°. Combine first six ingredients. Add the squash cubes; toss to coat. Transfer to a foil-lined 15x10x1-in. baking pan. Bake, stirring occasionally, until tender, 30-35 minutes.

2. Divide squash evenly among tortillas. Top with queso fresco, avocado and red onion. If desired, serve with pico de gallo.

**2 TACOS:** 353 cal., 13g fat (3g sat. fat), 13mg chol., 322mg sod., 54g carb. (7g sugars, 13g fiber), 11g pro.

# SALMON WITH CARIBBEAN SALSA

Salmon fillets smothered in tropical fruit salsa make an elegant main dish recipe. The cinnamon-spiced seasoning is a wonderful complement to grilled chicken, too.
—Mary Jones, Athens, OH

**PREP:** 25 min. + chilling • **BAKE:** 25 min. • **MAKES:** 8 servings (5 cups salsa)

**SEASONING**
- 1 Tbsp. salt
- 1 Tbsp. ground nutmeg
- 1 Tbsp. pepper
- 1½ tsp. each ground ginger, cinnamon and allspice
- 1½ tsp. brown sugar

**SALMON**
- 1 salmon fillet (3 lbs.)
- 4½ tsp. olive oil

**SALSA**
- 1 medium mango
- 1 medium papaya
- 1 medium green pepper
- 1 medium sweet red pepper
- 1 cup finely chopped fresh pineapple
- ¼ cup finely chopped red onion
- 3 Tbsp. minced fresh cilantro
- 2 Tbsp. lime juice
- 1 Tbsp. olive oil
- ½ tsp. salt

1. Combine the seasoning ingredients. Place the fillet in a greased 15x10x1-in. baking pan; sprinkle fillet with 1 Tbsp. seasoning. (Save remaining seasoning for another use.) Drizzle salmon with oil. Cover and refrigerate for at least 2 hours.

2. Peel and finely chop mango and papaya; place in a large bowl. Finely chop peppers; add to bowl. Add the remaining salsa ingredients and gently stir until blended. Cover mixture and refrigerate for at least 2 hours.

3. Bake salmon at 350° until fish flakes easily with a fork, 25-30 minutes. Serve with salsa.

**1 SERVING:** 402 cal., 23g fat (4g sat. fat), 100mg chol., 473mg sod., 14g carb. (9g sugars, 2g fiber), 35g pro.

## HOW TO DICE A MANGO

Lay washed fruit on the counter, then turn so the top and bottom are now the sides. Using a sharp knife, make a lengthwise cut as close to the long, flat seed as possible to remove each side of the fruit. Trim fruit away from seed.

Score each side of the fruit lengthwise and widthwise, without cutting through the skin.

Using your hand, push the skin up, turning the fruit out. Cut fruit off at the skin with a knife.

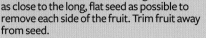

# SHEET-PAN CHICKEN PARMESAN

Saucy chicken, melty mozzarella and crisp-tender broccoli, all in one pan. What could be better?
—*Becky Hardin, Saint Peters, MO*

**PREP:** 15 min. • **BAKE:** 25 min. • **MAKES:** 4 servings

1 large egg
½ cup panko (Japanese) bread crumbs
½ cup grated Parmesan cheese
½ tsp. salt
1 tsp. pepper
1 tsp. garlic powder
4 boneless skinless chicken breast halves (6 oz. each)
Olive oil-flavored cooking spray
4 cups fresh or frozen broccoli florets (about 10 oz.)
1 cup marinara sauce
1 cup shredded mozzarella cheese
¼ cup minced fresh basil, optional

1. Preheat the oven to 400°. Lightly coat a 15x10x1-in. baking pan with cooking spray.

2. In a shallow bowl, whisk egg. In a separate shallow bowl, stir together the next five ingredients. Dip chicken breast in egg; allow excess to drip off. Then dip in crumb mixture, patting to help coating adhere. Repeat with the remaining chicken. Place the chicken breasts in center third of baking sheet. Spritz with cooking spray.

3. Bake 10 minutes. Remove from oven. Spread broccoli in a single layer along both sides of baking pan (if the broccoli is frozen, break pieces apart). Return to the oven; bake 10 minutes longer. Remove from oven.

4. Preheat broiler. Spread marinara sauce over chicken; top with shredded cheese. Broil chicken and broccoli 3-4 in. from heat until cheese is golden brown and the vegetables are tender, 3-5 minutes. If desired, sprinkle with the basil.

**1 SERVING:** 504 cal., 17g fat (7g sat. fat), 147mg chol., 1151mg sod., 27g carb. (10g sugars, 8g fiber), 52g pro.

### ✳ TEST KITCHEN TIP

Try serving this on a bed of riced cauliflower. A number of brands are available in the vegetable section of the freezer case. Like most Italian-inspired dishes, this would pair wonderfully with a thick slice of garlic bread.

# CHILI DOG PIZZA

My girls love it when I make this mash-up pizza with hot dogs and chili. It's a marvelous way to use up leftover chili.
—*Jennifer Stowell, Deep River, IA*

**TAKES:** 25 min. ● **MAKES:** 8 servings

1 tube (11 oz.) refrigerated thin pizza crust
½ cup yellow mustard
1 can (15 oz.) chili with beans
6 hot dogs, sliced
2 cups shredded cheddar cheese
Chopped onion and sweet pickle relish, optional

**1.** Preheat oven to 425°. Unroll and press dough into bottom of a greased 15x10x1-in. baking pan. Bake for 5-7 minutes or until the edges are lightly browned.

**2.** Spread with mustard; top with chili, hot dogs and cheese. Bake until the crust is golden and cheese is melted, 10-15 minutes. If desired, sprinkle with onion and relish.

**1 SERVING:** 404 cal., 25g fat (11g sat. fat), 54mg chol., 1113mg sod., 28g carb. (4g sugars, 3g fiber), 18g pro.

# MAKE-A-MONSTER PIZZA

Creepy creatures have completely taken over this playful meal! Since you can create a different design for each square, it's easy to cater to every diner's individual preferences.
—*Marie Louise Ludwig, Phoenixville, PA*

**PREP:** 30 min. ● **BAKE:** 20 min. ● **MAKES:** 6 servings

1 tube (13.8 oz.) refrigerated pizza crust
1 can (8 oz.) pizza sauce
4 cups shredded part-skim mozzarella cheese
2 oz. sliced deli ham, cut into ½-in. strips
  Optional toppings: asparagus, sweet peppers, tomatoes, mushrooms, ripe olives, pineapple, pepperoni and red onion

**1.** Preheat oven to 425°. Unroll pizza crust and press to fit into a greased 15x10x1-in. baking pan, pinching edges to form a rim. Bake until the edges are lightly browned, 8-10 minutes.

**2.** Spread crust with pizza sauce; top with mozzarella cheese. Using ham strips, outline 12 sections. Arrange toppings of your choice in each section to create individual designs. Bake until the crust is golden brown and cheese is melted, 10-15 minutes.

**2 PIECES:** 413 cal., 18g fat (9g sat. fat), 52mg chol., 1193mg sod., 39g carb. (7g sugars, 2g fiber), 25g pro.

## ✳ TEST KITCHEN TIP

Look to salad and olive bars for tiny treasures to boost the cuteness factor. Peppadew peppers, pickled garlic and cocktail onions are fun options. Use cookie cutters to cut sliced cheeses, meats and vegetables.

# PINEAPPLE CHICKEN FAJITAS

*I used chicken and pineapple for a different fajita flavor combination. It's more on the sweet side but my family loved them!*
—*Nancy Heishman, Las Vegas, NV*

**PREP:** 20 min. ● **COOK:** 20 min. ● **MAKES:** 6 servings

- 2 Tbsp. coconut oil, melted
- 3 tsp. chili powder
- 2 tsp. ground cumin
- 1 tsp. garlic powder
- ¾ tsp. kosher salt
- 1½ lbs. chicken tenderloins, halved lengthwise
- 1 large red or sweet onion, halved and sliced (about 2 cups)
- 1 large sweet red pepper, cut into ½-in. strips
- 1 large green pepper, cut into ½-in. strips
- 1 Tbsp. minced seeded jalapeno pepper
- 2 cans (8 oz. each) unsweetened pineapple tidbits, drained
- 2 Tbsp. honey
- 2 Tbsp. lime juice
- 12 corn tortillas (6 in.), warmed
  Optional toppings: pico de gallo, sour cream, shredded Mexican cheese blend and sliced avocado
  Lime wedges, optional

**1.** Preheat oven to 425°. In a large bowl, mix first five ingredients; stir in chicken. Add the onion, peppers, pineapple, honey and lime juice; toss to combine. Spread evenly in two greased 15x10x1-in. baking pans.

**2.** Roast 10 minutes, rotating pans halfway through cooking. Remove pans from oven; preheat broiler.

**3.** Broil chicken mixture, one pan at a time, 3-4 in. from heat until vegetables are lightly browned and chicken is no longer pink, 3-5 minutes. Serve in the tortillas, with toppings and the lime wedges as desired.

**2 FAJITAS:** 359 cal., 8g fat (4g sat. fat), 56mg chol., 372mg sod., 45g carb. (19g sugars, 6g fiber), 31g pro. **DIABETIC EXCHANGES:** 3 starch, 3 lean meat, 1 fat.

**✱ TEST KITCHEN TIP**

If you don't have coconut oil on hand, substitute canola or vegetable oil.

# SPICY ROASTED SAUSAGE, POTATOES & PEPPERS

I love to share my cooking, and this hearty sheet-pan dinner has gotten a tasty reputation. People have actually approached me in public to ask for the recipe.
—*Laurie Sledge, Brandon, MS*

**PREP:** 20 min. • **BAKE:** 30 min. • **MAKES:** 4 servings

- 1 lb. potatoes (about 2 medium), peeled and cut into ½-in. cubes
- 1 pkg. (12 oz.) fully cooked andouille chicken sausage links or flavor of your choice, cut into 1-in. pieces
- 1 medium red onion, cut into wedges
- 1 medium sweet red pepper, cut into 1-in. pieces
- 1 medium green pepper, cut into 1-in. pieces
- ½ cup pickled pepper rings
- 1 Tbsp. olive oil
- ½ to 1 tsp. Creole seasoning
- ¼ tsp. pepper

**1.** Preheat oven to 400°. In a large bowl, combine potatoes, sausage, onion, red pepper, green pepper and pepper rings. Mix oil, Creole seasoning and pepper; drizzle over potato mixture and toss to coat.

**2.** Transfer to a 15x10x1-in. baking pan coated with cooking spray. Roast until vegetables are tender, stirring occasionally, 30-35 minutes.

**1½ CUPS:** 257 cal., 11g fat (3g sat. fat), 65mg chol., 759mg sod., 24g carb. (5g sugars, 3g fiber), 17g pro. **DIABETIC EXCHANGES:** 3 lean meat, 1 starch, 1 vegetable, 1 fat.

# SOUTHERN-STYLE OVEN-FRIED CHICKEN

I call this America's best-loved oven-fried chicken. The secret is in the breading, which makes the chicken super moist and flavorful, herby and golden brown.
—*Elaina Morgan, Rickman, TN*

**PREP:** 15 min. • **BAKE:** 35 min. • **MAKES:** 6 servings

2 cups crushed Ritz crackers (about 50)
1 Tbsp. minced fresh parsley
1 tsp. garlic salt
1 tsp. paprika
½ tsp. pepper
¼ tsp. ground cumin
¼ tsp. rubbed sage
2 large eggs
1 broiler/fryer chicken (3 to 4 lbs.), cut up

1. Preheat oven to 400°. Place a rack in a 15x10x1-in. baking pan; coat the rack with cooking spray.

2. In a shallow bowl, mix the first seven ingredients. In a separate shallow bowl, whisk eggs. Dip the chicken pieces in eggs, then in cracker mixture, patting to help the coating adhere. Place on prepared rack.

3. Bake 20 minutes. Turn the chicken; bake or until chicken is golden brown and juices run clear, 15-25 minutes longer.

**4 OZ. COOKED CHICKEN:** 418 cal., 22g fat (5g sat. fat), 123mg chol., 638mg sod., 21g carb. (3g sugars, 1g fiber), 31g pro.

# TILAPIA & VEGETABLE DINNER

Unlike some one-pan dinners that require some precooking in a skillet
or pot, this one—loaded with fish and healthy veggies—uses just the sheet pan, period.

*—Judy Batson, Tampa, FL*

**PREP:** 10 min. ● **BAKE:** 25 min. ● **MAKES:** 2 servings

2 medium Yukon Gold potatoes, cut into wedges
3 large fresh Brussels sprouts, thinly sliced
3 large radishes, thinly sliced
1 cup fresh sugar snap peas, cut into ½-in. pieces
1 small carrot, thinly sliced
2 Tbsp. butter, melted
½ tsp. garlic salt
½ tsp. pepper
2 tilapia fillets (6 oz. each)
2 tsp. minced fresh tarragon or ½ tsp. dried tarragon
⅛ tsp. salt
1 Tbsp. butter, softened
Lemon wedges and tartar sauce, optional

1. Preheat oven to 450°. Line a 15x10x1-in. baking pan with foil; grease foil.

2. In a large bowl, combine the first five ingredients. Add melted butter, garlic salt and pepper; toss to coat. Place vegetables in a single layer in prepared pan; bake until potatoes are tender, about 20 minutes.

3. Remove from oven; preheat broiler. Arrange vegetables on one side of sheet pan. Add the fish to other side. Sprinkle fillets with tarragon and salt; dot with softened butter. Broil 4-5 in. from heat until fish flakes easily with a fork, about 5 minutes. If desired, serve with lemon wedges and tartar sauce.

**1 SERVING:** 555 cal., 20g fat (12g sat. fat), 129mg chol., 892mg sod., 56g carb. (8g sugars, 8g fiber), 41g pro.

### ✳ TEST KITCHEN TIP

Feel free to try any mild herb, such as dill, chervil or parsley, instead of the tarragon.

# SHEET-PAN CHIPOTLE-LIME SHRIMP BAKE

I like to make this seafood dinner for company because it tastes amazing, but takes very little effort to throw together. Use asparagus, Broccolini or a mix of the two. It's all about what's available for a decent price.
—Colleen Delawder, Herndon, VA

**PREP:** 10 min. ● **BAKE:** 45 min. ● **MAKES:** 4 servings

1½ lbs. baby red potatoes, cut into ¾-in. cubes
1 Tbsp. extra virgin olive oil
¾ tsp. sea salt, divided
3 medium limes
¼ cup unsalted butter, melted
1 tsp. ground chipotle pepper
½ lb. fresh asparagus, trimmed
½ lb. Broccolini or broccoli cut into small florets
1 lb. uncooked shrimp (16-20 per lb.), peeled and deveined
2 Tbsp. minced fresh cilantro

1. Preheat oven to 400°. Place potatoes in a greased 15x10x1-in. baking pan; drizzle with the olive oil. Sprinkle with ¼ tsp. sea salt; stir to combine. Bake 30 minutes. Meanwhile, squeeze ⅓ cup juice from the limes, reserving fruit. Combine lime juice, melted butter, chipotle and remaining sea salt.

2. Remove sheet pan from oven; stir potatoes. Arrange the asparagus, Broccolini, shrimp and reserved limes on top of potatoes. Pour lime juice mixture over vegetables and shrimp.

3. Bake until shrimp turn pink and vegetables are tender, about 10 minutes. Sprinkle with cilantro.

**1 SERVING:** 394 cal., 17g fat (8g sat. fat), 168mg chol., 535mg sod., 41g carb. (4g sugars, 6g fiber), 25g pro.

**✱ TEST KITCHEN TIP**

Don't throw out the squeezed limes. You'll be surprised by how much juice comes out of them after they're roasted.

# SWEET & TANGY SALMON WITH GREEN BEANS

I'm always up for new ways to cook salmon. In this dish, a sweet sauce gives the fish and green beans some down-home barbecue tang. Even our kids love it.
—Aliesha Caldwell, Robersonville, NC

**PREP:** 20 min. ● **BAKE:** 15 min. ● **MAKES:** 4 servings

4  salmon fillets (6 oz. each)
1  Tbsp. butter
2  Tbsp. brown sugar
2  Tbsp. reduced-sodium soy sauce
2  Tbsp. Dijon mustard
1  Tbsp. olive oil
½  tsp. pepper
⅛  tsp. salt
1  lb. fresh green beans, trimmed

1. Preheat oven to 425°. Place fillets in a 15x10x1-in. baking pan coated with cooking spray. In a small skillet, melt butter; stir in brown sugar, soy sauce, mustard, oil, pepper and salt. Brush half of the mixture over salmon.

2. Place green beans in a large bowl; drizzle with remaining brown sugar mixture and toss to coat. Arrange green beans around fillets. Roast until fish just begins to flake easily with a fork and green beans are crisp-tender, 14-16 minutes.

**1 FILLET WITH ¾ CUP GREEN BEANS:**
394 cal., 22g fat (5g sat. fat), 93mg chol., 661mg sod., 17g carb. (10g sugars, 4g fiber), 31g pro.
**DIABETIC EXCHANGES:** 5 lean meat, 1½ fat, 1 vegetable, ½ starch.

**❋ TEST KITCHEN TIP**
Craving Asian flavors? Add ½ tsp. minced fresh ginger to the sauce and use sesame oil instead of olive oil.

# ZESTY HORSERADISH MEAT LOAF

You'll love the bit of heat in this tasty meat loaf. Make sandwiches out
of the leftovers to get double duty out of the classic comfort food.
—*Nancy Zimmerman, Cape May Court House, NJ*

**PREP:** 15 min. ● **BAKE:** 45 min. + standing ● **MAKES:** 8 servings

4 slices whole wheat bread, crumbled
¼ cup fat-free milk
½ cup finely chopped celery
¼ cup finely chopped onion
¼ cup prepared horseradish
2 Tbsp. Dijon mustard
2 Tbsp. chili sauce
1 large egg, lightly beaten
1½ tsp. Worcestershire sauce
½ tsp. salt
¼ tsp. pepper
1½ lbs. lean ground beef (90% lean)
½ cup ketchup

1. Soak bread in milk for 5 minutes. Drain and discard milk. Stir in next nine ingredients. Crumble the beef over mixture and mix well.

2. Shape into a loaf in an 15x10x1-in. baking pan coated with cooking spray. Spread top with ketchup. Bake meat loaf at 350° until a thermometer inserted in the center reads 160°, 45-55 minutes. Let meat loaf stand for 10 minutes before cutting.

**FREEZE OPTION:** Omitting ketchup, bake as directed. Securely wrap the cooled meat loaf in plastic wrap and foil, then freeze. To use, partially thaw in refrigerator overnight. Unwrap and spread top with ketchup. Reheat on a greased 15x10x1-in. baking pan in a preheated 350° oven until a thermometer inserted in center reads 160°. Let stand 10 minutes before cutting.

**1 SLICE:** 207 cal., 8g fat (3g sat. fat), 79mg chol., 640mg sod., 14g carb. (7g sugars, 1g fiber), 19g pro. **DIABETIC EXCHANGES:** 2 lean meat, 1 starch.

# MUFFIN TIN

You can bake a lot more than gorgeous berry muffins with a versatile muffin tin. Use it to make cute-as-a-button pecan tarts, tiny quiches, elegant appetizers and herby Italian rolls. And don't forget the single-serving casseroles, meat loaves, pizzas and meat pies that freeze like a dream.

FOIL LINERS MAKE CLEANUP FAST

TINY TARTS AND PIES ARE CROWD FAVORITES

# MUFFIN-TIN TIPS & TRICKS

Muffin tins are great for making individual portions of recipes both savory and sweet. Here's what you should know about these versatile pans.

- Sizes available include regular (usually 12 cups per tin at ½-cup volume per cup), mini (generally 24 cups per tin) and jumbo (six per tin).

- The most versatile size is regular. Most recipes in this book call for regular tins.

- Buy two muffin tins so you have enough to accommodate most recipes.

- Muffins bake up more quickly than recipes made in loaf and full-size cake pans. There isn't much that can go wrong in such a short cook time, so there's no need to spend a lot of money on premium pans and finishes.

- Pans with a dark finish tend to promote browning more than shiny pans. You may need to adjust the bake time accordingly.

- We don't recommend using insulated muffin tins.

- Most pans come with a nonstick coating (you'll still want to lightly grease them, according to the recipe). To help protect a nonstick finish, you may want to hand-wash the muffin tins.

- For easy cleanup, use paper or foil liners when baking muffins, breads and desserts. Soak the muffin tin in hot soapy water for 30 minutes before cleaning with a scrubbing pad.

- When choosing muffin tins, consider ease of storing and washing the tins. "Bargain" tins can sometimes be found for a really low price—but do you really want to wash and store a giant 24-cup muffin tin that doesn't fit into your cabinet, sink or dishwasher?

# GENIUS WAYS TO USE A MUFFIN TIN

**PREP QUICK INGREDIENTS.** If you have a platter of grilled burgers or hot dogs set up, corral toppings and condiments nearby in a standard muffin tin. Put some ketchup, mustard, onions, pickles, mayo and more into the individual cups. Add small serving spoons to each cup so your guests can customize their burgers, dogs and more to their delight.

**BIGGER, BETTER ICE.** Fill your muffin tray with water and freeze it for quick access to large ice cubes. These cubes are ideal for keeping punch bowls and other large containers colder for longer. For added appeal, freeze water with lemon or lime slices or peels inside to add color and flavor.

**FREEZE YOUR SOUPS/STOCKS.** Proud of a soup you recently made? Have extra stock that you don't want to go to waste? Use a large-diameter muffin tin and pour your leftovers in. Freeze, covered, and you'll have easy access to serving-sized portions.

**FREEZE OATMEAL IN PORTIONS.** Love oatmeal in the morning? Here's how to make it in a jiff: Find a muffin tin with cups that are just the right portions for a single serving of oatmeal, fill the cups with oatmeal, and put it in the freezer. Now you have breakfast at the ready for the rest of the week!

**DECORATING FUN.** Shake different colors of sugar crystals, sanding sugar, nonpareils, jimmies and pearls into separate cups of a muffin tin. Set it out for the kids to scoop up the items they want to use for decorating cookies, cakes and other treats.

**FLIP IT AND BAKE TORTILLA BOWLS.** Flip your muffin tray over and lay small tortillas between the cups so they fold into four sections. Bake the tortillas this way, and they will stay in that shape so you have the perfect tortilla bowls for holding ingredients—and they're just the right size for hand-held foods when necessary.

## HOW TO CHECK MUFFINS FOR DONENESS

Use a kitchen timer and check muffins for doneness 5-7 minutes before the end of the recommended bake time. Muffins are done when a toothpick inserted in the center comes out clean. For muffins with a filling, make sure the toothpick is inserted into the muffin and not the filling.

Tips for perfect muffins:
- Don't overmix ingredients.
- Either use liners or grease only the bottoms and halfway up the sides of each cup. (The ungreased portion will allow the muffin to climb, making a higher muffin.)
- Fill only ⅔ full or as the recipe directs.

# EGG BASKETS BENEDICT

A little puff pastry turns Canadian bacon and eggs into a tasty update on eggs Benedict.
We use a packaged hollandaise or cheese sauce for the finish.
—*Sally Jackson, Fort Worth, TX*

**TAKES:** 30 min. • **MAKES:** 1 dozen (1 cup sauce)

1 sheet frozen puff pastry, thawed
12 large eggs
6 slices Canadian bacon, finely chopped
1 envelope hollandaise sauce mix

**1.** Preheat oven to 400°. On a lightly floured surface, unfold the puff pastry. Roll into a 16x12-in. rectangle; cut into twelve 4-in. squares. Place in greased muffin cups, pressing gently onto the bottoms and up sides, allowing corners to point up.

**2.** Break and slip an egg into center of each pastry cup; sprinkle with the Canadian bacon. Bake until the pastry is golden brown and the egg whites are completely set and the yolks begin to thicken but are not hard, 10-12 minutes. Meanwhile, prepare the hollandaise sauce according to the package directions.

**3.** Remove pastry cups to wire racks. Serve warm with hollandaise sauce.

**1 PASTRY CUP WITH ABOUT 1 TBSP. SAUCE:**
237 cal., 15g fat (6g sat. fat), 201mg chol., 355mg sod., 14g carb. (1g sugars, 2g fiber), 10g pro.

## HOW TO JUDGE DONENESS OF HOLLANDAISE

Hollandaise sauce is fully cooked when it is thick enough to coat the back of a spoon. To determine doneness, dip a spoon in the mixture and run your finger across the back of the spoon. The cooked sauce will hold a firm line and not run down onto the stripe you've made. A mixture that's not fully cooked will be too thin to hold the line.

WHAT CAN I COOK IN MY...MUFFIN TIN

# BROCCOLI QUICHE CUPS

Make this crustless quiche in muffin cups or in a regular-size pie tin.
Either way, there's plenty of bacon-y, cheesy goodness to go around.
—Angela Lively, Conroe, TX

**TAKES:** 25 min. • **MAKES:** 1 dozen

1 cup chopped fresh broccoli
1 cup pepper jack cheese
6 large eggs, lightly beaten
¾ cup heavy whipping cream
½ cup bacon bits
1 shallot, minced
¼ tsp. salt
¼ tsp. pepper

1. Preheat oven to 350°. Divide the broccoli and cheese among 12 greased muffin cups.

2. Whisk together the remaining ingredients; pour into cups. Bake until set, 15-20 minutes.

**2 QUICHE CUPS:** 291 cal., 24g fat (12g sat. fat), 243mg chol., 523mg sod., 4g carb. (2g sugars, 0 fiber), 16g pro.

**❊ TEST KITCHEN TIP**

Swap half-and-half for whipping cream and save more than 60 calories and 6g saturated fat per serving.

# HAM & CHEESE MINI STRATAS

Almost too cute to eat, these mini egg bakes make a handy portable meal.
Even with a creamy texture, they hold their shape and have the perfect amount of mix-ins.
—Shirley Warren, Thiensville, WI

**PREP:** 20 min. • **BAKE:** 25 min. • **MAKES:** 1 dozen

1 small onion, chopped
1 tsp. canola oil
5 large eggs
1½ cups 2% milk
1 cup shredded cheddar cheese
2 tsp. Dijon mustard
¼ tsp. salt
⅛ tsp. pepper
3 cups cubed day-old Italian bread
(½-in. cubes)
1 cup cubed fully cooked ham
1 plum tomato, seeded and chopped

1. Preheat oven to 350°. In a small skillet, saute onion in oil until tender. In a large bowl, whisk eggs, milk, cheese, mustard, salt and pepper. Stir in bread cubes, ham, tomato and onion.

2. Spoon into greased or foil-lined muffin cups. Bake, uncovered, until a knife inserted in the center comes out clean, 22-26 minutes.

**1 STRATA:** 128 cal., 7g fat (3g sat. fat), 96mg chol., 359mg sod., 7g carb. (2g sugars, 0 fiber), 9g pro.

# HASH BROWN NESTS WITH PORTOBELLOS & EGGS

Hash browns make a fabulous crust for these individual egg quiches. They look fancy but are actually easy to make. They've been a hit at holiday brunches and other special occasions.
—*Kate Meyer, Brentwood, TN*

**PREP:** 30 min. • **BAKE:** 15 min. • **MAKES:** 1 dozen

2 Tbsp. butter
½ lb. sliced baby portobello mushrooms, chopped
¼ cup chopped shallots
1 garlic clove, minced
½ tsp. salt
¼ tsp. pepper
  Dash cayenne pepper
2 Tbsp. sour cream
1 Tbsp. minced fresh basil or 1 tsp. dried basil
4 cups frozen shredded hash brown potatoes (about 1 lb.), thawed
7 large eggs, lightly beaten
¼ cup shredded Swiss cheese
2 bacon strips, cooked and crumbled

1. Preheat oven to 400°. In a large skillet, heat butter over medium-high heat; saute mushrooms and shallots until tender. Add garlic and seasonings; cook and stir 1 minute. Remove from heat; stir in sour cream and basil.

2. Press about ¼ cup potatoes onto the bottoms and up sides of greased muffin cups. Fill each cup with about 2 Tbsp. eggs. Top with mushroom mixture, cheese and bacon.

3. Bake until the eggs are set, 15-18 minutes.

**1 NEST:** 105 cal., 7g fat (3g sat. fat), 118mg chol., 191mg sod., 6g carb. (1g sugars, 1g fiber), 6g pro. **DIABETIC EXCHANGES:** 1 medium-fat meat, ½ starch, ½ fat.

# ARTICHOKE DIP BITES

Love artichoke dip? This recipe gives you the dip and dippers together in one appetizer. My friends can't get enough of the yummy baked bread cups and creamy filling.
—*Nikkole Vanyo, West Fargo, ND*

**PREP:** 25 min. ● **BAKE:** 20 min. ● **MAKES:** 2 dozen

1 can (14 oz.) water-packed artichoke hearts, rinsed, drained and chopped
½ cup grated Parmesan cheese
½ cup mayonnaise
½ cup sour cream
2 Tbsp. canned chopped green chilies
1 garlic clove, minced
1 loaf (1 lb.) frozen bread dough, thawed
1 cup shredded part-skim mozzarella cheese
Thinly sliced green onions

1. In a large bowl, combine the first six ingredients; set aside.

2. Shape the dough into twenty-four 1-in. balls. With floured fingers, press onto the bottoms and ½ in. up the sides of greased muffin cups.

3. Fill cups with tablespoonfuls of the artichoke mixture; sprinkle with the mozzarella cheese. Bake at 350° until golden brown, 18-22 minutes. Garnish with onions. Serve warm.

**1 APPETIZER:** 122 cal., 6g fat (2g sat. fat), 9mg chol., 224mg sod., 11g carb. (1g sugars, 1g fiber), 4g pro.

# ANTIPASTO CUPS

Experience Italian antipasto in a whole new way! Put it inside little cups of salami for deliciously different finger foods.
—*Melissa Obernesser, Utica, NY*

**PREP:** 20 min. ● **BAKE:** 10 min./batch ● **MAKES:** 2 dozen

24 slices Genoa salami (3½ in.)
1 can (14 oz.) water-packed artichoke hearts
1 jar (8 oz.) marinated whole mushrooms
1 jar (8 oz.) roasted sweet red peppers
½ lb. fresh mozzarella cheese, cut into ½-in. cubes
3 Tbsp. olive oil
2 Tbsp. red wine vinegar
½ tsp. garlic salt
⅛ tsp. pepper

1. Preheat oven to 400°. Press half of the salami into 12 muffin cups. Loosely crumple aluminum foil to form twelve 2-in. balls; place in cups to keep salami from sliding. Bake until the edges begin to brown, 6-8 minutes. Using tongs, remove from pans and invert onto paper towels to drain. Wipe the muffin cups clean. Repeat with remaining salami, reusing foil balls.

2. Meanwhile, drain and coarsely chop artichoke hearts, mushrooms and red peppers; transfer to a small bowl. Stir in cheese. In another bowl, whisk the oil, vinegar, garlic salt and pepper until blended. Drizzle over vegetable mixture; toss to coat. Using a slotted spoon, fill salami cups with vegetable mixture.

**1 APPETIZER:** 87 cal., 6g fat (3g sat. fat), 16mg chol., 325mg sod., 2g carb. (1g sugars, 0 fiber), 5g pro.

# CURRIED CHICKEN & RICE TARTLETS

These simple starters feature a yummy curried chicken filling that guests will love!
—Taste of Home *Test Kitchen*

**PREP:** 30 min. ● **BAKE:** 10 min. ● **MAKES:** 2 dozen

½ cup reduced-sodium chicken broth
¼ cup uncooked long grain rice
¾ cup cubed cooked chicken breast
½ cup frozen peas and carrots, thawed and drained
3 Tbsp. reduced-fat mayonnaise
1 green onion, chopped
½ tsp. salt
¼ tsp. pepper
¼ tsp. curry powder
⅛ tsp. garlic powder
⅛ tsp. ground turmeric
⅛ tsp. ground coriander
8 sheets phyllo dough (14x9 in.)
Butter-flavored cooking spray
Minced chives, optional

1. In a small saucepan, bring broth and rice to a boil. Reduce heat; cover and simmer until liquid is absorbed and rice is tender, 15-18 minutes.

2. In a large bowl combine the rice, chicken, peas and carrots, mayonnaise, green onion and seasonings.

3. Place one sheet of phyllo dough on a work surface; spritz with the butter-flavored spray. Top with another sheet of phyllo; spritz with spray. (Keep the remaining phyllo dough covered with a damp towel to prevent it from drying out.) Cut into 12 squares. Repeat three times, making 48 squares.

4. Stack two squares of layered phyllo in each of 24 muffin cups coated with cooking spray, rotating the squares so corners do not overlap. Spoon 1 Tbsp. rice mixture into each cup. Bake at 375° for 8-10 minutes or until golden brown. Garnish with chives if desired. Serve warm.

**1 TARTLET:** 35 cal., 1g fat (0 sat. fat), 4mg chol., 96mg sod., 4g carb. (0 sugars, 0 fiber), 2g pro.

# HAM-SPINACH CREPE CUPS

Using ingredients you likely already have on hand, these savory crepes will add fun to your celebration for mere pennies. Plus, by changing the filling to something sweet, such as berries and whipped cream, you can create a gorgeous dessert.
—*Kathi Grenier, Auburn, ME*

**TAKES:** 30 min. • **MAKES:** 6 crepe cups

1 cup whole milk
1 large egg
1 Tbsp. canola oil
⅔ cup all-purpose flour
¼ tsp. baking powder
¼ tsp. salt
**FILLING**
2 Tbsp. butter
3 Tbsp. all-purpose flour
1¼ cups whole milk
⅔ cup shredded Swiss cheese
½ tsp. salt
⅛ tsp. pepper
    Pinch ground nutmeg
2 drops hot pepper sauce
2 cups diced fully cooked ham
5 oz. frozen chopped spinach, thawed and squeezed dry (about ½ cup)

1. In a bowl, combine the milk, egg and oil; mix well. Combine flour, baking powder and salt; add to milk mixture and mix until smooth. Heat a lightly greased 8-in. skillet; add ¼ cup batter. Lift and turn pan to evenly coat the bottom. Cook until lightly browned; turn and brown the other side. Place each crepe in a greased muffin cup or custard cup, arranging the top edge in flutes. Place a small ball of foil in the center of each cup to hold the shape. Bake at 350° for 10 minutes. Remove the foil.

2. Meanwhile, for filling, melt butter in a saucepan over medium heat. Stir in flour until smooth. Gradually add milk; bring to a boil. Cook until thickened, about 2 minutes. Add the cheese, salt, pepper, nutmeg and hot pepper sauce; stir until smooth. Stir in the ham and spinach; heat through. Spoon into the hot crepe cups and serve immediately.

**TO MAKE AHEAD:** Stack cooled unfilled crepes with waxed paper between. Cover them tightly and refrigerate for up to 24 hours. Then shape and bake as directed.

**1 CREPE CUP:** 262 cal., 12g fat (5g sat. fat), 79mg chol., 963mg sod., 19g carb. (5g sugars, 1g fiber), 20g pro.

# MINI MAC & CHEESE BITES

Young relatives were coming for a Christmas party, so I wanted something fun for them to eat. Instead, the adults devoured my mini mac and cheese bites.
—*Kate Mainiero, Elizaville, NY*

**PREP:** 35 min. ● **BAKE:** 10 min. ● **MAKES:** 3 dozen

2 cups uncooked elbow macaroni
1 cup seasoned bread crumbs, divided
2 Tbsp. butter
2 Tbsp. all-purpose flour
½ tsp. onion powder
½ tsp. garlic powder
½ tsp. seasoned salt
1¾ cups 2% milk
2 cups shredded sharp cheddar cheese, divided
1 cup shredded Swiss cheese
¾ cup biscuit/baking mix
2 large eggs, lightly beaten

1. Preheat oven to 425°. Cook macaroni according to package directions; drain.

2. Meanwhile, sprinkle ¼ cup bread crumbs into 36 greased mini-muffin cups. In a large saucepan, melt butter over medium heat. Stir in flour and seasonings until smooth; gradually whisk in milk. Bring to a boil, stirring constantly; cook and stir mixture until thickened, 1-2 minutes. Stir in 1 cup cheddar cheese and Swiss cheese until melted.

3. Remove from heat; stir in biscuit mix, eggs and ½ cup bread crumbs. Add macaroni; toss to coat. Spoon about 2 Tbsp. macaroni mixture into prepared mini-muffin cups; sprinkle with remaining cheddar cheese and bread crumbs.

4. Bake until bites are golden brown, 8-10 minutes. Allow to cool in pans for 5 minutes before serving.

**1 APPETIZER:** 91 cal., 5g fat (3g sat. fat), 22mg chol., 162mg sod., 8g carb. (1g sugars, 0 fiber), 4g pro.

**✱ TEST KITCHEN TIP**

Customize these bites by adding mix-ins like chopped jalapenos, crumbled bacon or minced garlic. Also, hand-grating the cheese for any mac and cheese tends to result in the smoothest, tastiest sauce.

# INDIVIDUAL SHEPHERD'S PIES

These cute little pies make a fun St. Patrick's Day surprise for the family.
Extras are easy to freeze and eat later on busy weeknights.
—*Ellen Osborne, Clarksville, TN*

**PREP:** 30 min. ● **BAKE:** 20 min. ● **MAKES:** 10 mini pies

1 lb. ground beef
3 Tbsp. chopped onion
½ tsp. minced garlic
⅓ cup chili sauce or ketchup
1 Tbsp. cider vinegar
2 cups hot mashed potatoes (with added milk and butter)
3 oz. cream cheese, softened
1 tube (12 oz.) refrigerated buttermilk biscuits
½ cup crushed potato chips
Paprika, optional

**1.** Preheat oven to 375°. In a large skillet, cook the beef and onion over medium heat until beef is no longer pink, 5-7 minutes, breaking up beef into crumbles. Add the garlic; cook 1 minute or until tender. Drain. Stir in chili sauce and vinegar.

**2.** In a small bowl, mix the mashed potatoes and cream cheese until blended. Press one biscuit dough onto bottom and up sides of each of 10 greased muffin cups. Fill with beef mixture. Spread potato mixture over tops. Sprinkle with crushed potato chips, pressing down lightly.

**3.** Bake until pies are golden brown, 20-25 minutes. If desired, sprinkle the tops with paprika.

**FREEZE OPTION:** Freeze cooled shepherd's pies in a single layer in freezer containers. To use, partially thaw in refrigerator overnight. Bake on a baking sheet in a preheated 375° oven until heated through, 15-18 minutes.

**2 MINI PIES:** 567 cal., 30g fat (12g sat. fat), 84mg chol., 1378mg sod., 51g carb. (9g sugars, 2g fiber), 23g pro.

# MINI SAUSAGE PIES

The simple ingredients and family-friendly flavor of these little sausage cups make them a go-to dinner favorite. The fact that every person gets his or her own little pie makes them even better!
—*Kerry Dingwall, Wilmington, NC*

**PREP:** 35 min. ● **BAKE:** 30 min. ● **MAKES:** 1 dozen

1 pkg. (17.3 oz.) frozen puff pastry, thawed
1 lb. bulk sage pork sausage
6 green onions, chopped
½ cup chopped dried apricots
¼ tsp. pepper
⅛ tsp. ground nutmeg
1 large egg, lightly beaten

**1.** Preheat oven to 375°. On a lightly floured surface, unfold pastry sheets; roll each into a 16x12-in. rectangle. Using a floured cutter, cut twelve 4-in. circles from one sheet; press onto bottoms and up sides of ungreased muffin cups. Using a floured cutter, cut twelve 3½-in. circles from remaining sheet.

**2.** Mix sausage, green onions, apricots and spices lightly but thoroughly. Place ¼ cup mixture into each pastry cup. Brush the edges of the smaller pastry circles with egg; place over the pies, pressing edges to seal. Brush with egg. Cut slits in top.

**3.** Bake until pies are golden brown and a thermometer inserted in filling reads 160°, 30-35 minutes. Cool 5 minutes before removing from pan to a wire rack.

**2 MINI PIES:** 551 cal., 36g fat (10g sat. fat), 82mg chol., 784mg sod., 42g carb. (5g sugars, 5g fiber), 16g pro.

# MUFFIN-TIN LASAGNAS

This is a super-fun way to serve lasagna, and a great way to surprise everyone at the table. Easy and quick, these little cups can also be made with ingredients your family likes best.

—*Sally Kilkenny, Granger, IA*

**TAKES:** 30 min. ● **MAKES:** 1 dozen

1 large egg, lightly beaten
1 carton (15 oz.) part-skim ricotta cheese
2 cups shredded Italian cheese blend, divided
1 Tbsp. olive oil
24 wonton wrappers
1 jar (24 oz.) garden-style pasta sauce
   Minced fresh parsley, optional

**1.** Preheat oven to 375°. In a bowl, mix egg, ricotta cheese and 1¼ cups Italian cheese blend.

**2.** Generously grease 12 muffin cups with oil; line each cup with a wonton wrapper. Fill each with 1 Tbsp. ricotta mixture and 1½ Tbsp. pasta sauce. Top each with a second wrapper, rotating corners and pressing down centers. Repeat the ricotta and sauce layers. Sprinkle with remaining cheese blend.

**3.** Bake until the cheese is melted, 20-25 minutes. If desired, sprinkle with parsley.

**2 MINI LASAGNAS:** 414 cal., 19g fat (9g sat. fat), 83mg chol., 970mg sod., 36g carb. (8g sugars, 2g fiber), 22g pro.

## HOW TO MAKE HOMEMADE RICOTTA

**YOU'LL NEED:**
2 quarts whole milk
1 cup heavy whipping cream
½ teaspoon salt
3 tablespoons white vinegar
Strainer inside another bowl and with two layers of cheesecloth over top

**POINTERS:** The milk needs to separate into curds and whey, so you actually need fat to make ricotta. It's important to use milk with a higher fat content. Whole or 2% will do the trick.

Use the leftover whey in baked goods like muffins or biscuits, where it provides a tanginess akin to buttermilk.

● To make ricotta, start by straining the whey and collecting the curds. Get your setup together. First, line a large strainer with two layers of cheesecloth dampened with water. This creates a superfine filter for the ricotta mixture. Next, place the strainer over a large bowl.

● In a Dutch oven, bring the milk, cream and salt just to a boil over medium heat. Stir occasionally to prevent scorching. Once it's bubbling, remove from heat and gently stir in vinegar. Then let the mixture stand, allowing time for curds to form. This will take about 5 minutes. Resist the urge to poke or stir.

● Slowly pour the curdled mixture into a cheesecloth-lined strainer. Let drain 30-60 minutes. What's left in the strainer—soft curds of lightly tangy cheese—is the ricotta. It should be soft and spreadable, but not watery. (If it's watery, let it strain a while longer.) Store in the fridge up to 5 days.

# LOADED CHICKEN CARBONARA CUPS

Spaghetti cupcakes with a chicken carbonara twist make for a tasty, fun family dinner. Whole wheat pasta and reduced-fat ingredients make these quick and easy little pasta cakes nutritional winners, too.

—*Jeanne Holt, Mendota Heights, MN*

**PREP:** 30 min. ● **BAKE:** 15 min. ● **MAKES:** 1 dozen

4   oz. uncooked whole wheat spaghetti
1   large egg, lightly beaten
5   oz. frozen chopped spinach, thawed and squeezed dry (about ½ cup)
½   cup 2% cottage cheese
½   cup shredded Parmesan cheese, divided
¼   tsp. lemon-pepper seasoning
6   bacon strips, cooked and crumbled, divided
½   cup reduced-fat reduced-sodium condensed cream of chicken soup, undiluted
¼   cup reduced-fat spreadable chive and onion cream cheese
1   cup chopped cooked chicken breast
⅓   cup shredded part-skim mozzarella cheese
¼   cup finely chopped oil-packed sun-dried tomatoes

1. Preheat oven to 350°. In a large saucepan, cook spaghetti according to package directions; drain, reserving ⅓ cup pasta water.

2. In a large bowl, mix egg, spinach, cottage cheese, ¼ cup Parmesan cheese, lemon-pepper seasoning and half of the bacon. Add the spaghetti; toss to combine. Divide among 12 greased muffin cups. Using a greased tablespoon, make an indentation in the center of each.

3. In a large bowl, whisk together the soup, cream cheese and the reserved pasta water. Stir in chicken, mozzarella cheese and tomatoes; spoon into the cups. Sprinkle cups with the remaining bacon and Parmesan cheese.

4. Bake until set, about 15 minutes. Cool for 5 minutes before removing from pan.

**2 PASTA CUPS:** 266 cal., 12g fat (5g sat. fat), 74mg chol., 553mg sod., 20g carb. (4g sugars, 3g fiber), 21g pro. **DIABETIC EXCHANGES:** 2 lean meat, 1½ fat, 1 starch.

# BUFFALO CHICKEN BISCUITS

These spicy, savory muffins are always a hit at parties.
We love them as a simple snack on game day, too.
*—Jasmin Baron, Livonia, NY*

**PREP:** 20 min. ● **BAKE:** 25 min. ● **MAKES:** 1 dozen

3 cups chopped rotisserie chicken
¼ cup Louisiana-style hot sauce
2 cups biscuit/baking mix
¼ tsp. celery seed
⅛ tsp. pepper
1 large egg
½ cup 2% milk
¼ cup ranch salad dressing
1½ cups shredded Colby-Monterey
    Jack cheese, divided
2 green onions, thinly sliced
    Additional ranch dressing and
      hot sauce, optional

**1.** Preheat oven to 400°. Toss the chicken with the hot sauce. In large bowl, whisk together baking mix, celery seed and pepper. In another bowl, whisk together egg, milk and dressing; add to dry ingredients, stirring just until moistened. Fold in 1 cup cheese, green onions and chicken mixture.

**2.** Spoon into 12 greased muffin cups. Sprinkle with remaining cheese. Bake until a toothpick inserted in center comes out clean, 25-30 minutes.

**3.** Cool 5 minutes before removing from pan to a wire rack. Serve warm. If desired, serve with additional dressing and hot sauce. Refrigerate leftovers.

**2 MUFFIN BITES:** 461 cal., 24g fat (10g sat. fat), 121mg chol., 1180mg sod., 29g carb. (3g sugars, 1g fiber), 31g pro.

# LOADED PULLED PORK CUPS

Potato nests are simple to make and surprisingly handy for pulled pork, cheese, sour cream and other toppings. Make, bake and collect the compliments.
—*Melissa Sperka, Greensboro, NC*

**PREP:** 40 min. ● **BAKE:** 25 min. ● **MAKES:** 1½ dozen

1 pkg. (20 oz.) refrigerated shredded hash brown potatoes
¾ cup shredded Parmesan cheese
2 large egg whites, beaten
1 tsp. garlic salt
½ tsp. onion powder
¼ tsp. pepper
1 carton (16 oz.) refrigerated fully cooked barbecued shredded pork
1 cup shredded Colby-Monterey Jack cheese
½ cup sour cream
5 bacon strips, cooked and crumbled
Minced chives

**1.** Preheat oven to 450°. In a large bowl, mix hash browns, Parmesan cheese, egg whites and seasonings until blended. Divide the potatoes among 18 well-greased muffin cups; press onto bottoms and up sides to form cups.

**2.** Bake until edges are dark golden brown, 22-25 minutes. Carefully run a knife around sides of each cup. Cool 5 minutes before removing cups from pans to a serving platter. Meanwhile, heat the pulled pork according to the package directions.

**3.** Sprinkle cheese into cups. Top with pork, sour cream and bacon; sprinkle with chives. Serve warm.

**1 HASH BROWN CUP:** 129 cal., 6g fat (3g sat. fat), 19mg chol., 439mg sod., 11g carb. (4g sugars, 0 fiber), 8g pro.

# MUFFIN-PAN MEAT LOAVES

I used to have a catering business, and my specialty was comfort food. I once needed a gluten-free meat loaf, and my clients went nuts over this recipe. I often use an 8x8-in. pan or a loaf pan, but a muffin tin really cuts the cooking time.

—Vangie Panagotopulos, Moorestown, NJ

**TAKES:** 30 min. • **MAKES:** 1 dozen

2 large eggs, lightly beaten
¾ cup shredded Mexican cheese blend
1 Tbsp. chili powder
1 Tbsp. Worcestershire sauce
2 garlic cloves, minced
1½ tsp. hot pepper sauce
1 tsp. dried parsley flakes
½ tsp. salt
¼ tsp. pepper
¾ lb. lean ground beef (90% lean)
¾ lb. ground turkey
TOPPING
½ cup ketchup
3 Tbsp. brown sugar
1 tsp. prepared mustard

1. Preheat oven to 375°. In a large bowl, combine first nine ingredients. Add beef and turkey; mix lightly but thoroughly. Place ⅓ cup mixture into each of 12 ungreased muffin cups, pressing lightly.

2. In a small bowl, mix the topping ingredients; spoon over meat loaves. Bake, uncovered, until a thermometer reads 165°, 15-20 minutes.

**FREEZE OPTION:** Bake meat loaves without topping. Cool meat loaves, and freeze, covered, on a waxed paper-lined baking sheet until firm. Transfer meat loaves to an airtight container; return to freezer. To use, partially thaw in refrigerator overnight. Place meat loaves on a greased shallow baking pan. Prepare topping as directed; spread over tops. Bake in a preheated 350° oven until heated through.

**2 MINI MEAT LOAVES:** 304 cal., 15g fat (6g sat. fat), 147mg chol., 706mg sod., 14g carb. (13g sugars, 1g fiber), 27g pro.

### HOW TO MAKE PERFECTLY TENDER MEAT LOAF

The secret to tender meat loaf and meatballs is to not overwork the meat. After mixing the other ingredients, gently crumble the ground meat over the top (this makes it faster to mix without overhandling). Mix the ingredients just until blended.

# MUFFIN-TIN PIZZAS

I just baked these mini pizzas and the kids are already demanding more. The no-cook pizza sauce and refrigerated dough make this meal a snap.

*—Melissa Haines, Valparaiso, IN*

**PREP:** 25 min. ● **BAKE:** 10 min. ● **MAKES:** 16 pizzas

1  can (15 oz.) tomato sauce
1  can (6 oz.) tomato paste
1  tsp. dried basil
½  tsp. garlic salt
¼  tsp. onion powder
¼  tsp. sugar
1  tube (11 oz.) refrigerated thin pizza crust
1½  cups shredded part-skim mozzarella cheese
½  cup finely chopped fresh mushrooms
½  cup finely chopped fresh broccoli
16  slices pepperoni, halved

**1.** Preheat oven to 425°. In a small bowl, mix the first six ingredients.

**2.** Unroll the pizza crust; cut into 16 squares. Press the squares onto bottoms and up sides of 16 ungreased muffin cups, allowing corners to hang over the edges.

**3.** Spoon 1 Tbsp. sauce mixture into each cup. Top with the cheese, mushrooms, broccoli and pepperoni. Bake until crusts are golden brown, 10-12 minutes. Serve the remaining sauce mixture, warmed if desired, with the pizzas.

**FREEZE OPTION:** Freeze cooled baked pizzas in an airtight container. To use, reheat the pizzas on a baking sheet in a preheated 425° oven until they are heated through.

**2 PIZZAS WITH 2 TBSP. SAUCE:** 233 cal., 9g fat (4g sat. fat), 16mg chol., 755mg sod., 26g carb. (5g sugars, 2g fiber), 12g pro.

# SLOPPY JOE BISCUIT CUPS

I'm a busy teacher and mom, so meals with shortcuts are a huge help.
These savory cups are a fun way to change up the ever-popular sloppy joe.
—*Julie Ahern, Waukegan, IL*

**TAKES:** 30 min. ● **MAKES:** 5 servings

- **1 lb. lean ground beef (90% lean)**
- **¼ cup each finely chopped celery, onion and green pepper**
- **½ cup barbecue sauce**
- **1 tube (12 oz.) refrigerated flaky biscuits (10 count)**
- **½ cup shredded cheddar cheese**

**1.** Heat oven to 400°. In a large skillet, cook the beef and vegetables over medium heat until beef is no longer pink, 5-7 minutes, breaking up the beef into crumbles; drain. Stir in barbecue sauce; bring mixture to a boil. Reduce heat; simmer, uncovered, 2 minutes, stirring occasionally.

**2.** Separate dough into 10 biscuits; flatten to 5-in. circles. Press onto the bottoms and up sides of greased muffin cups. Fill with beef mixture.

**3.** Bake until biscuits are golden brown, 9-11 minutes. Sprinkle with cheese; bake until cheese is melted, 1-2 minutes longer.

**2 BISCUIT CUPS:** 463 cal., 22g fat (8g sat. fat), 68mg chol., 1050mg sod., 41g carb. (16g sugars, 1g fiber), 25g pro.

# LASAGNA CUPS

I love lasagna and garlic bread, so it only made sense to put them together in these fun little cups. Have one as an appetizer or two for a meal!
—*Angelique Douglas, Maryville, IL*

**PREP:** 40 min. ● **BAKE:** 15 min. ● **MAKES:** 16 lasagna cups

- 3 individual lasagna noodles
- ½ lb. ground turkey or beef
- 1 cup meatless pasta sauce
- ⅓ cup 2% cottage cheese
- ¼ tsp. garlic powder
- 2 tubes (8 oz. each) refrigerated crescent rolls
- 2 cups shredded Italian cheese blend or cheddar cheese
- 1 cup grape tomatoes, halved

1. Preheat oven to 375°. Cook lasagna noodles according to the package directions. Drain and rinse with water; cut each noodle into six squares.

2. In a large skillet, cook and crumble the turkey over medium heat until no longer pink, 5-7 minutes. Stir in sauce, cottage cheese and garlic powder; bring to a boil. Remove from heat.

3. Unroll both tubes of crescent dough and separate each into eight triangles. Press one triangle of dough onto the bottom and up sides of each greased muffin cup. Layer each muffin cup with 1 Tbsp. cheese, one noodle piece and 1 rounded Tbsp. meat sauce (discard extra noodle pieces). Sprinkle with remaining cheese.

4. Bake on a lower oven rack until crust is golden brown, 15-20 minutes. Let stand 5 minutes before removing from pan. Top with tomatoes.

**2 LASAGNA CUPS:** 412 cal., 21g fat (9g sat. fat), 39mg chol., 839mg sod., 34g carb. (7g sugars, 1g fiber), 18g pro.

# SOUR CREAM BLUEBERRY MUFFINS

When we were growing up, my mom made these delicious muffins on chilly mornings. I'm now in college and I enjoy baking them for friends.
—Tory Ross, Cincinnati, OH

**PREP:** 15 min. • **BAKE:** 20 min. • **MAKES:** 1 dozen

2  cups biscuit/baking mix
¾  cup plus 2 Tbsp. sugar, divided
2  large eggs
1  cup sour cream
1  cup fresh or frozen blueberries

1. Preheat oven to 375°. In a large bowl, combine biscuit mix and ¾ cup sugar. In a small bowl, combine the eggs and sour cream; stir into the dry ingredients just until combined. Fold in the blueberries.

2. Fill greased muffin cups three-fourths full. Sprinkle with remaining sugar. Bake 20-25 minutes or until a toothpick inserted in muffin comes out clean. Cool 5 minutes before removing from pan to a wire rack.

**NOTE:** If using frozen blueberries, use without thawing to avoid discoloring the batter.

**1 MUFFIN:** 195 cal., 7g fat (3g sat. fat), 48mg chol., 272mg sod., 29g carb. (16g sugars, 1g fiber), 3g pro.

## ✱ DID YOU KNOW?

Many muffin recipes are made using the stirred batter technique. Dry and wet ingredients are combined in separate bowls, then mixed just until blended. The batter may even have some lumps. Mix-ins such as berries or cheese are gently folded in with as little mixing as possible. Light mixing ensures a tender muffin with a fine crumb, not one that is tough or chewy.

# QUICK & EASY HERB FOCACCIA ROLLS

Yeast rolls speckled with fresh thyme and rosemary are a breeze to make without kneading and long wait times. Break out the good butter for these adorable rolls!
—*Linda Schend, Kenosha, WI*

**PREP:** 15 min. + rising ● **BAKE:** 20 min. ● **MAKES:** 1½ dozen

- 3 **cups all-purpose flour**
- 1 **pkg. (¼ oz.) quick-rise yeast**
- 2 **Tbsp. minced fresh thyme, divided**
- 2 **Tbsp. minced fresh rosemary, divided**
- 1 **Tbsp. sugar**
- 1½ **tsp. kosher salt, divided**
- 1½ **cups warm water (120° to 130°)**
- 6 **Tbsp. extra-virgin olive oil, divided**

**1.** Combine flour, yeast, 1 Tbsp. thyme, 1 Tbsp. rosemary, sugar and 1 tsp. salt. Add the water and 2 Tbsp. oil; beat 1 minute (the dough will be very sticky).

**2.** Divide dough among 18 greased muffin cups. Let rise in a warm place until doubled, about 30 minutes.

**3.** Preheat oven to 375°. In a small saucepan over medium-low heat, stir together remaining seasonings and oil just until herbs are fragrant and oil is hot, about 1½ minutes. Remove from heat; cool.

**4.** Gently spoon cooled herb mixture over each roll. Bake until golden brown, 20-25 minutes.

**1 ROLL:** 120 cal., 5g fat (1g sat. fat), 0 chol., 161 mg sod., 17g carb. (1g sugars, 1g fiber), 2g pro.

## ✱ TEST KITCHEN TIP

For standard focaccia, spread dough in a greased 13x9-in. pan. Let rise in a warm place until doubled, about 30 minutes. Top with herb mixture; bake at 375° until golden brown, 25-30 minutes.

# EASY MINI CARAMEL APPLE CHEESECAKES

Cheesecake is the ultimate comfort food, but a big slice can be too rich. These muffin-sized cheesecakes topped with apples and creamy caramel dazzle the senses without overwhelming them.

—*Brandie Cranshaw, Rapid City, SD*

**PREP:** 30 min. ● **BAKE:** 15 min. + cooling ● **MAKES:** 1 dozen

1 cup graham cracker crumbs
2 Tbsp. sugar
¼ tsp. ground cinnamon
3 Tbsp. butter, melted

**CHEESECAKE**

2 pkg. (8 oz. each) cream cheese, softened
½ cup sugar
1 tsp. vanilla extract
2 large eggs, lightly beaten

**TOPPING**

1 large apple, peeled and finely chopped
1 Tbsp. butter
1 Tbsp. sugar
¼ tsp. ground cinnamon
Dash ground cloves
½ cup butterscotch-caramel ice cream topping

1. Preheat oven to 350°. Line 12 muffin cups with paper liners.

2. In a small bowl, mix cracker crumbs, sugar and cinnamon; stir in melted butter. Spoon 1 rounded Tbsp. crumb mixture into each muffin cup; press down with a narrow glass or spoon.

3. In a large bowl, beat cream cheese and sugar until smooth. Beat in vanilla. Add eggs; beat on low speed just until blended. Pour over crusts.

4. Bake 15-18 minutes or until centers are set (do not overbake). Cool in pan on a wire rack 30 minutes.

5. Right before serving, in a small skillet, cook and stir the apple with the butter, sugar, cinnamon and cloves over medium heat until tender, 4-5 minutes; stir in caramel topping. Spoon over cheesecakes. Refrigerate any leftovers.

**1 CHEESECAKE WITH ABOUT 1 TBSP. TOPPING:** 307 cal., 19g fat (10g sat. fat), 84mg chol., 244mg sod., 31g carb. (23g sugars, 0 fiber), 4g pro.

# PECAN BUTTER TARTS

I searched for the perfect butter tart for ages. After many attempts, I discovered this favorite that begs for a scoop of ice cream on top.
—*Susan Kieboam, Streetsboro, OH*

**PREP:** 30 min. ● **BAKE:** 10 min. + cooling ● **MAKES:** 1 dozen

1 pkg. (14.1 oz.) refrigerated pie pastry
FILLING
½ cup raisins
1 cup water
1 large egg, lightly beaten
½ cup packed dark brown sugar
½ cup packed light brown sugar
⅓ cup butter, melted
1½ tsp. vanilla extract
¼ tsp. salt
⅓ cup coarsely chopped pecans
Vanilla ice cream, optional

1. Preheat the oven to 425°. Line 12 muffin cups with foil liners. (Do not use paper-lined foil liners.)

2. On a work surface, unroll pastry sheets. Cut 12 circles with a floured 4-in. round cookie cutter (save remaining pastry for another use). Gently press pastry circles onto bottom and up sides of foil liners. Refrigerate while preparing filling.

3. In a microwave-safe bowl, combine raisins and water; microwave on high 2 minutes. Drain; cool slightly.

4. In a small bowl, mix the egg, brown sugars, melted butter, vanilla and salt until blended; stir in the pecans and raisins. Spoon into the pastry cups, dividing evenly.

5. Bake on a lower oven rack until the filling just begins to bubble up and crusts are light golden brown, 7-9 minutes (do not overbake). Cool completely in pan on a wire rack. If desired, serve with ice cream.

**1 TART:** 252 cal., 13g fat (6g sat. fat), 33mg chol., 177mg sod., 33g carb. (22g sugars, 1g fiber), 2g pro.

### ✳ TEST KITCHEN TIP

Don't have two different shades of brown sugar? Don't fret; use 1 cup of whichever brown sugar you happen to have on hand.

# CAST-IRON SKILLET

The old, reliable ovenproof skillet like the one our great-grandparents used is in style again! For stovetop-to-oven (and even broiling and grilling) cooking convenience, you just can't beat the practical beauty of cast iron.

# TYPES OF HEAVY METAL

The two most common types of cast iron are traditional bare cast iron and enameled cast iron. They behave similarly, but there are some notable differences. Here's the rundown to help you rock your cast-iron cooking.

### TRADITIONAL CAST IRON

**PROS**

- Inexpensive
- Can be used over an open flame, such as a grill or campfire
- Practically indestructible and will last a lifetime (maybe longer!) if properly seasoned and cared for
- Food not likely to stick if the iron is properly seasoned

**CONS**

- Prone to rust; needs to be seasoned every once in a while
- Not practical for all foods; tomatoes and other acidic ingredients will cause seasoning to wear off
- May retain flavors of foods, such as fried fish, after using

### ENAMELED CAST IRON

**PROS**

- Available in a variety of attractive colors
- Can cook acidic ingredients without harming surface
- Beautiful oven-to-table presentation
- Does not retain flavors of foods after using

**CONS**

- Can be expensive
- Not as durable as traditional cast iron; enamel coating can chip if mishandled
- Food more likely to stick than on traditional cast iron
- Takes a little longer to heat up than traditional cast iron

## CARING FOR YOUR CAST IRON

**DO** clean immediately after use (after the pan cools).

**DO** wait until the pan is cool to the touch before washing it in the sink. Submerging hot cast iron in cold water can cause it to crack.

**DO** use hot water and soap if you like. It's a common misconception that soap will strip the seasoning from cast iron.

**DON'T** let it soak too long. Cast iron + extended exposure to water = rust.

# HOW TO CLEAN A CAST-IRON SKILLET

**CLEAN.** Wash the skillet after each use with hot water and, if desired, a little dish soap. A scrubbing pad works great for this.

**RINSE & DRY.** Rinse with plenty of hot water. Air-dry the skillet, upside-down, or wipe dry with paper towels (cast iron may leave marks on towels).

**SEASON.** Moisten a paper towel with cooking oil and wipe all over the pan, inside and out, including the handle. Wipe away excess oil with another paper towel. The skillet should be just lightly greased. Now place in a hot oven as shown below right to fully dry.

# HOW TO SAVE A RUSTY SKILLET

**GIVE IT A TOUCH-UP.** If a pan has just a small amount of rust, try wiping it away with cooking oil and a paper towel; then pop it in the oven as shown at right to fully dry.

**SCOUR.** Get the pan wet, add a little dish soap, then scrub with a piece of steel wool or a tough scrubber. Scrub in small circles, focusing on the rusty parts. Scrub until the original black iron emerges, then rinse.

**HEAT.** Set the oven to 350°. Place the skillet, upside-down, on the upper rack for about an hour, letting it heat up with the oven. Turn the oven off; leave the pan inside until it's cool. The oil bakes into the pores of the pan, creating a nonstick finish.

# DINER CORNED BEEF HASH

I created my hash to taste like a dish from a northern Arizona restaurant we always loved. We round it out with eggs and toast made from homemade bread.
—*Denise Chelpka, Phoenix, AZ*

**PREP:** 10 min. ● **COOK:** 25 min. ● **MAKES:** 4 servings

1¼ lbs. potatoes (about 3 medium), cut into ½-in. cubes
3 Tbsp. butter
¾ cup finely chopped celery
¾ lb. cooked corned beef, cut into ½-in. cubes (about 2½ cups)
4 green onions, chopped
¼ tsp. pepper
Dash ground cloves
2 Tbsp. minced fresh cilantro

**1.** Place potatoes in a saucepan; add water to cover. Bring to a boil. Reduce the heat; cook, uncovered, just until tender, 6-8 minutes. Drain.

**2.** In a large cast-iron skillet, heat butter over medium-high heat. Add celery; cook and stir until crisp-tender, 4-6 minutes. Add the potatoes; cook until they are lightly browned, turning occasionally, 6-8 minutes. Stir in the corned beef; cook mixture until heated through, 1-2 minutes. Sprinkle with green onions, pepper and cloves; cook 1-2 minutes longer. Stir in cilantro.

**1 CUP:** 407 cal., 25g fat (11g sat. fat), 106mg chol., 1059mg sod., 27g carb. (2g sugars, 4g fiber), 19g pro.

# CREAMY EGGS & MUSHROOMS AU GRATIN

When I want a brunch recipe that has the crowd appeal of scrambled eggs but is a little more special, I turn to this dish. The Parmesan sauce is simple but rich and delicious.
—*Deborah Williams, Peoria, AZ*

**PREP:** 15 min. • **COOK:** 25 min. • **MAKES:** 8 servings

2 Tbsp. butter
1 lb. sliced fresh mushrooms
1 green onion, chopped
**SAUCE**
2 Tbsp. butter, melted
3 Tbsp. all-purpose flour
½ tsp. salt
⅛ tsp. pepper
1 cup 2% milk
½ cup heavy whipping cream
2 Tbsp. grated Parmesan cheese
**EGGS**
16 large eggs
¼ tsp. salt
⅛ tsp. pepper
¼ cup butter, cubed
½ cup grated Parmesan cheese
1 green onion, finely chopped

1. In a large broiler-safe skillet, heat butter over medium-high heat. Add mushrooms; cook and stir until browned, 4-6 minutes. Add green onion; cook 1 minute longer. Remove from pan with a slotted spoon. Wipe the skillet clean.

2. For sauce, in a small saucepan, melt butter over medium heat. Stir in flour, salt and pepper until smooth; gradually whisk in the milk and cream. Bring to a boil, stirring constantly; cook and stir until thickened, 2-4 minutes. Remove from heat; stir in cheese.

3. Preheat broiler. For eggs, in a large bowl, whisk eggs, salt and pepper until blended. In same skillet, heat butter over medium heat. Pour in the egg mixture; cook and stir just until the eggs are thickened and no liquid egg remains. Remove from heat.

4. Spoon half of the sauce over the eggs; top with mushrooms. Add the remaining sauce; sprinkle with cheese. Broil 4-5 in. from heat until top is lightly browned, 4-6 minutes. Sprinkle with green onion.

**1 SERVING:** 363 cal., 29g fat (15g sat. fat), 431mg chol., 591mg sod., 8g carb. (3g sugars, 1g fiber), 18g pro.

# GARDEN CHEDDAR FRITTATA

The potato crust on this pretty fritatta is so easy to make, and everyone will love the taste. I've made it with goat cheese, too, and it's delicious. You can also use other vegetables if you like.
—*Eva Amuso, Cheshire, MA*

**PREP:** 30 min. • **BAKE:** 15 min. • **MAKES:** 6 servings

2 small potatoes, peeled and cut into ½-in. cubes
8 large eggs, lightly beaten
2 Tbsp. water
¼ tsp. salt
⅛ tsp. garlic powder
⅛ tsp. chili powder
⅛ tsp. pepper
1 small zucchini, chopped
¼ cup chopped onion
1 Tbsp. butter
1 Tbsp. olive oil
2 plum tomatoes, thinly sliced
1 cup shredded sharp cheddar cheese
  Minced chives and additional shredded cheddar cheese

**1.** Preheat oven to 425°. Place the potatoes in a small saucepan and cover with water. Bring to a boil. Reduce heat; cover and simmer 5 minutes. Drain. In a large bowl, whisk eggs, water, salt, garlic powder, chili powder and pepper; set aside.

**2.** In a 10-in. cast-iron or other ovenproof skillet, saute zucchini, onion and potatoes in butter and oil until tender. Reduce heat. Pour 1½ cups of the egg mixture into skillet. Arrange half of the tomatoes over top; sprinkle with ½ cup cheese. Top with remaining the egg mixture, tomatoes and cheese.

**3.** Bake, uncovered, until eggs are completely set, 12-15 minutes. Let stand 5 minutes. Sprinkle with chives and additional cheddar cheese. Cut frittata into wedges.

**1 SLICE:** 251 cal., 16g fat (8g sat. fat), 307mg chol., 325mg sod., 13g carb. (3g sugars, 2g fiber), 14g pro.

# OLD-WORLD PUFF PANCAKE

My grandmother taught my mom how to make this dish, which was popular during the Depression. At that time, cooks measured ingredients as pinches, dashes and dibs. But through the years, accurate amounts were noted. My wife and I continue to enjoy this dish today, particularly for brunch.
—*Auton Miller, Piney Flats, TN*

**TAKES:** 30 min. ● **MAKES:** 4 servings

2   **Tbsp. butter**
3   **large eggs**
¾   **cup whole milk**
¾   **cup all-purpose flour**
2   **tsp. sugar**
1   **tsp. ground nutmeg**
    **Confectioners' sugar**
    **Lemon wedges**
    **Syrup, optional**
    **Fresh raspberries, optional**

**1.** Place butter in a 10-in. ovenproof skillet; place in a 425° oven until melted, 2-3 minutes. In a blender, process the eggs, milk, flour, sugar and nutmeg until smooth. Pour into prepared skillet.

**2.** Bake at 425° until puffed and browned, 16-18 minutes. Dust with confectioners' sugar. Serve with lemon and, if desired, syrup and raspberries.

**1 PIECE:** 178 cal., 5g fat (2g sat. fat), 144mg chol., 74mg sod., 23g carb. (5g sugars, 1g fiber), 9g pro.

### ✳ READER RAVE

*"This was easy and fantastic. I didn't change a thing except for using lemon wedges. After taking it out of the oven, I just sprinkled powdered sugar on it and served it with a berry compote. Excellent."*

— KIVEC, TASTEOFHOME.COM

# CHEESY SKILLET PIZZA DIP

This creamy dip is oozing with cheesy goodness thanks to the combination of cream cheese and mozzarella. We topped ours with pepperoni slices, but you can easily customize it with your favorite pizza toppings. This is just one more delicious way to use your cast-iron pan.
—*Taste of Home Test Kitchen*

**PREP:** 25 min. + rising ● **BAKE:** 25 min. ● **MAKES:** 18 servings

- 6 Tbsp. butter
- 1 tsp. garlic powder, divided
- ¼ tsp. crushed red pepper flakes
- 1 pkg. (16 oz.) frozen bread dough dinner rolls, thawed
- 1 pkg. (8 oz.) cream cheese, softened
- 1½ cups shredded part-skim mozzarella cheese, divided
- 1 cup mayonnaise
- 1 tsp. Italian seasoning
- ½ cup pizza sauce
- ¼ cup (¾ oz.) sliced pepperoni
- 2 Tbsp. shredded Parmesan cheese
- 2 Tbsp. minced fresh basil

1. Microwave butter, ½ tsp. garlic powder and red pepper flakes, covered, until butter is melted. Cut each roll into thirds; roll each piece into a ball. Dip dough balls in butter mixture; place along outer edge of a 10-in. cast-iron skillet, leaving center open. Gently stack remaining balls on top of bottom layer, leaving some space between them. Cover and let rise until almost doubled, about 30 minutes.

2. Preheat oven to 400°. Bake until dough balls are set and beginning to brown, 15-18 minutes.

3. Meanwhile, combine cream cheese, 1 cup mozzarella, mayonnaise, Italian seasoning and the remaining garlic powder; spoon into center of skillet. Layer with ¼ cup mozzarella and pizza sauce. Top with remaining mozzarella and pepperoni. Brush rolls with some of remaining butter mixture; sprinkle with Parmesan.

4. Bake until dip is heated through and the rolls are golden brown, about 10 minutes, covering loosely with foil as needed to prevent the rolls from becoming too dark. Sprinkle with basil.

**1 SERVING:** 258 cal., 20g fat (7g sat. fat), 29mg chol., 372mg sod., 15g carb. (2g sugars, 1g fiber), 6g pro.

# CHINESE SCALLION PANCAKES

Unlike true pancakes, *cong you bing* (or Chinese scallion pancakes) are made from a dough instead of a batter. The tasty appetizers are the perfect sponge for mopping up extra sauce and can be made ahead of time for convenience. Just wrap in foil and reheat in the oven.
—*Jenni Sharp, Milwaukee, WI*

**PREP:** 35 min. + standing ● **COOK:** 5 min./batch
**MAKES:** 8 pancakes (¼ cup sauce)

3 cups all-purpose flour
1⅓ cups boiling water
4 tsp. sesame oil
6 green onions, chopped
1 tsp. salt
½ cup canola oil
**DIPPING SAUCE**
3 Tbsp. reduced-sodium soy sauce
1 Tbsp. brown sugar
2 tsp. minced fresh gingerroot
2 tsp. rice vinegar
½ tsp. sesame oil
⅛ tsp. crushed red pepper flakes

**1.** Place flour in a large bowl; stir in boiling water until dough forms a ball. Turn onto a floured surface; knead until smooth and elastic, 4-6 minutes. Place in a large bowl; cover and let rest for 30 minutes.

**2.** Divide dough into eight portions; roll each portion into an 8-in. circle. Brush with ½ tsp. sesame oil; sprinkle with 1 heaping Tbsp. of green onion and ⅛ tsp. salt. Roll up jelly-roll style; holding one end of rope, wrap dough around, forming a coil, pinching to seal. Flatten slightly. Roll each coil to ⅛-in. thickness.

**3.** In a large cast-iron skillet, heat 1 Tbsp. canola oil. Cook pancakes, one at a time, over medium-high heat until golden brown, 2-3 minutes on each side.

**4.** Meanwhile, combine sauce ingredients. Serve with pancakes.

**1 PANCAKE WITH 1½ TSP. SAUCE:** 333 cal., 17g fat (1g sat. fat), 0 chol., 534mg sod., 39g carb. (2g sugars, 2g fiber), 5g pro.

# MAPLE-GLAZED PORK CHOPS

Everyone cleaned their plates when my mother made these succulent pork chops when I was growing up.
Now I get the same results when I serve them to my family alongside applesauce and au gratin potatoes.
—*Cheryl Miller, Fort Collins, CO*

**TAKES:** 25 min. ● **MAKES:** 4 servings

½ cup all-purpose flour
   Salt and pepper to taste
4 bone-in pork loin chops
   (7 oz. each)
2 Tbsp. butter
¼ cup cider vinegar
⅓ cup maple syrup
1 Tbsp. cornstarch
3 Tbsp. water
⅔ cup packed brown sugar

1. In a large shallow dish, combine the flour, salt and pepper. Add the pork chops and turn to coat. In a large ovenproof skillet, cook the chops in the butter over medium heat until a thermometer reads 145°, 4-5 minutes on each side. Remove and keep warm.

2. Meanwhile, in the same skillet, bring the vinegar to a boil. Reduce the heat; add maple syrup. Cover and cook for 10 minutes. Combine cornstarch and water until smooth; gradually add to maple mixture. Bring to a boil; cook and stir glaze mixture until thickened, about 2 minutes.

3. Place chops on a broiler pan; sprinkle with brown sugar. Broil 4 in. from the heat until sugar is melted, 1-2 minutes. Drizzle with maple glaze.

**1 SERVING:** 530 cal., 14g fat (7g sat. fat), 101mg chol., 121mg sod., 68g carb. (52g sugars, 0 fiber), 32g pro.

# PEAR PORK CHOPS & CORNBREAD STUFFING

You'll be tempted to eat this main dish straight out of the pan.
But save some for your guests! It's sure to wow them at the dinner table.
—*Taste of Home Test Kitchen*

**TAKES:** 30 min. ● **MAKES:** 4 servings

1 pkg. (6 oz.) cornbread stuffing mix
4 boneless pork loin chops (6 oz. each)
½ tsp. pepper
¼ tsp. salt
2 Tbsp. butter
2 medium pears, chopped
1 medium sweet red pepper, chopped
2 green onions, thinly sliced

1. Prepare stuffing mix according to package directions. Meanwhile, sprinkle chops with pepper and salt. In a large cast-iron skillet, brown pork chops in butter. Sprinkle with pears and red pepper.

2. Top with stuffing and onions. Cook, uncovered, over medium heat until a thermometer inserted in pork reads 145°, 8-10 minutes.

**1 PORK CHOP WITH ¾ CUP STUFFING MIXTURE:** 603 cal., 28g fat (14g sat. fat), 127mg chol., 1094mg sod., 47g carb. (14g sugars, 5g fiber), 38g pro.

# DEEP-DISH SAUSAGE PIZZA

My grandma made the tastiest snacks for us when we stayed the night at her farm. Her wonderful pizza, hot from the oven, was covered with cheese and had fragrant herbs in the crust. Now this pizza is frequently a meal for my husband and me and our two young daughters.
—*Michele Madden, Washington Court House, OH*

**PREP:** 30 min. + rising • **BAKE:** 30 min. + standing • **MAKES:** 8 slices

- 1 pkg. (¼ oz.) active dry yeast
- ⅔ cup warm water (110° to 115°)
- 1¾ to 2 cups all-purpose flour
- ¼ cup vegetable oil
- 1 tsp. each dried oregano, basil and marjoram
- ½ tsp. garlic salt
- ½ tsp. onion salt

**TOPPINGS**
- 4 cups shredded part-skim mozzarella cheese, divided
- 2 medium green peppers, chopped
- 1 large onion, chopped
- ½ tsp. each dried oregano, basil and marjoram
- 1 Tbsp. olive oil
- 1 cup grated Parmesan cheese
- 1 lb. bulk pork sausage, cooked and drained
- 1 can (28 oz.) diced tomatoes, well drained
- 2 oz. sliced pepperoni

**1.** In a large bowl, dissolve yeast in warm water. Add 1 cup flour, oil and seasonings; beat until smooth. Add enough remaining flour to form a soft dough.

**2.** Turn onto a floured surface; knead until smooth and elastic, 6-8 minutes. Place in a greased bowl; turn once to greased top. Cover dough and let rise in a warm place until doubled, about 1 hour.

**3.** Punch dough down; roll out into a 15-in. circle. Transfer to a well-greased 12-in. heavy ovenproof skillet or round baking pan, letting dough drape over edges. Sprinkle with 1 cup mozzarella.

**4.** In a skillet, saute the green peppers, onion and seasonings in the oil until tender; drain. Layer half of the mixture over the crust. Layer with half of the Parmesan, sausage and tomatoes. Sprinkle with 2 cups mozzarella. Repeat layers. Fold crust over to form an edge.

**5.** Bake pizza at 400° for 20 minutes. Sprinkle with pepperoni and remaining mozzarella. Bake until the crust is browned, 10-15 minutes longer. Let stand for 10 minutes before slicing.

**1 SLICE:** 548 cal., 34g fat (14g sat. fat), 68mg chol., 1135mg sod., 32g carb. (8g sugars, 4g fiber), 27g pro

## ✷ STAFF HACK

*"Usually I eat leftover pizza cold, because what's not to like there? But sometimes I want it hot. The best way? Toss a piece or two in a frying pan, turn the heat to medium (no need to preheat or grease the pan) and in a few minutes, when the cheese melts, the pizza is done and the crust is crispy."*

— CHRIS MCLAUGHLIN, COPY EDITOR

# MEATBALL CHILI WITH DUMPLINGS

My family enjoys this delicious recipe—it's like a spicy meatball stew with dumplings!
—*Sarah Yoder, Middlebury, IN*

**PREP:** 20 min. ● **COOK:** 50 min. ● **MAKES:** 6 servings

1 large egg, beaten
¾ cup finely chopped onion, divided
¼ cup dry bread crumbs or rolled oats
5 tsp. beef bouillon granules, divided
3 tsp. chili powder, divided
1 lb. ground beef
3 Tbsp. all-purpose flour
1 Tbsp. canola oil
1 can (28 oz.) diced tomatoes, undrained
1 garlic clove, minced
½ tsp. ground cumin
1 can (16 oz.) kidney beans, rinsed and drained

**CORNMEAL DUMPLINGS**

1½ cups biscuit/baking mix
½ cup yellow cornmeal
⅔ cup whole milk
   Minced chives, optional

**1.** In a large bowl, combine egg, ¼ cup onion, bread crumbs, 3 tsp. bouillon and 1 tsp. chili powder; crumble beef over mixture and mix well. Shape into twelve 1½-in. meatballs. Roll in flour.

**2.** Heat oil in a 12-in. cast-iron or other ovenproof skillet; brown meatballs. Drain on paper towels. Meanwhile, in a large saucepan, combine the tomatoes, garlic and cumin with the remaining onion, bouillon and chili powder. Add meatballs. Cover and cook over low heat about 20 minutes. Stir in beans. Combine the dumpling ingredients. Drop by spoonfuls onto chili; cook on low, uncovered, for 10 minutes. Cover and cook or until a toothpick inserted in dumpling comes out clean, 10-12 minutes longer. If desired, sprinkle with minced chives.

**1 SERVING:** 475 cal., 16g fat (6g sat. fat), 76mg chol., 1523mg sod., 56g carb. (8g sugars, 7g fiber), 26g pro.

## HOW TO SHAPE MEATBALLS

Shape the meat mixture into 1½-in. rounds, roughly the size of a pingpong ball. Wet your hands before rolling to keep the meat from sticking to your fingers. Re-wet them every two or three meatballs; keep a bowl of water nearby so you don't have to keep walking to the sink.

# CATFISH WITH MANGO-AVOCADO SALSA

A delightful and tasty rub makes this quick recipe fantastic. While the fish is sitting to allow the flavors to blend, you can easily assemble the salsa. My family thinks this is marvelous.
—*Laura Fisher, Westfield, MA*

**PREP:** 20 min. + chilling ● **COOK:** 10 min. ● **MAKES:** 4 servings (2 cups salsa)

2 tsp. dried oregano
2 tsp. ground cumin
2 tsp. paprika
2¼ tsp. pepper, divided
¾ tsp. salt, divided
4 catfish fillets (6 oz. each)
1 medium mango, peeled and cubed
1 medium ripe avocado, peeled and cubed
⅓ cup finely chopped red onion
2 Tbsp. minced fresh cilantro
2 Tbsp. lime juice
2 tsp. olive oil

1. Combine the oregano, cumin, paprika, 2 tsp. pepper and ½ tsp. salt; rub over fillets. Refrigerate for at least 30 minutes.

2. Meanwhile, in a small bowl, combine the mango, avocado, red onion, cilantro, lime juice and remaining salt and pepper. Chill until serving.

3. In a large cast-iron skillet, cook fillets in oil over medium heat until fish flakes easily with a fork, 5-7 minutes on each side. Serve with salsa.

**1 FILLET WITH ½ CUP SALSA:** 376 cal., 22g fat (4g sat. fat), 80mg chol., 541mg sod., 17g carb. (9g sugars, 6g fiber), 28g pro. **DIABETIC EXCHANGES:** 5 lean meat, 1 starch, ½ fat.

---

# BLACKENED HALIBUT

Serve these spicy fillets with garlic mashed potatoes, hot crusty bread and a crisp salad to lure in your crew. This is what my family eats when we want to celebrate.
—*Brenda Williams, Santa Maria, CA*

**TAKES:** 25 min. ● **MAKES:** 4 servings

2 Tbsp. garlic powder
1 Tbsp. salt
1 Tbsp. onion powder
1 Tbsp. dried oregano
1 Tbsp. dried thyme
1 Tbsp. cayenne pepper
1 Tbsp. pepper
2½ tsp. paprika
4 halibut fillets (4 oz. each)
2 Tbsp. butter

1. In a large shallow dish, combine the first eight ingredients. Add fillets, two at a time, and turn to coat.

2. In a large cast-iron skillet, cook fillets in butter over medium heat until fish flakes easily with a fork, 3-4 minutes on each side.

**1 FILLET:** 189 cal., 8g fat (4g sat. fat), 51mg chol., 758mg sod., 3g carb. (1g sugars, 1g fiber), 24g pro. **DIABETIC EXCHANGES:** 3 lean meat, 1 fat.

# SWEET POTATO FRIES WITH BLUE CHEESE

I hated sweet potatoes when I was a child—mostly because they came out of a can. When I learned of their many health benefits, I began trying fresh sweet potatoes with my husband. We like to make fries with different toppings like cinnamon sugar or cayenne pepper...and at some point, we discovered how awesome they are with blue cheese.

—Katrina Krumm, Apple Valley, MN

**TAKES:** 25 min. • **MAKES:** 2 servings

1 Tbsp. olive oil
2 medium sweet potatoes (about 1¼ lbs.), peeled and cut into ½-in.-thick strips
1 Tbsp. apricot preserves
¼ tsp. salt
3 Tbsp. crumbled blue cheese

In a large cast-iron skillet, heat oil over medium heat. Add sweet potatoes; cook until tender and lightly browned, turning occasionally, 12-15 minutes. Add preserves, stirring to coat; sprinkle with salt. Top with cheese.

**1 SERVING:** 246 cal., 11g fat (3g sat. fat), 9mg chol., 487mg sod., 34g carb. (15g sugars, 3g fiber), 5g pro.

# HOMEY MAC & CHEESE

I also call this "my grandson's mac and cheese." Zachary has been to Iraq and Afghanistan with both the Marines and Navy, and I've been privileged to make his favorite dish for him for more than 20 years.

—Alice Beardsell, Osprey, FL

**PREP:** 20 min. • **BAKE:** 25 min. • **MAKES:** 8 servings

2½ cups uncooked elbow macaroni
¼ cup butter, cubed
¼ cup all-purpose flour
½ tsp. salt
¼ tsp. pepper
3 cups 2% milk
5 cups shredded sharp cheddar cheese, divided
2 Tbsp. Worcestershire sauce
½ tsp. paprika

1. Preheat oven to 350°. Cook macaroni according to package directions for al dente.

2. Meanwhile, in a large saucepan, heat butter over medium heat. Stir in flour, salt and pepper until smooth; gradually whisk in milk. Bring to a boil, stirring constantly; cook and stir until thickened, 2-3 minutes.

3. Reduce heat. Stir in 3 cups cheese and Worcestershire sauce until cheese is melted.

4. Drain macaroni; stir into sauce. Transfer to a greased 10-in. ovenproof skillet. Bake, uncovered, 20 minutes. Top with remaining cheese; sprinkle with paprika. Bake until bubbly and cheese is melted, 5-10 minutes.

**1 CUP:** 447 cal., 28g fat (20g sat. fat), 97mg chol., 701mg sod., 28g carb. (6g sugars, 1g fiber), 22g pro.

# JALAPENO BUTTERMILK CORNBREAD

If you're from the South, you have to have a good cornbread recipe. Here's a healthier version of my mom's traditional cornbread.
—*Debi Mitchell, Flower Mound, TX*

**PREP:** 15 min. ● **BAKE:** 20 min. ● **MAKES:** 8 servings

1 cup self-rising flour
1 cup yellow cornmeal
1 cup buttermilk
¼ cup egg substitute
3 Tbsp. canola oil, divided
2 Tbsp. honey
1 Tbsp. reduced-fat mayonnaise
¼ cup fresh or frozen corn, thawed
3 Tbsp. shredded reduced-fat cheddar cheese
3 Tbsp. finely chopped sweet red pepper
½ to 1 jalapeno pepper, seeded and finely chopped

**1.** Preheat oven to 425°. In a large bowl, whisk flour and cornmeal. In another bowl, whisk the buttermilk, egg substitute, 2 Tbsp. oil, honey and mayonnaise. Pour remaining oil into an 8-in. ovenproof skillet; place skillet in oven 4 minutes.

**2.** Meanwhile, add the buttermilk mixture to flour mixture; stir just until moistened. Fold in corn, cheese and peppers.

**3.** Carefully tilt and rotate skillet to coat bottom with oil; add batter. Bake 20-25 minutes or until a toothpick inserted in center comes out clean.

**NOTE:** As a substitute for 1 cup of self-rising flour, place 1½ tsp. baking powder and ½ tsp. salt in a measuring cup. Add all-purpose flour to measure 1 cup. Also, wear disposable gloves when cutting hot peppers; the oils can burn skin. Avoid touching your face.

**1 WEDGE:** 180 cal., 4g fat (1g sat. fat), 4mg chol., 261mg sod., 32g carb. (6g sugars, 2g fiber), 6g pro. **DIABETIC EXCHANGES:** 2 starch, 1 fat.

# MUENSTER BREAD

My sister and I won blue ribbons in 4-H with this bread many years ago. The recipe makes a beautiful round golden loaf. With a layer of cheese peeking out of every slice, it's definitely worth the effort.

*—Melanie Mero, Ida, MI*

**PREP:** 20 min. + rising ● **BAKE:** 45 min. + cooling ● **MAKES:** 1 loaf (16 slices)

2 pkg. (¼ oz. each) active dry yeast
1 cup warm whole milk (110° to 115°)
½ cup butter, softened
2 Tbsp. sugar
1 tsp. salt
3¼ to 3¾ cups all-purpose flour
1 large egg plus 1 large egg yolk
4 cups shredded Muenster cheese
1 large egg white, beaten

1. In a large bowl, dissolve yeast in milk. Add the butter, sugar, salt and 2 cups flour; beat until smooth. Stir in enough remaining flour to form a soft dough.

2. Turn onto a floured surface; knead until smooth and elastic, 6-8 minutes. Place in a greased bowl, turning once to grease top. Cover dough and let rise in a warm place until doubled, about 1 hour.

3. In a large bowl, beat egg and yolk; stir in cheese. Punch down dough; roll into a 16-in. circle.

4. Place in a greased 10-in. cast-iron skillet or 9-in. round baking pan, letting dough drape over the edges. Spoon the cheese mixture into center of the dough. Gather dough up over filling in 1½-in. pleats. Gently squeeze pleats together at top and twist to make a top knot. Allow to rise 10-15 minutes.

5. Brush loaf with egg white. Bake at 375° for 40-45 minutes. Cool on a wire rack for 20 minutes. Serve warm.

**1 SLICE:** 273 cal., 16g fat (9g sat. fat), 71mg chol., 399mg sod., 22g carb. (3g sugars, 1g fiber), 11g pro.

# CHOCOLATE PECAN SKILLET COOKIE

Bake up the ultimate shareable cookie. For variety, swap out the chocolate chips for an equal quantity of M&M's or chocolate chunks. Or go super fancy by mixing the chocolate chips and pecans into the dough, then gently folding in 1½ cups fresh raspberries.

—James Schend, Pleasant Prairie, WI

**PREP:** 15 min. ● **BAKE:** 35 min. ● **MAKES:** 12 servings

1 cup butter
1 cup sugar
1 cup packed brown sugar
2 large eggs, room temperature
2 tsp. vanilla extract
3 cups all-purpose flour
1½ tsp. baking soda
½ tsp. kosher salt
1 cup 60% cacao bittersweet chocolate baking chips
1 cup chopped pecans, toasted
   Vanilla ice cream, optional

**1.** Preheat oven to 350°. In a 12-in. cast-iron skillet, heat butter in oven as it preheats. Meanwhile, in a large bowl, stir together sugar and brown sugar. When butter is almost melted, remove skillet from oven and swirl butter until completely melted. Stir butter into sugar mixture; set skillet aside.

**2.** Beat eggs and vanilla into sugar mixture. In another bowl, whisk together flour, baking soda and salt; gradually beat into sugar mixture. Stir in chocolate chips and nuts. Spread mixture into buttered skillet.

**3.** Bake until toothpick inserted in center comes out with moist crumbs and the top is golden brown, 35-40 minutes. Serve warm, with vanilla ice cream if desired.

**1 SERVING:** 528 cal., 27g fat (13g sat. fat), 72mg chol., 378mg sod., 69g carb. (43g sugars, 3g fiber), 6g pro.

## MINI COOKIE CRAZE

This cookie recipe may be prepared in four 6-in. cast-iron skillets. Just brush skillets with melted butter before adding dough. Bake mini cookies for 25-30 minutes.

# SKILLET CARAMEL APRICOT GRUNT

Here's an old-fashioned pantry dessert made with ingredients you can easily keep on hand.
Mix up a second batch of dry ingredients for the dumplings to save a few minutes next time you prepare it.
—*Shannon Roum, Cudahy, WI*

**PREP:** 20 min. + standing ● **BAKE:** 20 min. ● **MAKES:** 8 servings

2 cans (15¼ oz. each) apricot halves, undrained
2 tsp. quick-cooking tapioca
⅓ cup packed brown sugar
1 Tbsp. butter
1 Tbsp. lemon juice

**DUMPLINGS**
1½ cups all-purpose flour
½ cup sugar
2 tsp. baking powder
2 Tbsp. cold butter
½ cup whole milk

**TOPPING**
¼ cup packed brown sugar
1 Tbsp. water
Half-and-half cream, optional

**1.** In a large saucepan, combine apricots and tapioca; let stand for 15 minutes. Add the brown sugar, butter and lemon juice. Cook and stir until mixture comes to a full boil. Reduce heat to low; keep warm.

**2.** For dumplings, in a large bowl, combine the flour, sugar and baking powder; cut in butter until crumbly. Add the milk; mix just until combined. Pour the warm fruit mixture into an ungreased 9- or 10-in. cast-iron skillet. Drop the batter in six mounds onto fruit mixture.

**3.** Bake, uncovered, at 425° until a toothpick inserted into a dumpling comes out clean, about 15 minutes. Stir together brown sugar and water; microwave until sugar is dissolved, stirring frequently, about 30 seconds. Spoon over dumplings; bake 5 minutes longer. Serve with cream if desired.

**1 SERVING:** 336 cal., 5g fat (3g sat. fat), 13mg chol., 170mg sod., 71g carb. (51g sugars, 2g fiber), 4g pro.

**✳ TEST KITCHEN TIP**

Cutting butter into dry ingredients results in tiny bits of flour-coated butter throughout the batter, creating a dumpling that is both tender and crumbly at the same time. If you don't have a pastry blender, use two knives to cut in the cold butter.

# BANANA SKILLET UPSIDE-DOWN CAKE

My grandmother gave me my first cast-iron skillet, and I've been cooking and baking with it ever since. Sometimes I add drained maraschino cherries to this banana skillet dessert and serve it with ice cream.
—*Terri Lynn Merritts, Nashville, TN*

**PREP:** 25 min. ● **BAKE:** 35 min. ● **MAKES:** 10 servings

- 1  pkg. (14 oz.) banana quick bread and muffin mix
- ½  cup chopped walnuts
- ¼  cup butter, cubed
- ¾  cup packed brown sugar
- 2  Tbsp. lemon juice
- 4  medium bananas, cut into ¼-in. slices
- 2  cups sweetened shredded coconut

**1.** Preheat oven to 375°. Prepare banana bread batter according to package directions; stir in walnuts.

**2.** In a 10-in. ovenproof skillet, melt butter over medium heat; stir in brown sugar until dissolved. Add lemon juice; cook and stir until slightly thickened, 2-3 minutes longer. Remove from heat. Arrange the bananas in a single layer over brown sugar mixture; sprinkle with coconut.

**3.** Spoon the prepared batter over coconut. Bake until dark golden and a toothpick inserted in center comes out clean, 35-40 minutes. Cool 5 minutes before inverting onto a serving plate. Serve warm.

**1 SLICE:** 554 cal., 22g fat (10g sat. fat), 49mg chol., 459mg sod., 82g carb. (30g sugars, 2g fiber), 6g pro.

# OTHER GADGETS

You have 'em; you love 'em. But you might not use them as often as you'd like. Here are 27 tasty reasons to dig out that fondue pot, cocktail shaker, spiralizer, panini maker and stand mixer.

# CHOOSING A STAND MIXER

All serious home bakers want a stand mixer to call their own. Beautiful, strong and versatile, the stand mixer serves as a third hand in the kitchen, beating and whipping ingredients as you do other tasks. Consider these factors when choosing one.

- **Price.** Stand mixers can cost anywhere from around $200 to $700. The higher-end models are typically larger and more powerful, so they're mostly for people who would use them regularly and for mixing large batches.

- **Style.** There are two general styles to consider. A tilt-head model requires you to push the top of the mixer back so you have clear access to pour your ingredients directly into the bowl, and the bowl-lift design essentially picks up the bowl and moves it up to the beaters. The bowl-lift style gives you a bit more flexibility when mixing small batches.

- **Power and Speed.** The machine's power and speed settings will vary. Some models offer just three, while pricier models have as many as 12.

- **Attachments.** There are three common attachments: a paddle or flat beater for mixing cookies and cake, a wire whip for aerating meringue and whipped cream, and a dough hook for making bread. (The third one is a bit less common, so seek it out if you're a bread baker.)

- **Options.** Want a stand mixer that does more? Some models offer optional attachments, such as a meat grinder, ice cream maker, food processor, spiralizer and more. If having one workhorse appliance that does many jobs appeals to you, consider what optional attachments you may want for your machine.

- **Appearance.** Since the stand mixer will likely have a permanent home on your counter, choose a style and color that appeal to you.

**A.** Stand mixer
**B.** Spiralizer
**C.** Fondue
**D.** Panini maker
**E.** Cocktail shaker
**F.** Food processor

## PANINI MAKER

First came the George Foreman Grill, which was on everyone's Christmas lists in the mid-2000s. Next were enhancements like removable plates, which make cleaning a breeze, and interchangeable plates (even waffle iron plates) introduced by the Cuisinart Griddler a few years later.

You can you use your countertop grill (aka panini maker) to sear up grilled pork chops in the dead of winter and to make classic panini sandwiches.

# WHY NOT SPIRALIZE IT?

The spiral slicer, or spiralizer, burst into the kitchens of heath-conscious cooks a few years ago, and we're increasingly finding new ways to put this gadget to use.

**LIGHTEN UP.** Use veggie "noodles" in place of all—or some—regular noodles. This boosts the nutrition in a dish while lowering the overall carbs and calories.

**PLAY WITH YOUR FOOD.** Create cute restaurant-style curly fries or sweet potato fries.

**IT'S NOT JUST FOR VEGGIES.** Use it as an apple slicer for strudels, pies or other baking needs.

**FEAST YOUR EYES.** Craft pretty garnishes that are fun to eat, such as carrot, beet or cucumber ribbons atop a salad.

## FONDUE = FUN

The communal dish named for the French word "to melt" was popularized in America in the 1960s. It enjoys a resurgence in popularity every couple of decades, as demonstrated in 1985 by the start of The Melting Pot fondue restaurant franchise.

If you're a food lover, chances are your family has a fondue pot tucked away somewhere in the kitchen cabinet or basement storage.

There are three main types of fondue: the classic cheese; chocolate, from which other dessert fondues stemmed; and bourguignon, a style in which you cook meat in a fondue pot's hot oil. Mostly, though, we Americans love the fondue pot for keeping food warm, dipping and dunking goodies into a hot, delicious dip, and adding cozy ambiance to any get-together. When the weather turns cold, we sure do enjoy our fondue!

## COCKTAIL SHAKER

**Getting a cocktail shaker is a rite of passage for adulthood. Choosing a shaker often comes down to personal style. Also consider these points:**

- A classic **three-piece shaker** (consisting of shaker, strainer and lid), shown on facing page, is common and easy to use.

- The **two-piece Boston shaker**, shown left, consists of a large shaker and a smaller mixing glass that fits into and over the shaker. It's preferred by the pros because of its quick operation and versatility (the mixing glass serves as a separate drink mixer). It's a bit trickier to master and requires that you buy a separate strainer.

- Consider **the size;** you'll want a shaker that stores easily. For mixing multiple drinks at a time, you might consider a giant shaker.

# SANTA'S ORANGE-KISSED COCKTAIL

Refreshing but not overly sweet, this drink is a festive choice for Christmas get-togethers.
Serve it during cocktail hour, at dinner or even for brunch in place of mimosas.
—*Claire Beattie, Toronto, ON*

**TAKES:** 5 min. • **MAKES:** 1 serving

Ice cubes
¼ cup light rum
¼ cup unsweetened pineapple juice
1 Tbsp. lime juice
2 Tbsp. orange juice
1 tsp. grenadine syrup
3 Tbsp. lemon-lime soda

**1.** Fill a shaker three-fourths full with ice. Add rum, juices and the grenadine syrup.

**2.** Cover and shake until condensation forms on outside of shaker, 10-15 seconds. Strain into chilled glass. Top with soda.

**1 SERVING:** 209 cal., 0 fat (0 sat. fat), 0 chol., 7mg sod., 20g carb. (16g sugars, 0 fiber), 1g pro.

## HOW TO BUILD THE ESSENTIAL PARTY BAR

Every great party needs a few good cocktails. Here's what you'll need to make sure the bar's ready. Don't worry if you're missing a few items—basics go a long way.

**THE BASICS**
Classic spirits: rum, bourbon or whiskey, gin, vodka and tequila.

**BUILD ON THE BASE**
Keep a few secondary options around to help you customize your cocktails. Bitters and flavored liqueurs are usually used in small quantities, so a single bottle will log a lot of miles. Try some of these options:

Bitters: classic Angostura
Orange liqueur: Cointreau or Grand Marnier
Elderflower liqueur: St-Germain
Ginger liqueur: Domaine de Canton

**FROM THE FARMERS MARKET**
To take the flavor up a notch, incorporate fresh produce, especially celery, tomatoes, citrus fruits, seasonal stone fruits, berries or herbs.

**MIXERS**
Mixers are the nonalcoholic liquid ingredients added to cocktails.

These include club soda, tonic water, colas and ginger ale, juice and simple syrups.

**THE TOOLKIT**
An initial investment in a few key items will pay you back for years to come.

Keep these in your arsenal: cocktail shaker and strainer; muddler (or the handle of a wooden spoon); ice cube trays; paring knife; bottle/wine opener; peeler; hand-held citrus press; straws.

# BASIL CITRUS COCKTAIL

This irresistible cocktail is fruity, fantastic and low in calories. What's not to love?
—*Taste of Home Test Kitchen*

**TAKES:** 10 min. • **MAKES:** 1 serving

6  fresh basil leaves
1½ to 2 cups ice cubes
2  oz. white grapefruit juice
2  oz. mandarin orange juice
¾  oz. gin
½  oz. Domaine de Canton ginger
   liqueur

1. In a shaker, muddle basil leaves.

2. Fill shaker three-fourths full with ice. Add juices, gin and ginger liqueur; cover and shake until condensation forms on the outside of the shaker, 10-15 seconds. Strain into a chilled cocktail glass.

**1 SERVING:** 136 cal., 0 fat (0 sat. fat), 0 chol., 0 sod., 14g carb. (7g sugars, 0 fiber), 1g pro.

# WHISKEY SOUR

Some of the best libations are the simplest. With only three ingredients, the classic whiskey sour is far from pretentious, but still packs a punch.
—*Taste of Home Test Kitchen*

**TAKES:** 5 min. • **MAKES:** 1 serving

   Ice cubes
2  oz. whiskey
1½ oz. sour mix
GARNISH
   Orange wedge and maraschino
   cherry

Fill a shaker three-fourths full with ice. Add whiskey and sour mix. Cover and shake until condensation forms on the outside of the shaker, 10-15 seconds. Strain into a chilled wine or sour glass. Garnish as desired.

**⅔ CUP:** 213 cal., 0 fat (0 sat. fat), 0 chol., 2mg sod., 22g carb. (21g sugars, 0 fiber), 0 pro.

# CRANBERRY COCKTAIL

I adore the combination of flavors in this recipe. The secret is to thaw the lemonade so it's still slightly icy—this way the cocktail will be cool and refreshing. For a nonalcoholic option, use peach juice and lemon-lime soda instead of schnapps and vodka.
—*Julie Danler, Bel Aire, KS*

**TAKES:** 10 min. • **MAKES:** 4 servings

Ice cubes
4 oz. vodka
4 oz. peach schnapps liqueur
4 oz. thawed lemonade concentrate
4 oz. cranberry-raspberry juice
16 maraschino cherries

1. Fill a shaker three-fourths full with ice cubes.

2. Add vodka, schnapps, lemonade concentrate and juice to shaker; cover and shake until condensation forms on outside of shaker, 10-15 seconds. Strain into four cocktail glasses. Place a skewer with four cherries in each glass.

**1 SERVING:** 226 cal., 0 fat (0 sat. fat), 0 chol., 4mg sod., 33g carb. (31g sugars, 0 fiber), 0 pro.

# WHITE JAMAICAN

A tropical twist on the classic white Russian, my easy-to-drink cocktail blends the flavors of coffee, vanilla and coconut.
—*Mark Brown, Irvine, CA*

**TAKES:** 5 min. • **MAKES:** 1 serving

Crushed ice
1½ oz. vanilla vodka
1½ oz. coconut rum
1½ oz. coffee liqueur
¾ oz. heavy whipping cream

Fill a shaker three-fourths full with crushed ice. Add the vodka, rum, coffee liqueur and cream; cover and shake until condensation forms on outside of shaker, 10-15 seconds. Strain into glass, if desired, or serve over ice.

**1 SERVING:** 445 cal., 8g fat (5g sat. fat), 31mg chol., 13mg sod., 25g carb. (20g sugars, 0 fiber), 1g pro.

# PERFECT LEMON MARTINI

Time to relax with a refreshing cocktail! The combination of tart lemon and sweet liqueur will tingle your taste buds.
—*Marilee Anker, Chatsworth, CA*

**TAKES:** 5 min. • **MAKES:** 1 serving

1 lemon slice
Sugar
Ice cubes
2 oz. vodka
1½ oz. limoncello
½ oz. lemon juice

Using lemon slice, moisten the rim of a chilled cocktail glass; set lemon aside. Sprinkle sugar on a plate; hold glass upside down and dip rim into sugar. Discard remaining sugar on plate. Fill a shaker three-fourths full with ice. Add vodka, limoncello and lemon juice; cover and shake until condensation forms on the outside of the shaker, 10-15 seconds. Strain into prepared glass. Garnish with lemon slice.

**1 SERVING:** 286 cal., 0 fat (0 sat. fat), 0 chol., 1mg sod., 18g carb. (17g sugars, 0 fiber), 0 pro.

# MARTINI

Whether you're going for a Rat Pack or secret agent vibe, you can't have a cocktail party without a martini on the menu. The choice of gin or vodka is up to you, but either way, this queen-of-the-cocktail-hour drink comes shaken, not stirred.
—*Taste of Home Test Kitchen*

**TAKES:** 5 min. • **MAKES:** 1 serving

Ice cubes
3 oz. gin or vodka
½ oz. dry vermouth
Pimiento-stuffed olives

Fill a shaker three-fourths full with ice. Add gin and vermouth; cover and shake until condensation forms on outside of shaker. Strain into a chilled cocktail glass. Garnish with olives.

**NOTE:** This recipe makes a dry martini. Use less vermouth for an extra-dry martini; use more for a wet martini. You may also serve the martini over ice in a rocks glass.

**⅔ CUP:** 209 cal., 0 fat (0 sat. fat), 0 chol., 5mg sod., 0 carb. (0 sugars, 0 fiber), 0 pro.

**APPLE MARTINI:** Omit vermouth and olives. Reduce vodka to 2 oz. and use 1½ oz. sour apple liqueur and 1½ tsp. lemon juice. Garnish with a green apple slice.

**CHOCOLATE MARTINI:** Omit the vermouth and olives. Reduce vodka to 2 oz. and use 2 oz. creme de cacao or chocolate liqueur. Garnish with chocolate shavings.

# FUN-DO FONDUE

Fondues are a hit at our gatherings. The younger crowd dips bread cubes,
and the adults like apples and pears. Celery, cucumbers and bell peppers work, too.
—*Judy Batson, Tampa, FL*

**TAKES:** 20 min. ● **MAKES:** 3 cups

2   cups shredded Jarlsberg cheese
½   cup shredded Swiss cheese
¼   cup all-purpose flour
½   tsp. ground mustard
½   tsp. freshly ground pepper
1   cup heavy whipping cream
1   cup reduced-sodium chicken broth
1   Tbsp. honey
1   tsp. lemon juice
    Cubed French bread, sliced pears
       and assorted fresh vegetables

1. In a small bowl, combine the first five ingredients; toss to combine. In a saucepan, combine cream, broth and honey; bring just to a boil, stirring occasionally. Reduce heat to medium-low. Add ½ cup cheese mixture; stir constantly until almost completely melted. Continue adding cheese, ½ cup at a time, allowing cheese to almost melt completely between additions. Continue stirring until thickened and smooth. Stir in the lemon juice.

2. Transfer mixture to a heated fondue pot; keep fondue bubbling gently. Serve with bread, pears and vegetables for dipping. If fondue becomes too thick, stir in a little additional broth.

¼ CUP: 166 cal., 13g fat (8g sat. fat), 43mg chol., 151mg sod., 5g carb. (2g sugars, 0 fiber), 7g pro.

# CHOCOLATE RUM FONDUE

Who needs a fancy fondue restaurant when you can whip up a chocolate
sensation like this in just 10 minutes? You'll love the hint of rum flavor.
—*Angie Samples, Maysville, GA*

**TAKES:** 10 min. ● **MAKES:** 1½ cups

3   milk chocolate Toblerone candy
       bars (3.52 oz. each), coarsely
       chopped
⅔   cup heavy whipping cream
4   tsp. rum or ½ tsp. rum extract
    Pear slices, cubed cake, large
       marshmallows and/or macaroon
       cookies

1. In a small heavy saucepan, combine candy bars and cream. Cook and stir over medium-low heat until blended. Remove from the heat; stir in rum.

2. Transfer to a small fondue pot and keep warm. Serve fondue with dippers of your choice.

¼ CUP: 358 cal., 23g fat (14g sat. fat), 46mg chol., 35mg sod., 33g carb. (27g sugars, 1g fiber), 4g pro.

**CHOCOLATE AMARETTO FONDUE:** Substitute 2 Tbsp. amaretto or ½ tsp. almond extract for the rum.

GOOD TIMES
**EVERYONE LOVES TO
DIP & DUNK**

# TOMATO CHEDDAR FONDUE

I serve this cheesy fondue with shrimp and French bread cubes. Every bite tastes like a little gourmet grilled cheese sandwich. You can also use soft pretzel nuggets or tortilla scoops as dippers.
—*Roberta Rotelle, Honey Brook, PA*

**TAKES:** 30 min. ● **MAKES:** 3½ cups

1 garlic clove, halved
6 medium tomatoes, seeded and diced
⅔ cup dry white wine
6 Tbsp. butter, cubed
1½ tsp. dried basil
   Dash cayenne pepper
2 cups shredded cheddar cheese
1 Tbsp. all-purpose flour
   Cubed French bread and cooked shrimp

1. Rub garlic clove over the bottom and sides of a fondue pot; discard garlic and set pot aside.

2. In a large saucepan, combine the tomatoes, wine, butter, basil and cayenne; bring to a simmer over medium-low heat. Reduce heat to low. Toss cheese with flour; gradually add to tomato mixture, stirring after each addition until cheese is melted.

3. Transfer to prepared fondue pot and keep warm. Serve with bread cubes and shrimp.

**¼ CUP:** 118 cal., 10g fat (7g sat. fat), 30mg chol., 135mg sod., 4g carb. (2g sugars, 1g fiber), 4g pro.

# LEMON FONDUE

As pretty as it is luscious, this sunshiny sauce is a lovely complement to cubed angel food or pound cake. It's just right for a special luncheon.
—*Diane Hixon, Niceville, FL*

**TAKES:** 15 min. ● **MAKES:** 5 cups

1 cup sugar
½ cup cornstarch
½ tsp. salt
4 cups water
½ cup butter, cubed
½ cup lemon juice
2 Tbsp. grated lemon zest
   Strawberries, gingerbread and/or bite-sized meringues

1. In a large heavy saucepan, combine the sugar, cornstarch and salt. Stir in water until smooth. Bring to a boil over medium heat; cook and stir until thickened, 1-2 minutes. Remove from the heat; stir in butter, lemon juice and zest until butter is melted.

2. Transfer to a fondue pot and keep warm. Serve with strawberries, gingerbread and/or meringues.

**2 TBSP.:** 46 cal., 2g fat (1g sat. fat), 6mg chol., 53mg sod., 7g carb. (5g sugars, 0 fiber), 0 pro.

# CARAMEL APPLE FONDUE

I serve this yummy caramel dip with sliced apples while we're watching football games on Sunday afternoons. It warms us up on those chilly fall days and satisfies our craving for something sweet.
—*Katie Koziolek, Hartland, MN*

**TAKES:** 25 min. • **MAKES:** 3½ cups

½ cup butter, cubed
2 cups packed brown sugar
1 can (14 oz.) sweetened condensed milk
1 cup light corn syrup
2 Tbsp. water
1 tsp. vanilla extract
  Apple slices

1. In a heavy 3-qt. saucepan, combine the butter, brown sugar, milk, corn syrup and water; bring to a boil over medium heat. Cook and stir until a candy thermometer reads 230° (thread stage), 8-10 minutes. Remove from the heat; stir in vanilla.

2. Transfer to a small fondue pot or 1½-qt. slow cooker; keep warm. Serve with apple slices.

**NOTE:** We recommend that you test your candy thermometer before each use by bringing water to a boil; the thermometer should read 212°. Adjust your recipe temperature up or down based on your test.

**2 TBSP.:** 167 cal., 4g fat (3g sat. fat), 14mg chol., 71mg sod., 32g carb. (29g sugars, 0 fiber), 1g pro.

# BLACKENED TILAPIA WITH ZUCCHINI NOODLES

I love healthy, quick meals like this one-skillet wonder. Homemade pico de gallo is easy to make the night before, or use store-bought to keep prep even more simple.
—*Tammy Brownlow, Dallas, TX*

**TAKES:** 30 min. • **MAKES:** 4 servings

2 large zucchini (about 1½ lbs.)
1½ tsp. ground cumin
¾ tsp. salt, divided
½ tsp. smoked paprika
½ tsp. pepper
¼ tsp garlic powder
4 tilapia fillets (6 oz. each)
2 tsp. olive oil
2 garlic cloves, minced
1 cup pico de gallo

**1.** Trim ends of zucchini. Using a spiralizer, cut zucchini into thin strands.

**2.** Mix cumin, ½ tsp. salt, smoked paprika, pepper and garlic powder; sprinkle generously onto both sides of tilapia. In a large nonstick skillet, heat oil over medium-high heat. In batches, cook tilapia until fish just begins to flake easily with a fork, 2-3 minutes per side. Remove from pan; keep warm.

**3.** In same pan, cook the zucchini with garlic over medium-high heat until slightly softened, 1-2 minutes, tossing constantly with tongs (do not overcook). Sprinkle with remaining salt. Serve with the tilapia and pico de gallo.

**1 SERVING:** 203 cal., 4g fat (1g sat. fat), 83mg chol., 522mg sod., 8g carb. (5g sugars, 2g fiber), 34g pro. **DIABETIC EXCHANGES:** 5 lean meat, 1 vegetable, ½ fat.

## ✳ STAFF HACK

*"I substitute spiralized summer squash and carrots for about half the soba noodles in my homemade pad Thai. Brings down the carb count and boosts the nutrition, so even a hearty serving is guilt-free!"*
—DEB MULVEY, COPY CHIEF

# ARUGULA PESTO CHICKEN

I had an abundance of arugula in my garden, so I turned it into pesto and added it to this recipe. The bold green color reminds my son of something The Incredible Hulk would eat. Any way I can get him to eat veggies is a win for me!
—*Courtney Stultz, Weir, KS*

**TAKES:** 25 min. ● **MAKES:** 4 servings

- 4 **cups fresh arugula or spinach**
- 1 **cup fresh basil leaves**
- ¼ **cup pine nuts**
- 1 **garlic clove, minced**
- 1½ **tsp. sea salt, divided**
- ¼ **cup plus 1 Tbsp. olive oil, divided**
- 4 **medium zucchini**
- 1 **rotisserie chicken, skin removed, shredded**
- 2 **plum tomatoes, chopped**
- ¼ **tsp. pepper**
  **Grated Parmesan cheese, optional**

1. Pulse arugula, basil, pine nuts, garlic and 1 tsp. salt in a food processor until chopped. While processing, gradually add ¼ cup oil in a steady stream until mixture is smooth. Using a shredder or spiralizer, shred zucchini lengthwise into long strands.

2. In a large skillet, heat remaining oil over medium heat. Add zucchini strands and chicken. Cook and stir until zucchini is crisp-tender, about 4 minutes.

3. Remove from heat. Add tomatoes, pesto, pepper and remaining salt; toss mixture to coat. If desired, sprinkle with Parmesan cheese. Serve using a slotted spoon.

**1½ CUPS:** 488 cal., 32g fat (5g sat. fat), 110mg chol., 836mg sod., 10g carb. (6g sugars, 3g fiber), 41g pro.

## HOW TO MAKE ZUCCHINI NOODLES

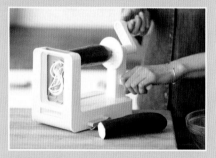

**YOU'LL NEED:**
Spiralizer, vegetable peeler or box grater
2 large zucchini (about 1½ pounds)
1 teaspoon olive oil
2 garlic cloves, minced
¼ teaspoon salt

Trim off the ends of zucchini. Depending on your preference, you can keep the skin on or peel it off before turning the vegetable into noodles.

Align zucchini so one end meets the blade, then poke the claw insert into the opposite end to hold it in place. Crank the spiralizer handle, applying light pressure to feed the zucchini into the grating blades. Keep turning until the zucchini is completely spiralized...and that's it! The strands you've created are zucchini noodles.

Add oil to a large nonstick skillet over medium-high heat. Toss in the zucchini noodles (with minced garlic if you want more flavor). Cook for 1-2 minutes. Make sure the zucchini cooks only slightly, to preserve its fresh, crunchy texture. As the zoodles cook, toss them constantly with tongs so they don't overcook. When finished, sprinkle with salt.

# OMELET PANINI

When you're in a hurry to get out the door in the morning, this speedy breakfast will fill you up without slowing you down. The recipe makes two crispy, flavorful sandwiches. It's also a fun change of pace for dinner.
—*Dorothy McClinton, North Chicago, IL*

**TAKES:** 20 min. • **MAKES:** 2 servings

4 slices sourdough bread
  (½ in. thick)
2 tsp. stone-ground mustard
2 slices Havarti cheese (1 oz. each)
4 thin slices prosciutto or deli ham
5 tsp. butter, softened, divided
2 large eggs
1 Tbsp. finely chopped onion
2 tsp. grated Parmesan cheese
1 tsp. minced chives
1 tsp. 2% milk

**1.** Spread two slices of bread with mustard. Top with Havarti cheese and prosciutto; set aside.

**2.** In a small nonstick skillet, melt 1 tsp. butter over medium-high heat. In a small bowl, whisk the eggs, onion, Parmesan cheese, chives and milk. Pour into skillet (mixture should set immediately at edges). As eggs set, push cooked edges toward the center, letting uncooked portion flow underneath.

**3.** Invert omelet onto a plate; cut in half. Place over prosciutto; top with remaining bread. Lightly spread the remaining butter over outsides of sandwiches.

**4.** Cook on a panini maker or indoor grill for 1-2 minutes or until bread is browned and cheese is melted.

**1 SERVING:** 487 cal., 26g fat (14g sat. fat), 279mg chol., 1084mg sod., 37g carb. (4g sugars, 3g fiber), 25g pro.

# CUBAN PANINI

The Cuban sandwich is a twist on the traditional ham and cheese, typically piled high with ham, Swiss, pickles and condiments, and sometimes, as in this hearty version, smoked turkey.
—Janet Sanders, Pine Mountain, GA

**PREP:** 20 min. • **COOK:** 5 min./batch • **MAKES:** 4 servings

- 2 garlic cloves, minced
- ½ tsp. olive oil
- ½ cup reduced-fat mayonnaise
- 8 slices artisan bread
- 8 thick slices deli smoked turkey
- 4 slices deli ham
- 8 slices Swiss cheese
- 12 dill pickle slices
- 1 cup fresh baby spinach

**1.** In a small skillet, cook and stir garlic in oil over medium-high heat until tender. Cool.

**2.** Stir garlic into mayonnaise; spread over bread slices. Layer four slices of bread with turkey, ham, cheese, pickles and spinach; close sandwiches.

**3.** Cook on a panini maker or indoor grill until browned and cheese is melted, 2-3 minutes.

**1 PANINI:** 545 cal., 27g fat (12g sat. fat), 85mg chol., 1526mg sod., 41g carb. (4g sugars, 2g fiber), 33g pro.

# MEDITERRANEAN TURKEY PANINI

A panini is a sandwich that is pressed and toasted. I love making these for my fellow teachers and friends. For potlucks, make several and cut them into fourths to serve as tasty hot appetizers.
—Martha Muellenberg, Vermillion, SD

**TAKES:** 25 min. • **MAKES:** 4 servings

- 4 ciabatta rolls, split
- 1 jar (24 oz.) marinara or spaghetti sauce, divided
- 1 container (4 oz.) crumbled feta cheese
- 1 jar (7½ oz.) marinated quartered artichoke hearts, drained and chopped
- 2 plum tomatoes, sliced
- 1 lb. sliced deli turkey

**1.** Spread each ciabatta bottom with 2 Tbsp. marinara sauce. Top with the cheese, artichokes, tomato and turkey. Spread each ciabatta top with 2 Tbsp. marinara sauce; place over turkey.

**2.** Cook on a panini maker or indoor grill for 4-5 minutes or until cheese is melted. Place remaining marinara sauce in a small microwave-safe bowl; cover and microwave on high until sauce is heated through. Serve with sandwiches.

**1 PANINI WITH ⅓ CUP SAUCE:** 701 cal., 18g fat (5g sat. fat), 55mg chol., 2314mg sod., 98g carb. (18g sugars, 8g fiber), 40g pro.

# CAESAR CHICKEN BURGERS

We love these grilled chicken sandwiches so much they've become a regular part of the dinner rotation. They're easy to make on the barbecue during summer and on the indoor grill during winter.
—*Andrea VanDinter, Prince George, BC*

**TAKES:** 20 min. • **MAKES:** 4 servings

4 boneless skinless chicken breast halves (4 oz. each)
¼ tsp. salt
¼ tsp. pepper
4 slices red onion
2 Tbsp. butter, softened
4 hamburger buns, split
2 cups torn romaine
1 Tbsp. grated Parmesan cheese
½ cup creamy Caesar salad dressing, divided

1. Sprinkle the chicken with salt and pepper. Grill on an indoor grill coated with cooking spray until juices run clear, for 4-5 minutes. Grill onion slices until tender, 4-5 minutes.

2. Meanwhile, spread butter over cut sides of buns. Place buttered side up on an ungreased baking sheet. Broil 3-4 in. from the heat until golden brown, about 1 minute.

3. Toss romaine with cheese and ¼ cup dressing; spoon onto bun bottoms. Top with onions, chicken and the remaining dressing. Replace bun tops.

**1 SERVING:** 416 cal., 22g fat (7g sat. fat), 89mg chol., 760mg sod., 24g carb. (3g sugars, 2g fiber), 29g pro.

# QUICK APPLE-GLAZED PORK CHOPS

These succulent pork chops are nicley seasoned with everyday spices you likely have stocked in your pantry or spice rack. The rub is versatile, so give it a try on any meat, poultry or fish.
—*Taste of Home Test Kitchen*

**TAKES:** 20 min. • **MAKES:** 4 servings

2 Tbsp. brown sugar
2 tsp. paprika
1 tsp. salt
1 tsp. onion powder
1 tsp. garlic powder
1 tsp. ground mustard
1 tsp. dried thyme
½ tsp. pepper
4 boneless pork loin chops (1 in. thick and 6 oz. each)
2 Tbsp. apple jelly

1. Combine the first eight ingredients; rub over both sides of pork chops. Cook in batches on an indoor grill coated with cooking spray until a thermometer inserted into chops reads 145°, 3-4 minutes on each side. Let pork chops stand for 5 minutes before serving.

2. In a microwave-safe bowl, heat jelly until warmed; brush over pork chops.

**1 SERVING:** 283 cal., 10g fat (4g sat. fat), 82mg chol., 522mg sod., 14g carb. (12g sugars, 1g fiber), 33g pro. **DIABETIC EXCHANGES:** 5 lean meat, 1 starch.

# HAZELNUT MACARONS

The renowned chef Julia Child had a passion for life and French cooking as she and Alex Prud'homme described in the book *My Life in France*. The woman who introduced Americans to the delights of French cuisine most likely would have found these crispy, French-style cookies a delight, too.

—*Taste of Home Test Kitchen*

**PREP:** 50 min. ● **BAKE:** 10 min./batch ● **MAKES:** about 5 dozen

6 **large egg whites**
1½ **cups hazelnuts, toasted**
2½ **cups confectioners' sugar**
 **Dash salt**
½ **cup superfine sugar**
**COFFEE BUTTERCREAM**
1 **cup sugar**
6 **Tbsp. water**
6 **large egg yolks**
4 **tsp. instant espresso powder**
1 **tsp. vanilla extract**
1½ **cups butter, softened**
6 **Tbsp. confectioners' sugar**

## HOW TO WHIP EGG WHITES TO STIFF PEAKS

- For maximum volume, use a very clean bowl and beaters.

- Let egg whites stand at room temperature 30 minutes.

- Lift beater out of the whites to test the peaks. Stiff peaks form a point, rather then a soft or curving mound.

1. Place egg whites in a small bowl; let stand at room temperature for 30 minutes.

2. Preheat oven to 350°. Place the hazelnuts and confectioners' sugar in a food processor; pulse until nuts are finely ground.

3. Add salt to egg whites; beat on medium speed until soft peaks form. Gradually add superfine sugar, 1 Tbsp. at a time, beating on high until stiff peaks form. Fold in hazelnut mixture.

4. With a reusable pastry bag, pipe 1-in.-diameter cookies 2 in. apart onto parchment paper-lined baking sheets. Bake until lightly browned and firm to the touch, 9-12 minutes. Transfer cookies on the parchment paper to wire racks; cool completely.

5. For the buttercream, in a heavy saucepan, combine sugar and water. Bring to a boil; cook over medium-high heat until sugar is dissolved. Remove from heat. In a small bowl, whisk a small amount of hot syrup into the egg yolks; return all to pan, whisking constantly. Cook until thickened, 2-3 minutes, stirring constantly; remove from heat. Stir in espresso powder and vanilla; cool completely.

6. In a stand mixer with the whisk attachment, beat the butter until creamy. Gradually beat in cooled syrup. Beat in confectioners' sugar until fluffy. Refrigerate until mixture firms to a spreading consistency, about 10 minutes.

7. Spread about 1½ tsp. buttercream onto the bottom of each of half of the cookies; top with remaining cookies. Store in airtight containers in the refrigerator.

**NOTE:** To toast whole hazelnuts, bake in a shallow pan in a 350° oven until fragrant and lightly browned, stirring occasionally, 7-10 minutes. To remove skins, wrap hazelnuts in a tea towel; rub with towel to loosen skins.

**1 SANDWICH COOKIE:** 117 cal., 8g fat (3g sat. fat), 31mg chol., 67mg sod., 12g carb. (11g sugars, 0 fiber), 1g pro.

# HOMEMADE MANGO MARSHMALLOWS

You'll never go back to bagged store-bought marshmallows after trying homemade ones. I achieved yummy results when I flavored mine with mango nectar. Look for it in your store's Mexican food section.
—*Deirdre Cox, Kansas City, MO*

**PREP:** 25 min. ● **COOK:** 20 min. + cooling ● **MAKES:** 1½ lbs.

2  envelopes unflavored gelatin
1¼ cups chilled mango nectar, divided
1½ cups sugar
¾ cup light corn syrup
1  tsp. almond extract
2  cups sweetened shredded coconut, toasted

### ✱ STAFF HACK

*"I use my stand mixer to make the cream cheese and sour cream base for my taco dip. I don't like that mixture to be lumpy, and the stand mixer is great for taking the work out of it. It's my 'elbow-grease saver' in the kitchen."*

**—RAEANN THOMPSON, SENIOR ART DIRECTOR**

1. Line a 8-in. square pan with foil; grease foil with cooking spray. In a heatproof bowl of a stand mixer, sprinkle gelatin over ½ cup nectar.

2. In a large heavy saucepan, combine the sugar, corn syrup and remaining nectar. Bring mixture to a boil, stirring occasionally. Cook, without stirring, over medium heat until a candy thermometer reads 240° (soft-ball stage).

3. Remove from heat; slowly drizzle into gelatin, beating on high speed. Continue beating until very stiff and doubled in volume, about 10 minutes. Immediately beat in extract. Spread into prepared pan. Cover and let cool at room temperature for 6 hours or overnight.

4. Place coconut in a food processor; process until finely chopped. Using foil, lift candy out of pan. Using a lightly buttered kitchen scissors, cut into 1-in. pieces. Roll in coconut. Store in an airtight container in a cool, dry place.

**NOTE:** To toast coconut, bake in a shallow pan in a 350° oven for 5-10 minutes or cook in a skillet over low heat until golden brown, stirring occasionally.

**1 MARSHMALLOW:** 48 cal., 1g fat (1g sat. fat), 0 chol., 11mg sod., 10g carb. (10g sugars, 0 fiber), 0 pro.

# MINI CHOCOLATE CHIP SANDWICH COOKIES

I created these twice-as-nice sandwich cookies for my annual holiday cookie platter, and I also gift some to family and friends. If the filling doesn't come together after all of the butter has been incorporated, add some shortening one tablespoon at a time until the mixture starts to transform.
—*Julie Thomas, Saukville, WI*

**PREP:** 1 hour + chilling ● **BAKE:** 10 min. + cooling ● **MAKES:** about 5 dozen

1 cup shortening
1 cup packed light brown sugar
½ cup granulated sugar
2 large eggs
1 tsp. vanilla extract
2¼ cups all-purpose flour
1 tsp. baking soda
1 tsp. salt
1 pkg. miniature semisweet chocolate chips (10 oz.)

**FILLING**

1 vanilla bean
3 large egg whites
½ cup granulated sugar
½ tsp. vanilla extract
¾ cup unsalted butter, room temperature

**1.** Preheat oven to 350°. Cream the shortening and sugars until light and fluffy. Beat in the eggs and vanilla. In another bowl, whisk flour, baking soda and salt; gradually beat into creamed mixture. Stir in chocolate chips. Chill dough for 1 hour.

**2.** Shape teaspoonfuls of dough into 1-in. balls. Place 1½ in. apart on ungreased baking sheets. Bake until edges begin to brown, 8-10 minutes. Cool on pans 2 minutes. Remove to wire racks to cool completely.

**3.** Meanwhile, for filling, split vanilla bean lengthwise. Using a sharp knife, scrape seeds from center into top of a double boiler over simmering water; discard bean. Add the egg whites, granulated sugar and vanilla extract. Whisking constantly, heat mixture until sugar is dissolved and a thermometer reads 160°, 8-10 minutes. Transfer to a stand mixer fitted with a whisk attachment.

**4.** Whisk egg white mixture on high until it cools to room temperature, 8-10 minutes. Reduce speed to medium; gradually add butter, 1 Tbsp. at a time, beating well after each addition. Increase speed to high; beat until smooth.

**5.** To assemble, transfer filling to a reusable pastry bag. Pipe about 1 tsp. on bottoms of half of the cookies; cover with remaining cookies. Store in airtight containers.

**1 SANDWICH COOKIE:** 120 cal., 7g fat (3g sat. fat), 12mg chol., 67mg sod., 14g carb. (10g sugars, 0 fiber), 1g pro.

**❋ TEST KITCHEN TIP**

Make baking these cookies even easier by using a small ice cream scoop to keep the cookies a uniform size. No vanilla bean in the house? Use 1 tsp. vanilla extract in place of the bean.

# ORANGE-PISTACHIO DIVINITY

Old-fashioned divinity candy is even yummier with a hint of refreshing orange zest and bits of crunchy pistachios. Store-bought versions can't compare!
—*Lorri Reinhardt, Big Bend, WI*

**PREP:** 15 min. • **COOK:** 20 min. + standing • **MAKES:** about 4 dozen (1⅓ lbs.)

- 2 **large egg whites**
- 2⅔ **cups sugar**
- ⅔ **cup light corn syrup**
- ½ **cup water**
- 1 **tsp. grated orange zest**
- 1 **tsp. vanilla extract**
- ⅔ **cup pistachios, coarsely chopped**

### ❋ TEST KITCHEN TIP

Check the weather forecast before making divinity. Avoid humid days because the candy may not set up properly.

Beating divinity can be tricky. It's important to beat the egg whites and sugar syrup sufficiently, but if you overbeat, the whites will break down and the mixture will become grainy. When it just starts to lose its sheen, that's your cue to stop beating.

For best results, use a stand mixer. It beats more evenly than a hand mixer and will save wear and tear on your arm.

Work quickly while dropping the divinity onto prepared pans, adding a few drops of hot water if mixture stiffens.

**1.** Place egg whites in bowl of a stand mixer; let stand at room temperature for 30 minutes. Meanwhile, line two 15x10x1-in. pans with waxed paper.

**2.** In a large heavy saucepan, combine sugar, corn syrup and water; cook and stir until sugar is dissolved and mixture comes to a boil. Cook, without stirring, over medium heat until a thermometer reads 252° (hard-ball stage). Just before that temperature is reached, beat egg whites on medium speed until stiff peaks form.

**3.** Increase speed to high. As the mixer continues to run, slowly add the hot sugar mixture in a thin stream over egg whites, beating constantly and scraping sides of bowl occasionally. Add orange zest and vanilla. Beat until candy holds its shape and begins to lose its gloss, 5-6 minutes. (Do not overbeat, or candy will stiffen and crumble.) Immediately fold in the pistachios.

**4.** Quickly drop the mixture by tablespoonfuls onto prepared pans. Let stand at room temperature until dry to the touch. Store between layers of waxed paper in an airtight container at room temperature.

**1 PIECE:** 68 cal., 1g fat (0 sat. fat), 0 chol., 13mg sod., 15g carb. (15g sugars, 0 fiber), 1g pro.

# ICE CREAM KOLACHKES

These bite-sized pastries, sometimes also spelled *kolaches*, have Polish and Czech roots. They are usually filled with poppy seeds, nuts, jam or a mashed fruit mixture. I add vanilla ice cream to the dough for an extra-sweet twist. Use a square cookie cutter to to make quick work of cutting the dough.

—*Diane Turner, Brunswick, OH*

**PREP:** 1 hour + chilling ● **BAKE:** 15 min./batch ● **MAKES:** 10 dozen

- 2 cups butter, softened
- 1 pint vanilla ice cream, softened
- 4 cups all-purpose flour
- 2 Tbsp. sugar
- 2 cans (12 oz. each) apricot and/or raspberry cake and pastry filling
- 1 to 2 Tbsp. confectioners' sugar, optional

**✱ READER RAVE**

*"This recipe is the one that made me a loyal subscriber to Taste of Home. These were present at every holiday gathering I can remember as a child, and were a family favorite. My Gram always made them with apricot filling."*

—JENNYCROCKER, TASTEOFHOME.COM

**1.** In the bowl of a heavy-duty stand mixer, beat butter and ice cream until blended (mixture will appear curdled). Add flour and sugar; mix well. Divide dough into four portions; cover and refrigerate for 2 hours or until easy to handle.

**2.** Preheat oven to 350°. On a lightly floured surface, roll one portion of dough into a 12x10–in. rectangle; cut into 2-in. squares. Place a teaspoonful of filling in the center of each square. Overlap two opposite corners of dough over filling; pinch tightly to seal. Place 2 in. apart on ungreased baking sheets. Repeat with remaining dough and filling.

**3.** Bake kolachkes until bottoms are lightly browned, 11-14 minutes. Cool 1 minute before removing from pans to wire racks. Lightly sprinkle with confectioners' sugar if desired.

**NOTE:** This recipe was tested with Solo brand cake and pastry filling. Look for it in the baking aisle.

**1 PASTRY:** 60 cal., 3g fat (2g sat. fat), 9mg chol., 27mg sod., 7g carb. (2g sugars, 0 fiber), 1g pro.

# INDEX BY COOKING TOOL

Here are the recipes you'll find by appliance or cookware.

# ALPHABETICAL INDEX